BEST PRACTICE
THE PROS ON ADOBE ILLUSTRATOR

Toni Toland

THOMSON

DELMAR LEARNING   Australia Canada Mexico Singapore Spain United Kingdom United States

THOMSON

DELMAR LEARNING

Best Practice: The Pros on Adobe Illustrator

Toni Toland

Vice President, Technology and Trades ABU:
Dave Garza

Director of Learning Solutions:
Sandy Clark

Senior Acquisitions Editor:
James Gish

Product Manager:
Jaimie Weiss

Marketing Director:
Deborah Yarnell

Marketing Coordinator:
Mark Pierro

Production Director:
Patty Stephan

Editorial Assistant:
Niamh Matthews

Senior Production Manager:
Larry Main

Senior Content Project Manager:
Thomas Stover

Content Project Manager:
Nicole Stagg

Cover Design:
Toni Toland

For permission to use material from the text or product, contact us by

Tel. (800) 730-2214

Fax (800) 730-2215

www.thomsonrights.com

Library of Congress
Cataloging-in-Publication Data

ISBN: 1-4180-1144-4

NOTICE TO THE READER

For John Sellers and Rodger Mack:
their support and encouragement
will always inspire me.

TABLE OF CONTENTS

INTENDED AUDIENCE

This book is all about professional illustrators and designers who use Adobe Illustrator on a regular basis. Daily, in fact. And quite possibly dream about it!

The reason behind the book is that most artists and designers are usually interested in the "how" something was created, as much as the "why." In these pages, you'll learn a bit about the personality behind the images, as well as how they were created. Each chapter offers opportunities to try new techniques and tricks, and to incorporate them into your own work.

Anyone looking to add some spice to their work, or to test new "recipes" for developing illustrations, will find many intriguing approaches to creating images and working with type in Adobe Illustrator.

So, whether you're a beginner, or have some basic Illustrator skills, you should find something that whets your appetite, gets your creative juices flowing, or simply inspires you.

ORGANIZATION

The first chapter of this book is a result of the direct request from my students: a refresher course on the basics of Adobe Illustrator. As students, they are studying many diverse subjects and retain what they "need to know" to pass a course. This book, for them, was a welcome opportunity to hone their proficiencies in Illustrator, and they discovered that they needed a primer, if you will, to jog their memories and assist them in recalling what they learned the previous semester, or a year earlier.

Subsequent chapters are organized in terms of degrees of difficulty. The first several include interesting twists on basic Illustrator knowledge. "Use it or loose it" is a good phrase for working with any software program, and it's very true for Adobe Illustrator. The more you use something, the more adept you get. That's the goal of these chapters.

The later chapters become more challenging, building on the techniques and basics covered previously to introduce more sophisticated approaches. It's in these chapters that you'll find the artists and designers who are pushing the limits and using CS and CS2 features, like Live Trace, Live Paint, and 3D Revolve.

In writing this book, I've assumed that those interested in it already know, or are concurrently learning, the history and principles of design and illustration, such as composition, contrast, texture, color, and value.

There's a DVD at the back of the book that is as valuable as the text. It includes video interviews with several of the artists featured in this book, along with video demonstrations of how some of Adobe Illustrator CS2's new features work, and others that demonstrate a particular technique or trick.

The DVD also serves as your resource for the hands-on exercises in each chapter. Called "DIY" (for Do It Yourself), these exercises may call for one or more files. You'll find all the files you will need in the folder named for the artist you're reading about. I've included these files so that completing any particular exercise doesn't have to be about starting from scratch unless you want it to be.

Digital Deconstruction sections feature this vegetable peeler icon.

Once you've mastered the techniques in each chapter's DIY exercises, you have the opportunity to complete an assignment that incorporates your new skills. Many of these assignments were developed in concert with my students, and so should reflect contemporary design interests and venues. Wherever possible, I've included their completed assignments to give you some food for thought about how you might go about creating your own image or design.

The DIY (Do It Yourself) sections are represented by a whisk icon.

FEATURES

As mentioned, each chapter is broken down into three general areas. They all begin with some background about each artist, including where they came from, and any advice they have for aspiring professionals.

- There are at least two Digital Deconstructions in each chapter, where a particular image is dissected and analyzed in terms of how it was created, and what interesting techniques the artist used.

Sections that feature basic information about an option or technique are marked with measuring spoons.

- There are also at least two DIY (Do It Yourself) exercises in each chapter so that you can learn these techniques, step by step. Think of these as making a cake from a mix: some of the work is done for you, but you still have to add some ingredients and bake it before it's a real cake.

- There is a final assignment for each chapter, On Your Own, where you're challenged to create something that incorporates what you have learned. This is your opportunity to make the cake from scratch, as it were.

The key points for each chapter are indicated with this knife icon.

- Some chapters include FYI (For Your Information) sections that cover aspects of Adobe Illustrator, or reproduction issues, that are important to understand in order to attain professional standards and expertise.

Assignments at the end of each chapter are marked with a spatula.

- Finally, the interviews and video demonstrations on the DVD provide extra, special ingredients that should make using this book a rich and rewarding experience.

INGREDIENTS FOR SUCCESS

The first caveat for working successfully on any project is to keep your materials organized. Create a folder on your hard drive or portable hard drive (my students are all using their iPods!) where you can save your DIY files and final assignments. I'd recommend creating subfolders within that master folder for each chapter, just as they are organized on the DVD.

The second caveat is to save your work frequently! More than once in the past months, as my students worked alongside me to make sure the DIY sections were accurate and easy to follow, I received an IM saying, "The computer just crashed and I lost everything! What do I do now?"

My answer: start over. It's not as bad as it sounds. You'll find that doing something more than once makes your work better, and makes *you* work better. It's practice that makes perfect, after all.

E.RESOURCE

An instructor's guide on CD is available to assist instructors in planning and implementing their instructional programs. It includes sample syllabi for using this book in either an 11- or 15-week course. It also provides PowerPoint slides highlighting the main topics, and additional instructor resources.

ISBN: 1-4180-1145-2

ABOUT THE AUTHOR

Toni Toland earned her B.F.A and M.F.A from Syracuse University, where she is an Associate Professor in the Department of Design in the College of Visual and Performing Arts. Her twenty-five-year career at SU also includes stints as Department Chair, and Director of the School of Art + Design.

In between pursuing her degrees, she worked in advertising agencies as art director, and creative group head, in design studios, and for *Town and Country* magazine. Her work has won awards from The Society for Publication Designers and *Advertising Age*. She began teaching full time in 1981.

Toni started using the computer when Apple came out with the Mac 512 in 1984 and incorporated its use in her courses as an imaging and layout tool for designers in 1986, using a Mac Plus as a server.

When she's not in the classroom or creating her own work, Toni is sailing on one of the most beautiful lakes in New York—Skaneateles—in her sixteen-foot daysailer. During nonsailing months, she's an avid knitter and reader (cheap murder mysteries, mostly). She enjoys cooking all year long.

ACKNOWLEDGMENTS

I must first thank the artists who so graciously worked with me to make this book not only about Adobe Photoshop, but about them as well; they are very cool people, and professionals who create amazing digital art and design. I have thoroughly enjoyed getting to know each of you. Thank you for your patience. Thanks for teaching me things I didn't know, and for reminding me of things I had forgotten. I hope what I've put together here honors your immense talents and generous spirits.

I am also indebted to the students who bravely registered for an Independent Study with me. When I invited these Ad Design majors to participate, I anticipated that perhaps four or six students would be interested. Instead, I ended up working with twenty-six incredibly determined, helpful, enthusiastic, and talented kids. Their job was to read several chapters each, do the DIY's to make sure they were accurate, and help develop the final On Your Own projects for each chapter. Then, they got to do the assignments they'd created.

Because this was an independent study situation, there was no classroom, so we invented one. I created a screen name and (re)learned how to use AIM (AOL Instant Messaging). I had it on almost 24/7 to be available to answer questions and resolve issues. On Tuesday evenings, we met in a chat room to talk about their progress and mine.

I truly could not have completed this project without them. When I flagged, they were IM'ing me with encouraging words, and when they were exhausted, I gave them a break ;-). In all my years of teaching, I have never had the privilege to work with such amazing people. Thank you.

My husband, Hugh Phillips, has stood by me throughout the process, often behind me, massaging my shoulders as I typed. He indulged my need for technology and never winced when I decided I needed a new printer and a new digital camera. He also recognized when *I* needed a break and patiently waited on the lakeshore for me to return from sailing. He did the laundry, took out the garbage, and bought all the groceries. I love you, Hugh.

Zachary Phillips, my son, is the man behind the DVD. His talents with a camera and the computer are impressive. I am so proud of his accomplishments, and grateful for his efforts. Thanks, Zach.

THE ARTISTS:

Rocco Baviera
David Brooks
Mark Collins
Kenny Kiernan
David McCord
Colleen O'Hara
Daniel Pelavin
Heidi Schmidt
Peter Sinclair
Chris Spollen
Jack Tom

Thanks are also due to my daughter, Elizabeth Luttinger, who wrote the music for the DVD and whose photography I have used in several places in this book. She continues to amaze me with her many diverse talents. Thanks, Elizabeth!

Finally, the team at Thomson Delmar Learning, starting with Arthur Jones, who introduced me to Jim Gish and got the ball rolling. Jim, Jaimie Weiss, Niamh Matthews, Tom Stover, and Nicole Stagg were there when I got anxious or needed help. A huge thanks to all of you, for your belief in me and your support, the opportunity to write this book, and for allowing me to design it, as well.

Thomson Delmar Learning and I are also grateful to the following reviewers for their time and attention, their suggestions, and their expertise:

Donald Bevirt, Chair, Visual & Performing Arts Department
Southwestern Illinois College
Belleville, Illinois

Dawn Carlson, Graphic Design Department
International Academy of Design & Technology
Tampa, Florida

Phyllis Owens, Computer Graphics Department
Camden County College
Blackwood, New Jersey

Very special thanks to Melissa Cogswell for ensuring the technical accuracy of this text, and to Mardelle Kunz for her fantastic copyediting!

QUESTIONS AND FEEDBACK

Everyone involved in education at any level is always interested in ideas that might make the process more enjoyable and more rewarding for both teachers and students. We welcome your comments and suggestions for improving this text. You can let us know what you think by writing to us at:

Thomson Delmar Learning
Executive Woods
5 Maxwell Drive
Clifton Park, NY 12065
Attention: Media Arts and Design Team

Toni Toland / toni@tatoland.com

MY VERY SPECIAL STUDENTS:

Jeff Adams
Kate Ambis
Anna Bratslavskaya
Amanda Cohen
Caitlin Douglas
Melissa Evans
Laura Fontana
Kristen Hiegel
Lauren Honig
Tim Hsieh
John Intrater
Lauren Katz
Miriam Langsam
Erin Lustig
Natalie Mammone
Caitlyn McCarthy
Carolina Mendez
Deirdre Merrigan
Nicholas Panas
Megan Paradise
Noah Phillips
J. D. Proulx
Carolyn Rabiner
Jill Savage
Oliver Vignola
Lauren Zuckerman

1 BASIC INGREDIENTS

If you're fairly new to Adobe Illustrator, or if it's been a while since you've played around with it, consider this chapter a refresher course. It doesn't include every aspect of the software, since the rest of the book covers many of the newest and more interesting features.

If you're comfortable with the basic functions, such as opening a new file, saving images, and using the tools, including the Pen tool, use this chapter as a general review.

CREATING A NEW DOCUMENT

When you launch Illustrator, all the palettes, including the most important one, the Toolbar, open. However, you have to create a new document before you can begin to work.

File ➡ New (Command/Ctrl N) will open a dialog box that lets you specify the dimensions of your document, as well as the color mode in which you want to work (Figure 1.1). Setting the color mode is important, since you'll want CMYK for anything you are going to print, and RGB for anything that will be placed on the Web.

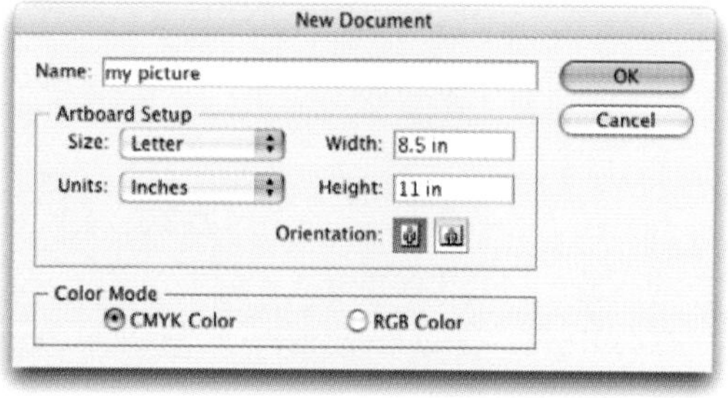

You can choose an artboard size from the pop-up menu, or type in your own dimensions in the width and height fields. You can also choose portrait, or landscape orientation. If you type in a width that's larger than the height, Illustrator automatically selects landscape orientation.

You'll also note an opportunity to set your unit of measure. You can type in any unit of measure in the width and height fields (for instance 51p by 66p for picas) and Illustrator will convert them to inches (8.5" x 11").

Figure 1.1 Choices you make in the New Document dialog box include size, orientation, and color mode.

Clicking OK opens your work area, which consists of the artboard—where you work—with space around it (the pasteboard) where you can work as well. Anything left outside your document margins (the artboard) won't print. It's a great place to experiment, and to place items you need to work with, but don't need in a final image (like a pattern tile).

New in CS2 is a palette across the top called the Control bar (Figure 1.3). Its purpose is to combine several characteristics of, and options for, any particular tool or object into one handy space. Because it's a "dynamic" palette, its options change as you select different tools and elements.

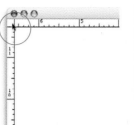

Figure 1.2 Set your ruler's zero point by clicking and dragging the + icon where the two rulers meet to a new location. If your rulers aren't showing, use Command/Ctrl R (or View ➡ Rulers).

Figure 1.3 Set your measurement units by Control/ right-clicking in the ruler.

Hide or show the artboard and/or page tiling, bounding box, and other aspects of the work area from the View menu.

Open palettes from the Window menu; collapse palettes by double-clicking in the gray bar across the top or clicking the green dot on a Mac, or clicking the x-box in the top right corner for PCs.

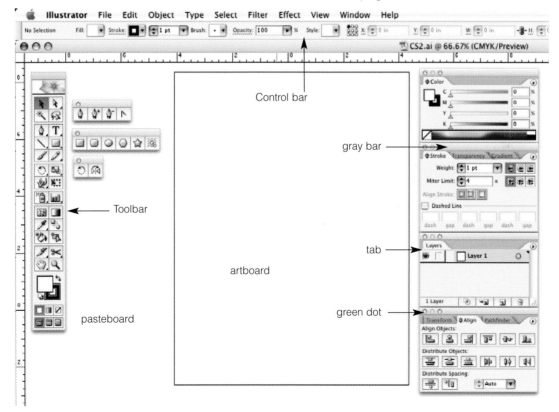

Control bar

gray bar

Toolbar

tab

artboard

green dot

pasteboard

The fill and stroke color options present the colors in your Swatches palette. Unless you've opened one of the Swatch Libraries first, your choices are limited to the default colors.

Open the various other palettes from the Window menu. Some palettes are grouped with others; you just need to click the tab within the palette set to bring the desired one to the front. You can also separate them by dragging the tab out of the palette set. This can be very convenient: regroup them, or reorganize them into different sets by dragging the tab of one palette into the gray space of another (Figure 1.4).

You can also "tear off" sets of tools from the Toolbar, which saves a lot of time unless you use the keystroke shortcuts to select your tools.

To separate a bar of tools from the Toolbar click and hold, then drag your mouse to the "tear-off" tab at the far right and let go (Figure 1.5). You'll notice a small dot at the top left of a torn-off tools palette (or top right x-box on PCs). Clicking that will snap the tools back to the Toolbar where they belong.

PREFERENCES

Preferences establish the ways in which you like to work. Understanding which Illustrator behaviors are affected by setting preferences is important. For instance, not knowing how to get rid of the blue smart guides and slices that follow your cursor around might make you crazy. Open the Preferences panel (Figure 1.6) using the Command/Ctrl K shortcut, or selecting Preferences from the Illustrator/Edit menu.

Here are the essentials:

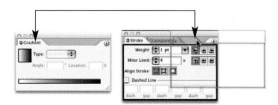
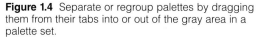

Figure 1.4 Separate or regroup palettes by dragging them from their tabs into or out of the gray area in a palette set.

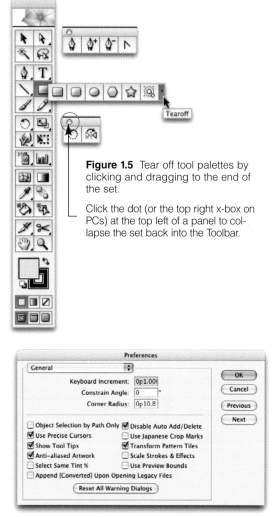

Figure 1.5 Tear off tool palettes by clicking and dragging to the end of the set.

Click the dot (or the top right x-box on PCs) at the top left of a panel to collapse the set back into the Toolbar.

Figure 1.6 Establishing your preferences for how Illustrator looks and works can streamline your efforts.

General: Set your preferences for selecting objects, how things display, and pen behavior, along with basic transformation options.

Smart Guides & Slices: Uncheck all the display options if you don't want blue lines and captions following the cursor's every move; also set your constrain angles and Snapping Tolerance here (Figure 1.7).

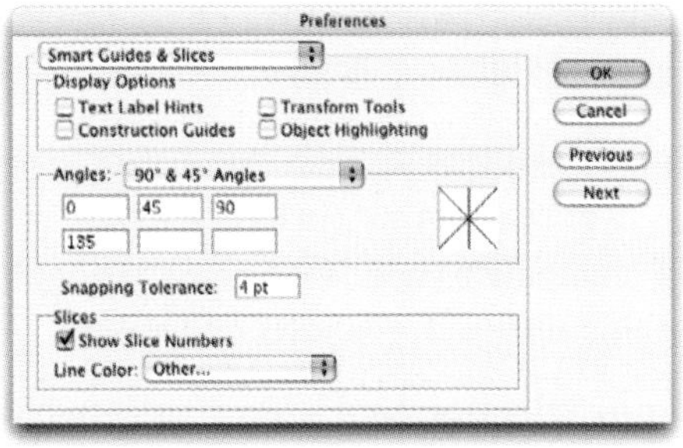

Type: One preference for type that many artists in this book prefer is to select type the Type Object Selection by Path (Baseline) Only option. This isolates the type from other objects and makes it easier to select. Other options can be modified using the Type palette.

File Handling & Clipboard: Establish whether or not to use Version Cue (Adobe's new file management system), how placed files are handled, and what to do with objects in your clipboard when you exit Illustrator.

TOOLS REVIEW

Most of you may be familiar with the tools in Illustrator. They haven't changed much over the last couple of versions (with the exception of the new Live Paint options). Here's a quick review of the tools and what they do (Figure 1.8).

Remember, to make something happen, you must first select the object (with a Selection tool), then perform the manipulation or transformation you want. If you want to manipulate the entire object, and not just part of it, make sure all the points on the object are solid.

Selection tool (solid arrow): Selects entire objects. If the object is part of a larger group, this tool selects the whole group.

Figure 1.7 If you don't like guide lines and label hints following your every move, turn them off in the Smart Guides & Slices preferences pane.

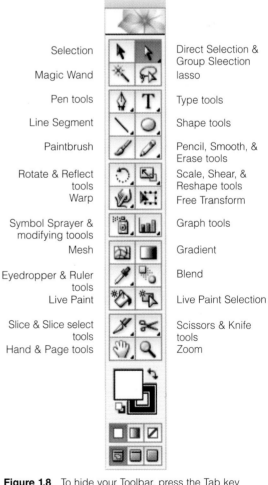

Figure 1.8 To hide your Toolbar, press the Tab key (which will hide all your palettes) or close it from the Window menu.

Direct Selection tool (hollow arrow, at left): selects only a point or portion of a path so you can manipulate parts of an object without disturbing other areas or parts of a group.

Group Selection tool (with plus sign, hidden behind the Direct Selection tool): Selects an entire object or path, exclusive of any other objects that may be part of the same group as the selected object.

NOTE: To shortcut or toggle between any other tool you may be using and a Selection tool (the one you used last), hold down the Command/Ctrl key. This will turn your tool into an arrow tool cursor as long as you hold it down. When you let go, the cursor will turn back into the icon for the tool you were using.

Magic Wand tool: Selects objects with the same characteristics as the one you click on—the same fill and stroke colors. If you have the same stroke applied to various objects but different fills, the Magic Wand will only select the ones that are identical (Figure 1.9). To add to a selection, hold the Shift key and click on something else. To subtract from a selection, hold the Option/Alt key and click on the object you want to deselect.

Lasso tool: Select a portion of an object by encircling it with this freeform tool (Figure 1.10).

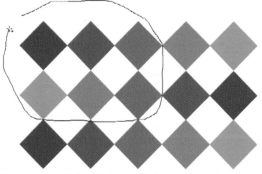

Figure 1.9 Use the Magic Wand to select objects with the same fill and stroke colors.

Figure 1.10 Click and drag with the Lasso tool to select parts of things.

Pen tool: This works in a click, or click and drag behavior. Click to place corner points (points which define sharp corners) or click and drag to place curve points (those which define a curved portion of a line).

Add Anchor Point tool (with plus sign): Click on the path where you want an additional anchor point.

Delete Anchor Point tool (with minus sign): Select the path from which you want to delete a point and click on the point you want eliminated.

Convert Anchor Point tool: With the path selected, click on the point that you want to change. If you are changing a corner point to a curve point, drag your mouse in the direction of the curve you want. To change a smooth (curve) point to a corner point, just click on it.

There's a section after this that describes using the Pen tool, as well as a video you can watch in the "intro" folder on your DVD.

Type tools: Click and drag to create a text box, or click to create an insertion point, and type. Triple-clicking on top of existing type will select the entire paragraph for editing or changing the typeface, size, and so forth. When you're finished typing, click on another tool. If you want to type something separate from the first text object, click the Type tool again. To access this tool without selecting it from the Toolbar, double-click on any existing text.

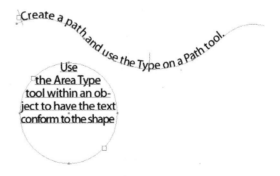

Figure 1.11 The Type tools allow you to create text in a variety of ways. Click and drag with the Type tool to create a bounding box.

Area Type tool (in shape): Draw a shape with any tool, then use this tool to type within that shape: click on the edge of the shape to start.

Type on a Path tool (with wavy line): This allows you to position type along a previously drawn path.

NOTE: The last three Type tools will generate your type the same as the first three, except with the letters stacked vertically rather than horizontally.

Line Segment tool: Click and drag to create a straight line in any direction; click once to specify length and direction.

Arc tool: This draws quarter circles (arcs). Click and drag, or click once to specify your parameters.

Spiral tool: Create spirals by clicking and dragging (Figure 1.12). Or, click once to specify how may whorls you want and how big.

Rectangular Grid tool: Either click and drag, or click once to specify the dimensions of the grid, and the number of rows and columns. The resulting grid will have the stroke and fill colors currently selected (which, of course, can be changed at any time).

Polar Grid tool: Create concentric circles with pie shapes intersecting it. Either click and drag, or click once to access the options for this tool.

NOTE: To create shapes with specific dimensions, click once with the tool (rather than clicking and dragging) and a dialog box will appear; you can type in dimensions and attributes in the dialog box, click OK, and the object will be drawn to your specifications.

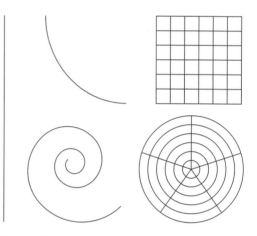

Figure 1.12 With the Arc, Spiral, Rectangular Grid, and Polar Grid tools, click and drag to create the object, or click once to specify dimensions, direction, and angle.

Rectangle tool: This draws rectangles from the corner. Constrain to a square by holding down the Shift key. Toggle from drawing from a corner to drawing from the middle by double-clicking on the tool icon itself, or hold down the Option/Alt key while you click and drag.

Rounded Rectangle tool: This draws a TV shape from the corner. You can change the radius of the corner by clicking once with the tool to get a dialog box.

Ellipse tool: As with the Rectangle tool, constrain to circles using the Shift key, and resize and/or reshape a drawn oval with the Scale tool.

Polygon tool: Click and drag to create a polygon. Just click once to specify the number of sides and the size you want (a great way to make triangles!).

Star tool: Click and drag to create a five-pointed star (the default). Click once to specify the number of points and the size of the star. Radius 1 equals the outer dimensions of the star. Radius 2 establishes the distance between the center of the star and the inner angles (Figure 1.14).

Flare tool: Click once to specify the number of rays and other parameters. This creates the illusion of a lens flare, so it works best when you use it on top of an existing element.

NOTE: Draw from the center of any of these shapes (rather than from a corner) by holding down the Option/Alt key. Constrain the shape to a perfect square or circle by holding the Shift key as you drag your shape.

Figure 1.13 Click and drag with the shape tools.

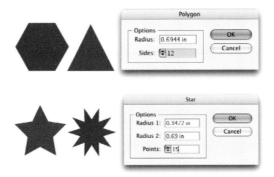

Figure 1.14 Click once with a shape tool to specify size, number of sides, or points.

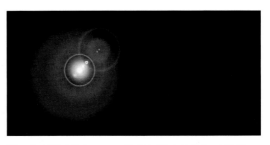

Figure 1.15 Click once with the Flare tool to access the various options for setting the effect.

Paintbrush tool: This allows you to "paint" freeform lines, which are actually paths that imitate calligraphy or other brush styles. Never make the mistake of using it to color the interior of a shape!

Pencil tool: Click and drag to draw any shape/contour. You can set the frequency that anchor points occur along your path by double-clicking the tool in the Toolbar.

Smooth tool: After you've drawn a shape with the Pencil, click and drag over portions of the edge to smooth them out a bit.

Erase tool: Drag across any portion of a line to delete it. You can turn one line into several by erasing parts in the middle.

NOTE: To get a dialog box with any of the following transformation tools, choose the tool you want, and hold down the Option/Alt key when you click on a selected object. A dialog box will allow you to specify what you want the tool to do. Or, double-click on the tool in the Toolbar.

Rotate tool: Make sure to select your object first, then choose the Rotate tool. Click first to create a registration point, then click and drag the tool to rotate your object (Figure 1.18). You can rotate an object 45° or 90° by holding down the Shift key as you drag the object. To rotate an object to a specific degree, hold the Option/Alt key down as you click to place your origin; a dialog box will allow you to specify the degree of rotation.

Figure 1.16 Click and drag with the Paintbrush to create a path. Use the Brushes palette to specify the size and style of the brush stroke.

Figure 1.17 Use the Pencil tool by clicking and dragging. Select a path and drag with the Smooth tool to soften edges. Click and drag along a selected path to delete parts with the Eraser.

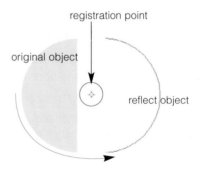

Figure 1.18 Click to create your registration point, then click and drag to reflect (above) or rotate your object (below). The unfilled outline reflects your new position.

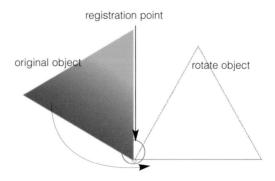

Reflect tool: This tool creates a mirror image of the selected element—it can also rotate that element, as the mirror image is being created. Be careful! Clicking on or near a selected element using the Option/Alt key pulls up a dialog box that allows you to specify the direction of the reflection.

Scale tool: Click once near your selected object to place the registration point. Then click and drag your mouse. The outline of your resized element will appear. Let go of the mouse button when the object is the desired size (Figure 1.19). Or hold down the Option/Alt key and click once to get a dialog box where you can specify the exact percentage you want to scale the selected object.

Shear tool: Again, click to place an origin for the skew, then click and drag to slant your object. Hold the Shift key to skew in only one direction.

Reshape tool: This adds anchor points to the edges of an object where you click, or moves existing anchor points when you click and drag them.

Warp tools: These effects are also available under the Effects menu. Either click and hold on the edge of a shape, or click and drag to create these effects (Figure 1.20).

Warp tool: Click and drag on an object to distort it in weird blobby ways.

Twirl tool: Click on an area of an object to make twirly shapes appear at the edges.

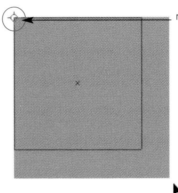

registration point

Figure 1.19 Click to establish the point from which you want to scale, then click and drag. Hold the Shift key to constrain your proportions.

Pucker tool: Click on an object to have it contract in weird places.

Bloat tool: This tool makes edges expand in blobs—click and drag over the selected object.

Scallop tool: Click on an object to create a scalloped edge.

Crystallize tool: This is similar to the scallop tool, but the edges are more rounded.

Wrinkle tool: Use this tool to create a nicely wrinkled look to an edge.

NOTE: These tools all appear as a huge round cursor. To change the shape of the cursor, hold down the Option/Alt key and click and drag to create a new shape and/or size.

Free Transform tool: Select an object first. This tool allows you to distort it in several ways (rotate, scale, etc.), including making something appear in perspective. To distort your shape using individual anchor points, place the cursor at the corner of the bounding box and after you begin to drag, hold down the Command/Ctrl key.

Symbol tools: In the Symbols palette, you will find a variety of predefined symbols. The symbol tools are used to place these images in your document as you click and drag. You can even make your own symbols by creating something, selecting it, and dragging it to the Symbols palette (Figure 1.21).

First, you have to use the Symbol Sprayer tool—select a symbol from the Symbols palette, which may be hidden beneath the Swatches or

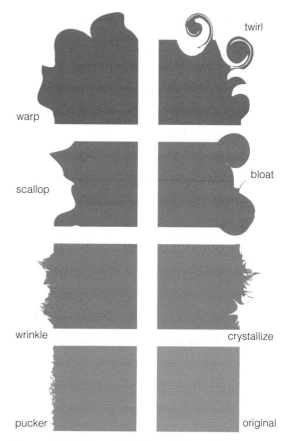

Figure 1.20 Click and hold for a bit, then drag to distort an object.

Brushes palette. If you can't find it, click on the Window menu, and select Symbols. Next, click and drag with the Symbol Sprayer—it looks like an aerosol can. A bounding box surrounds the area where your symbols appear.

Use any of the other tools to modify the symbol "instance." The bounding box must be selected in order for these to work.

The tools behind the Symbol Sprayer shift, scrunch, resize, spin (change the rotation of the symbols at random), stain (select a different fill color first), screen (make the symbols lighter), and style (choose a predefined style from the Graphic Styles palette first) selected symbols.

Graph tools: These tools create different kinds of graphs and charts. You must have data to enter into the dialog box that will appear when you click or click and drag with this tool. The numbers you enter are automatically plotted along the X or Y axis, and translated into the selected chart format. This set of tools is especially valuable for annual reports.

Mesh tool: This creates a grid-like substructure within an existing object and fills the object with a gradient (Figure 1.23). It's a great way to add unusual (i.e., not linear or radial) color gradients to your work. More control over this tool is available using the Object menu.

Figure 1.21 Click and drag with the Symbol Sprayer to lay down a series of symbols (select a symbol from the Symbols palette first). Use the modifying tools to distort the symbols.

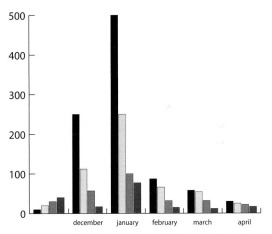

Figure 1.22 Click and drag to establish the size and shape of your graph, then enter the X and Y coordinates. You can change the default colors once you've finished entering information. Use the Direct Selection tool to select individual elements.

Gradient tool: After you've applied a gradient fill to an object, you can alter the direction of the gradient by clicking and dragging inside the selected object with this tool.

Eyedropper tool: This will change your stroke and/or fill color to the color of the object you click on. It's particularly useful if you want to use a color again, but forgot the CMYK values. If something is selected when you click on another object, the fill and stroke of the selected object will change to match. Use the Option/Alt key to change this into a filled Eyedropper cursor you can use to fill an unselected object.

Measure tool: Click two different places to see how far apart the clicks were, and at what angle they were to each other. Holding the Shift key as you click will give you the measurement of just one direction (horizontal, or vertical). These measurements then appear in the Info palette, which opens automatically when you first click with the ruler icon.

Live Paint Bucket tool: Click on an object within a Live Paint group to fill it. Use the Option/Alt key to change this into an Eyedropper (Figure 1.24).

Live Paint Selection tool: Use this to select areas of a Live Paint group so you can then fill

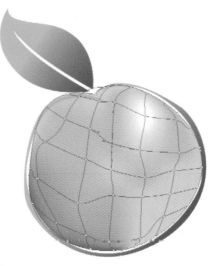

Figure 1.23 The Mesh tool divides an object into a grid that you can then color individually using the mesh points.

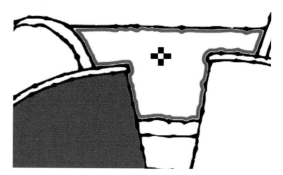

Figure 1.24 To fill a Live Paint object, select your fill color and click with the Live Paint Bucket wherever you want that color. A large red outline appears as your cursor moves over Live Paint areas.

them using the Swatches palette or Color palette (Figure 1.25).

Blend tool: This creates a series of steps between objects or paths. Click on a point in the first object, then click on a point in the second object to create the blend (Figure 1.26). Use Object ➡ Blend ➡ Blend Options to specify the number of intermediary steps or smooth color blends, or simply double-click the tool in the Toolbar.

Slice tool: Use this to create slices used to divide an image into individual rectangular shapes for the Web, or to add interactivity to an image for a web site.

Slice Selection tool: Once you have slices in your file, use this to select them.

Scissors tool: This snips a path into parts. Just click on the path of the object you want to cut.

Knife tool: Slice one or more objects into bits and pieces by dragging this tool across it (Figure 1.27).

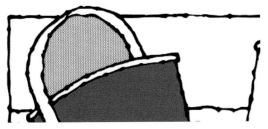

Hand tool: This allows you to grab and move your viewing area around in the Window (known as "scrolling").

Page tool: This adjusts the page grid—which is the printable area as defined by the page size you specify for your document and your current

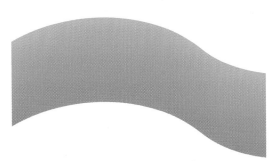

Figure 1.25 Use the Live Paint Selection tool to select Live Paint areas. Fill them with color using the Color or Swatches palettes.

Figure 1.26 Use the Blend tool to create color shifts that are not radial or linear.

Figure 1.27 Click and drag across objects with the Knife tool to slice them into bits.

printer—indicated by the dotted lines around the page margins (Figure 1.28).

NOTE: To shortcut using the Hand tool, hold the Spacebar and click and drag around in the document window to scroll. Double-click on the hand icon in the Toolbar to get the "fit in window" view. Or type Command/Ctrl 0 (zero).

Zoom tool: Click on the portion of the image you want enlarged (this gives you a closer view, but does not change the actual size of the object). Toggle between zoom-in and zoom-out by holding the Option/Alt key.

NOTE: To shortcut using this tool, hold the Spacebar Option/Spacebar Alt keys. Your cursor will change into a magnifying glass icon. Click the area you wish to view closer (or click and drag).

The shortcut for zooming out is to hold down the Spacebar Command Option/Spacebar /Ctrl Alt keys, and then clicking.

Many tools have options that you can set by double-clicking the tool in the Toolbar. These include:

Selection and **Direct Selection tools**: Determine move options.

Magic Wand tool: Set the tolerance, fill, and stroke characteristics to select.

Line Segment tool: Establish the line length and angle.

Paintbrush and **Pencil tools**: Set the tolerances for placing anchor points and editing options.

Rotate and **Reflect tools**: Specify the direction, angle, and whether you want a copy.

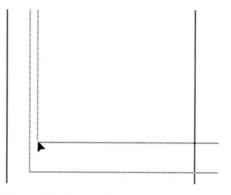

Figure 1.28 Use the Page tool to establish the printable area within a document.

Figure 1.29 Double-clicking a tool in the Toolbar lets you set your preferences for how that tool works.

Scale tool: Specify uniform or nonproportional percentages, and the object's characteristics to scale (stroke weight and effects, object, and pattern fills).

Shear tool: Determine the shear angle and axis, along with characteristics.

Warp tools: Set the dimensions and warp options, plus whether to use a precise or brush size cursor, and the option to use a stylus and pressure sensitive tablet (Figure 1.29).

Symbol Sprayer tool: Select the kind, along with the diameter and intensity (how many symbols occur along a given length) of the symbols sprayed.

Graph tools: Select the type of graph you want, and specify where Illustrator should place the legend. You can also specify column width and add a drop shadow to your graph.

Eyedropper tool: Establish which characteristics it selects and/or applies.

Blend tool: Decide whether to blend in steps or smooth color and whether to orient the blend to the page or to a path.

Live Paint Bucket tool: The Live Paint feature in CS2 allows you to choose to fill paths and/or strokes and set the highlight color and weight of selected objects. In CS, the Paint Bucket fills the characteristics you check in the list.

Live Paint Selection tool: Choose to select fills and/or strokes.

Hand: Double-clicking this sets your view to fit the window.

Zoom: Sets your view to 100%.

You can also access the options for several tools by holding Option/Alt and clicking once

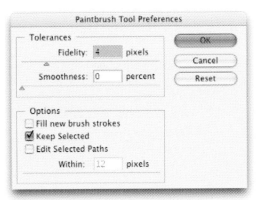

Figure 1.30 Set your Paintbrush and Live Paint Bucket options by double-clicking those tools in the Toolbar.

KEYSTROKE SHORTCUTS WORTH MEMORIZING

TO DO THIS	MAC	WINDOWS
Scroll around workspace	Spacebar	Spacebar
Zoom in	Spacebar Command, click & drag	Spacebar Ctrl, click & drag
Zoom out	Spacebar Command option, click	Spacebar Ctrl Alt, click
Enlarge view	Command +	Ctrl +
Reduce view	Command -	Ctrl -
Fit in window	Command 0	Ctrl 0
100% view	Command 1	Ctrl 1
Show/hide rulers	Command R	Ctrl R
New	Command N	Ctrl N
Open	Command O	Ctrl O
Close window	Command W	Ctrl W
Save	Command S	Ctrl S
Print	Command P	Ctrl P
Quit	Command Q	Ctrl Q
Undo	Command Z	Ctrl Z
Redo	Command Shift Z	Ctrl Shift Z
Cut	Command X	Ctrl X
Copy	Command C	Ctrl C
Paste	Command V	Ctrl V
Paste in front	Command F	Ctrl F
Paste in back	Command B	Ctrl B
Select all	Command A	Ctrl A
Deselect all	Command Shift A	Ctrl Shift A
Join	Command J	Ctrl J
Average + join	Command Option Shift J	Ctrl Alt Shift J
Make guide	Command 5	Ctrl 5
Release guide	Command Option Shift, double-click guide	Ctrl Alt Shift. double-click guide
Make compound path	Command 8	Ctrl 8
Make mask	Command 7	Ctrl 7
Show Type palettes	Command T	Ctrl T
Preview/artwork mode	Command Y	Ctrl Y
Transform again	Command D	Ctrl D
Group	Command G	Ctrl G
Constrain	Shift	Shift
Create from center	Option	Alt
Add or subtract from selection	Shift	Shift
Toggle to Selection tool	Command	Ctrl
Duplicate while dragging	Option	Alt

Figure 1.31 Print this list of shortcuts from the file in the "basic ingredients" folder on your DVD.

with the tool in the artboard or pasteboard area. This can be more efficient since you're setting the options and creating or transforming your object at the same time.

KEYSTROKE SHORTCUTS

There is a printable PDF file of the keystroke shortcuts in the "basic ingredients" folder on your DVD. In the meantime, each chapter highlights several so that you should be very comfortable with them by the time you're finished.

There are several shortcuts worth mentioning now, however.

The Direct Selection tool is a very powerful beast. It can do almost anything you need it to do, including select a group.

To be most effective, get in the habit of clicking on the Direct Selection tool (the hollow arrow) when you first launch Illustrator. This makes it the "last" Selection tool you used. (Another good habit is to show your rulers: Command/Ctrl R.)

Once you've highlighted the Direct Selection tool, go on about your work. Whenever you need to select something, just hold the Command/Ctrl key to access the Direct Selection tool without having to go get it from the Toolbar. If you didn't select it before trying this shortcut, you'll toggle to the Selection tool instead. Nice, but not when you want to adjust anchor points.

If you need the Group Selection tool (hidden behind the Direct Selection tool) to select an entire group, hold Command Option/Ctrl Alt together. Click once on an object in the group, then click again to select the rest of it.

You'll be amazed how easy this is to remember after some conscious practice, and it's a huge time saver. You'll notice in the how-to videos on the DVD that the artist is using this technique almost all the time.

Another shortcut that you'll use often is the drag/copy feature. Hold the Option/Alt key as you move something to create a copy of it. If you're using another tool, hold the Command/Ctrl key to toggle to the Selection tool, along with the Option/Alt key when you drag your object.

And here's one you won't find on any of the menus: average two points and join them in one step—Command Option Shift J/Ctrl Alt Shift J. Very nice.

NOTE: When using Command Option Shift/Ctrl Alt Shift and double-clicking to release a guide, make sure you delete it right away. If you don't, you've essentially created an invisible path the entire width or height of the workspace—a bit over 224"! This can really mess things up later on!

 THE LAYERS PALETTE

The power of using the Layers palette to select, and to rearrange, elements should never be underestimated. Creating layers to separate and label different objects within a complex image is the mark of a true professional. There's a file called "layers.eps" in the "basic ingredients" folder for you to play with as we review this important piece of Illustrator.

To select everything on one layer, click the circle next to the layer name.

To see all the objects on a layer, click the gray triangle to the left of the layer name.

Any grouped objects are displayed with a <Group> name and a gray triangle. You can select the entire group by clicking the circle, or open it by clicking the gray triangle to see each element in the group.

To select random elements, click and shift-click the circles to the right of the layers or sublayers you want.

Remember, too, that you can reorder objects by dragging the sublayers, and layers themselves, up or down in the palette. Watch for a grey bar between two layers to indicate that's where you're dragging something before letting go of the mouse button.

Something most of the artists featured in this text do is scan a sketch or tight drawing to use as a template to help them re-create their idea. The Layers palette is one place where you can designate a layer as a template. After placing or opening a scan directly into Illustrator, use the Layer palette's submenu to turn it into a template. This dims the scan to 50% (double-click the Template layer's name to change that percentage, if you want), and locks it so you can't inadvertently move your scan or otherwise mess with it.

If you've already got an Illustrator document open and you want to place an image to use as a template, make sure you click the Template option at the bottom of the Place dialog box. This makes the placed image a Template layer automatically, and adds a layer for you to draw on all in one step.

Note that you can unlock and draw on a Template layer, but that can be dangerous. If you need to unlock your Template layer to modify your scan (enlarge it, or rotate it, for instance), make sure you lock it again right away.

One huge advantage to creating Template layers is that when you switch to Outline view, you can still see the placed image. If you mere-

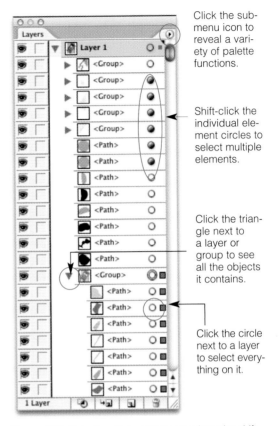

Click the submenu icon to reveal a variety of palette functions.

Shift-click the individual element circles to select multiple elements.

Click the triangle next to a layer or group to see all the objects it contains.

Click the circle next to a layer to select everything on it.

Figure 1.32 Select multiple objects on a layer by shift-clicking the circles on the right. The blue boxes indicate what's selected.

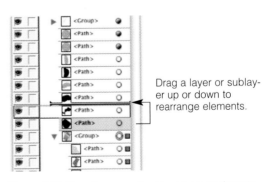

Drag a layer or sublayer up or down to rearrange elements.

Figure 1.33 Drag layers and sublayers up or down to rearrange the stacking order.

ly lock the layer, outline view will only show you the rectangle where the image exists (Figure 1.34).

THE KEY TO TRUE MASTERY: THE PEN TOOL

The Pen tool is perhaps the most difficult, and most valuable, drawing tool you have to work with in Illustrator. It deserves a review here to remind you of the power of the pen.

First, a brief note about the concept behind this amazing tool.

You probably remember (and perhaps not too fondly) dealing with geometry somewhere along your academic career. There was this exercise about doing calculations with the answers resulting in plotting points along X and Y axes. When you had enough points plotted, you could connect the dots, so to speak. That's essentially how the Pen tool works (Figure 1.35 and 1.36).

Fortunately for us, Pierre Bézier (bez' e ay) pioneered the equation that allowed for curved connections between those plotted points. It's his discovery that is the basis for the Pen tool, along with Adobe's PostScript language.

And, while corner points are single points, curve points have control handles that can be adjusted in and out, and up and down, to influence the nature of the curved path before it and after it.

First, take a look at the phases of the Pen tool. It's important to recognize the symbols next to the pen icon so you know what's happening.

Before you place any points, the Pen will have an X next to it. As you continue to click and drag, you will see solid arrowheads. In between clicks, the Pen tool is plain.

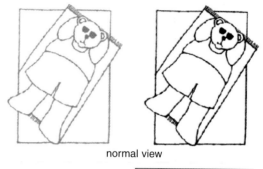

normal view

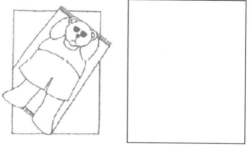

outline view

Figure 1.34 Making a Template layer vs. just locking a layer to trace from has advantages. When you switch to outline view, your locked image disappears (below) if you don't make the layer a Template layer.

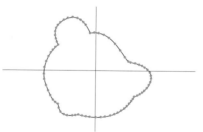

Figure 1.35 If you do enough math, eventually you might be able to create something by plotting the points. Why bother when the Pen tool can do it for you?

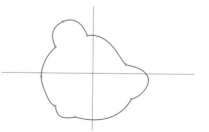

Figure 1.36 Bézier points now describe curved and linear shapes in fewer points.

If you've deselected a path and want to continue working on it, move the Pen tool to the end of the path until you see the slash mark. Click on the last point of the path and continue drawing.

When you're about to close a path, you'll see a circle icon. Since Illustrator fills objects from the first to last point, it's important to close your paths if you want a completely filled shape.

You'll note that there are both normal and precise icons for the Pen tool. Which one you use is an individual preference, and can be set in the General Preferences pane. Or, you can toggle back and forth between the two by using the Caps Lock key.

There are several little QuickTime movies that demonstrate using the Pen tool in the "movFiles" folder within the "basic ingredients" folder on your DVD. You might want to take a minute to look at them.

In the meantime, here's how it works.

To create corner points, you just click, move your cursor, and click again. Illustrator creates a path between the two points. Continue around until you see a little circle icon next to the Pen tool cursor to indicate you're about to complete your shape.

Curve points can be a bit trickier. To create curves, you click and drag in one smooth motion. The dragging action pulls handles out from the points you place. These handles, their length and relationship to the path, are what create a curved path.

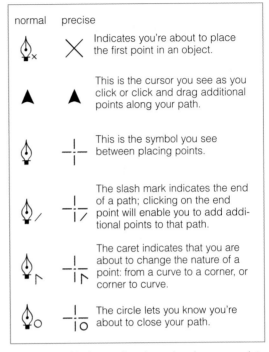

Figure 1.37 Understanding the various icons associated with the Pen tool will help you work more efficiently.

normal   precise

- Indicates you're about to place the first point in an object.
- This is the cursor you see as you click or click and drag additional points along your path.
- This is the symbol you see between placing points.
- The slash mark indicates the end of a path; clicking on the end point will enable you to add additional points to that path.
- The caret indicates that you are about to change the nature of a point: from a curve to a corner, or corner to curve.
- The circle lets you know you're about to close your path.

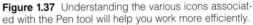

Figure 1.38 Click with the Pen tool to place a point at strategic corners. When you're drawing straight lines, you only need to place a point at each corner.

Figure 1.39 As you click and drag, you pull handles from the point. These handles determine the shape of the curve you're making, as well as the one to come.

NOTE: Most people have a tendency, when just starting out, to click on the end of a handle to create another point. Don't go there! Move your pen some distance away before placing another point.

Longer handles create smoother curves, and shorter handles create more severe curves. The distance between curve points also influences the shape of the curve (Figure 1.41).

While it would be nice if every shape you needed was a simple curve or straight line, there are many occasions when you need a combination: a straight line moving into a curve and vice versa, or a broken curve, like a scallop.

Here's where that little caret symbol comes into play.

When you place a corner point that needs to move into a curved portion of a path, click and drag on the corner point to pull out one handle. Notice as you move the Pen over the last point you created, that the little caret icon pops up to let you know you're going to convert the point.

To have a curved path move into a straight one, you need to delete the front half of the handle. Instead of clicking and dragging on the last point, simply click once and that handle will disappear (Figure1.42).

Finally, breaking curve point handles (which typically work in a seesaw way) allows you to create reverse curves or scallops. This requires a keystroke: Option/Alt.

To break a curve handle, hold Option/Alt and move the cursor to the end of the *handle*—not the point itself. It will look like a caret, without any Pen tool cursor next to it. Click and drag the end of the handle where you want it.

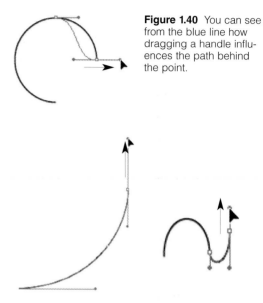

Figure 1.40 You can see from the blue line how dragging a handle influences the path behind the point.

Figure 1.41 Longer handles create smooth curves; shorter handles create more severe curves. The shape of a curve is also influenced by the distance between curve points.

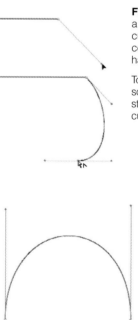

Figure 1.42 To move from a straight segment to a curved one, click on the corner point and drag a handle out.

To eliminate a curve handle so you can create a straight line, click on the curve point once.

Figure 1.43 Hold the Option/Alt key and drag the end of the handle to a new position to create a reverse curve or scallop.

These basic tips should serve you well as you perfect your Pen tool techniques. But what if you've created and finished a shape that isn't quite right? There are several Pen tools available, along with the Direct Selection tool, that can edit existing points and paths.

If you need to add a point to a path to fine-tune it, use the Add Anchor Point tool. Click anywhere on the path; it doesn't have to be selected first.

If you have too many points (which can sometimes happen when you draw with the Pencil or Paintbrush), delete the unnecessary ones with the Delete Anchor Point tool. Select the path first, and click directly on the point.

NOTE: Selecting a point and deleting it using the Delete key will break the path into parts, not eliminate an extra point, unless it's the first or last point on a path.

The Convert Anchor Point tool is used to turn corner points into curves. Click and drag on a corner point to pull out handles (Figure 1.45). To change a curve point to a corner point, just click. If you need to reverse a curve, use this tool on the end of the handle to drag it somewhere else.

If you're not confident with your skills with the Pen tool, there are some scanned leaves and other exercises on the DVD in the "basic ingredients" folder (Figure 1.46). Use them as templates to practice using the Pen tool, adjusting handles, and creating reverse curves.

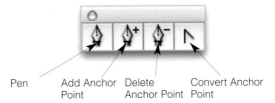

Pen   Add Anchor Point   Delete Anchor Point   Convert Anchor Point

Figure 1.44 Use the Pen tools to add or delete points, to convert one type to another, and to "break" the handles on curve points.

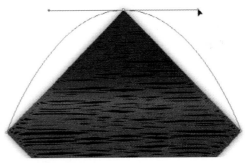

Figure 1.45 Click and drag a corner point with the Convert Anchor Point tool point to turn it into a curve. To change a curve point to a corner, just click.

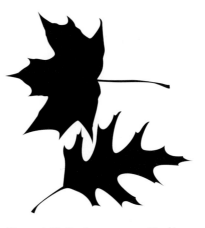

Figure 1.46 Tracing a scanned leaf is a great way to practice using both the Direct Selection tool using the Command/Ctrl key shortcut to modify curve handles, as well as the Option/Alt key to break handles for reversed curves.

> **NOTE:** Many of the artists and designers featured in this book use a pressure-sensitive tablet and pen to draw. The Pen tool works the same whether you are clicking with a mouse or a stylus. If at any point in your drawing you need to make an adjustment to a point or handle, toggle to the Direct Selection tool (hold the Command/Ctrl key), make the alteration, then toggle back to the Pen (let go of the Command/Ctrl key) and continue drawing.

Other tools that are worth reviewing include the transformation tools: Reflect, Rotate, and Scale.

TRANSFORMATIONS

Illustrator provides multiple ways—tools and menu items—to transform objects.

The Object menu offers Transform options including Move, Rotate, Reflect, Scale, and Shear. In addition, you can select several objects and transform them individually, rather than as a group, using Transform Each (Figure 1.47).

There are also tools for transforming; the Rotate and Reflect tools are together in one set, the Scale, Shear, and Reshape tools are right next to those. The key to using these tools is:

1. Select the object you want to transform.

2. Select the transform tool you want to use.

3. Click to set your registration point.

4. Click and drag to transform your object.

If you know how you want something rotated, sheared, reflected, or scaled numerically, hold Option/Alt as you click the registration point to open a dialog box where you can type in specific parameters.

Figure 1.47 Transforming a group by scaling (left), and transforming each using Transform ➡ Transform Each (right).

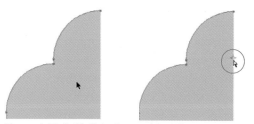

Figure 1.48 (left), Select your object then set your registration point (the place you want the transformation to occur) (right).

COLOR

There are a variety of ways to work with color in Illustrator. The Swatches palette provides basic crayon box colors, and the Color palette is where you can mix your own colors. Open these palettes from the Window menu. Each has a submenu offering several choices.

In Illustrator, you can choose any color system for creating colors (Figure 1.49). That means, even if you're creating an RGB image, you can still mix your colors using CMYK values in the Color palette.

In the upper left corner of the Color palette are the Fill and Stroke options. Click on the filled square to alter a fill color, or the outlined box to change a stroke color (Figure 1.50). The white square with a red slash is transparent—no color. Choose this if you don't want a stroke around something or an object with no fill.

You can also use the bottom portion of your Toolbar to reverse fill and stroke colors, reset the defaults to a black stroke and white fill (just type the letter "d" for "default"—how easy is that?), click on the last used color, and set something to transparent or a gradient fill (Figure 1.50).

The Swatches palette is fairly straightforward. Use the Color palette to focus on fill or stroke, and then click the swatch you want to use (Figure 1.51).

NOTE: You can't assign a gradient to a stroke.

Whenever you mix a new color in the Color palette, you can save it to your Swatches palette to use again one of three ways:

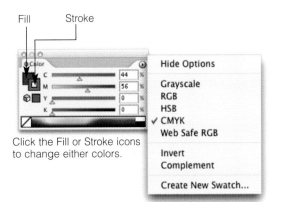

Fill   Stroke

Click the Fill or Stroke icons to change either colors.

Figure 1.49 Create colors by clicking in the spectrum at the bottom, by typing in percentages in the fields to the right of each color, or by dragging the sliders in the color bars.

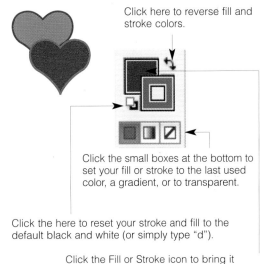

Click here to reverse fill and stroke colors.

Click the small boxes at the bottom to set your fill or stroke to the last used color, a gradient, or to transparent.

Click the here to reset your stroke and fill to the default black and white (or simply type "d").

Click the Fill or Stroke icon to bring it forward so you can change the color.

Figure 1.50 Select an object and use the Toolbar to reverse the fill and stroke colors by clicking on the arrow icon, or reset the colors to the defaults.

- Drag the fill or stroke icon from the Color palette to the Swatches palette.

- Select the object with the color you want to save, and then click the New Swatch icon at the bottom of the Swatches palette.

- Select New Swatch from the Swatches palette's submenu.

You can save gradients and patterns this way too.

Creating a gradient in Illustrator can be a bit confusing. Typically, you create the object you need, and then use the Gradient palette to fill it. By default, Illustrator fills your object with a black-to-white linear gradient. This, in turn, changes the mode of your Color palette from CMYK, or RGB, to Grayscale.

To change the colors in the gradient, click on one of the color stops in the gradient bar to focus on it. Then change the color mode back to CMYK (or RGB) in the Color palette and select a new color. Repeat this for the second color stop.

If you want to add more colors to a gradient, click below the gradient bar to add a color stop. Since you're already in CMYK (or RGB) mode at this point, just click the new color stop and then use the Color palette to select the color you want.

SAVING AND EXPORTING

You can save Illustrator files in several different file formats: the native AI, as an EPS (Encapsulated PostScript), as a PDF, as a template, or as an SVG (Scalable Vector Graphic) file. What you're going to do with the file determines which format to use.

Choose **AI** or **EPS** if you plan to continue working on the file in Illustrator.

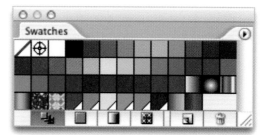

Figure 1.51 The Swatches palette contains the basic crayon colors, a couple of patterns, and some gradients. We'll be playing with this a lot in the coming chapters!

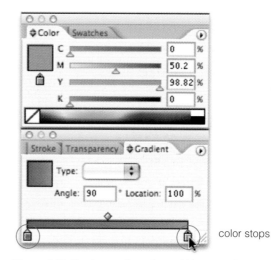

color stops

Figure 1.52 To change the colors within a gradient, click a color stop in the Gradient palette, then select a new color from the Color palette. If your colors are set to Grayscale, select CMYK from the Color palette's submenu.

Choose **EPS** if you plan to use the file in another application, like QuarkXPress.

PDF (Portable Document Format) is excellent if you need to share the file with someone via e-mail or FTP (File Transfer Protocol).

Select **SVG** (Scalable Vector Graphic) if the image is to be used on the Web.

In addition, you can export Illustrator files for other uses. When you choose File ➡ Export, you can choose from:

BMP (BitMaP): A bitmap format.

Targa: Another bitmap format.

PNG (Portable Network Graphic): Choose this if you're going to work on the image in Fireworks, or if you want to import it into Flash.

AutoCAD Drawing: This keeps the paths intact as vector information, and deletes any colors.

EMF (Enhanced Metafile): A standard Windows vector image.

Macromedia Flash: This saves the image in SWF (Shockwave Flash) format.

JPEG (Joint Photographers Expert Group): A lossy compression system that rasterizes the file and deletes some data to make it smaller. Choose this if you're placing the image on the Web, or want to e-mail it to someone for approval.

PICT (PICTure): another compression system appropriate for low resolution, flat graphic images—that is, those with no gradients, tints, or transparencies.

Photoshop: Use this if you want to retain layers and work further on your image in Photoshop.

Figure 1.53 Saving for AutoCAD applications retains the vector information, and deletes any colors.

Figure 1.54 You have several choices of file format when you export the file, rather than saving it.

TIFF (Tagged Image File Format): A bitmap image for use in other applications like QuarkXPress

Text Format: This will export any text in the image to a text file.

Windows Metafile: Choose this if someone using a PC will be working on the file (Adobe notes that EMF (above) is the preferred format).

PRINTING

Printing from Illustrator is relatively simple when you're printing for proofing purposes. Illustrator's new Print dialog box now includes options for printing when an image is going to be soft proofed or printed commercially.

See Chapter 13 for detailed information about soft-proofing, commercial printing, transparency issues, and other details associated with printing Illustrator files, as well as a couple of interesting DIY exercises.

KEY POINTS

- Illustrator will translate any unit of measure you use into the units used in the current document.

- Use Option/Alt to specify options for the different tools and selected objects.

- "Tear off" any tool sets that you use frequently to save time.

- Change your Preferences to have Illustrator look and behave according to your needs.

- Double-clicking some tools in the Toolbar lets you set their behavior.

- Option/Alt clicking with a tool allows you to specify options for the object you're about to create or transform.

- Draw from the center of a shape by holding the Option/Alt key as you draw.

- Constrain a shape to a perfect square or circle by holding the Shift key as you draw.

- Change the size of the Symbol Reshaping tools using the Option/Alt key.

- To free transform one point at a time, hold the Command/Ctrl key as you begin to drag with the Transform tool.

- Hold the Spacebar to scroll around your document window.

- Keystroke shortcuts save time.

- Select groups or whole layers by clicking the circle in the Layers palette.

- Drag layers up or down in the Layers palette to rearrange elements.

- Master the Pen tool.

2 PETER SINCLAIR

Blending Objects & Blending Modes

Peter Sinclair has developed a digital rendition of cut tissue paper, developing images rich with transparent, overlapping shapes.

Peter Sinclair is perhaps best known for his comic strip "Alex's Restaurant," which has appeared in more than fifty newspapers nationally and internationally, and can be found on the Web at *http://projects.alexsrestaurant.com/alex/*. While these cartoons where originally created in pen and ink with watercolors, Peter has successfully moved them into the digital universe by scanning in his line work and adding color using Painter.

His work in Illustrator is entirely different in style and has appeared in *The New York Times,* among other publications. His current clients include Sendo Ltd, Dow Chemical Co, AGP, Bolger and Battle, DTE Energy, and the Cook County Board of Elections (Chicago).

Peter earned his B. F. A. in painting from the University of Michigan. After graduation, he felt at loose ends, and had no interest in moving east or west. "New York just puts my senses on overload. I love it, but I couldn't survive there for more than five days."

He enrolled in a few first-aid courses, which he found fascinating. This led to a job as a paid paramedic in his hometown of Midland, Michigan.

"Being an EMT is great. I work for twenty-four hours, then have several days off. It gives me lots of time to work on my art."

At one point, Peter was so intrigued with the medical field that he completed the course work required for a nursing license. He worked

Figure 2.1 Peter's comic strip "Alex's Restaurant" has been hailed as "the next Doonesbury."

in an intensive care unit at a local hospital for several years.

"I thrive on stress, but I really thought it was going to kill me. I'd rather be an EMT."

His interest in healthcare also lead him to become certified to practice acupressure, which he's done for the past ten years. "I don't see a lot of clients at this point, though. I'm just too busy."

When he's not working in his studio, gardening, or assisting those in need, Peter practices yoga and tai chi. It's no surprise that he's also a firm believer in a holistic approach to healthcare.

His favorite activity, though, is curling up on the couch with a sketchpad. "Drawing is my touchstone. It keeps me centered."

Figure 2.2 Energy Man: this image was created to demonstrate the benefits of an herbal product for Tinge.

Figure 2.4 "The Further Adventures of Chad & Dimples" is an animated TV commercial Peter created for the Cook County Board of Elections.

Figure 2.3 One of Peter's favorite techniques includes gradients and overlapping, transparent shapes.

Figure 2.5 A series of package design for ShariAnn's organic soups.

He claims it's hard to develop a real style in the Midwest, since the clients are so diverse, and competent illustrators so few.

"Here, you have to be able to do a lot of different things." Which is why he's also involved with package and point-of-purchase design, logo and corporate identity systems, web site development, and television commercials.

Peter uses several different programs, including Flash, to produce animations. He's currently working on an animation project "that's going to take a lot more effort than it's going to pay,

but it's worth it." He's also done several animations in a variety of styles for Dow Chemical, and the Cook County Board of Elections.

Peter is a drawing evangelist. "One of the things that makes me different from a lot of cartoonists is that I can draw. If the drawing isn't good, then the writing better be."

Peter continues to pursue new comic strip ideas, believing that "making people laugh is an art form" in and of itself.

In the meantime, his work using Illustrator captures that belief. Whimsical freeform shapes, exaggerated and distorted features, and unique techniques permeate all his images, whether the client is a major chemical manufacturer or herbal products company.

DIGITAL DECONSTRUCTION: HAPPY MONKEY

This happy guy and many of Peter's other images sport some signature elements: a large grin, overlapping shapes set to Multiply blending mode, and big eyes.

One of the most basic aspects of the monkey is Peter's use of organic freeform shapes that make up the image.

Peter uses his Wacom tablet along with the Pencil tool to generate this spontaneous look. Because he loves to draw and is very skillful with these tools, he doesn't create a sketch or a scan to trace before he begins in Illustrator.

He starts with some fundamental shapes on the base layer: in this case, the tree, the monkey's body (head, arms, torso, tail, and legs), and the rock.

Adding layers as he focuses on developing detail and dimension, Peter stacks small overlapping shapes in a seemingly haphazard fashion to build up a particular area. He uses both flat color and gradient fills, and sets many of the shapes to Multiply in the Transparency palette to create an interplay between the overlapping colors. He also duplicates and offsets transparent objects to get the color density he wants, while also creating interesting "edges" around these shapes.

Other areas worth noting are his big teeth and eyes. Peter has used this technique in many of his images, and we'll take a look at how they're created in a bit.

Figure 2.6 Peter uses a Wacom tablet and the Pencil tool to generate his free-flowing shapes.

DIY:
BLENDING MODES
(AND A BIT MORE)

First, let's play with the Blending modes and Transparency features Illustrator has to offer. If you have a pressure-sensitive tablet, now's the time to pull it out and experiment.

1. In the "sinclair" folder on your DVD, there's a file called "basicmonkey.eps." Open that in Illustrator.

You'll note there are four layers: "monkey" and "tree" are templates for you to use as guides. The other two ("draw monkey" and "draw tree") are where you'll be working. Make sure to leave the "monkey" and "tree layers" locked so you don't move things or draw on them by mistake.

2. For now, hide the "tree" layer so you can work on the monkey without getting confused.

Click the eye in the left column of the Layers palette to hide it.

Notice in Figure 2.8 the number of random shapes Peter used to create the monkey's fur. Underlying all of them are the basic body shapes you'll see on the "monkey" layer.

3. Use the Pencil tool to re-create the head, body, arms, legs, and tail as separate elements. Don't worry about being perfect because you can always undo (Command/Ctrl Z), delete, or edit your shape with the Direct Selection tool.

Fill these shapes with a pale brown/taupe color. The shapes you draw on top will give the fur a darker color over time.

Figure 2.7 Use the "monkey" layer to create the basic body parts, then add the fur shapes.

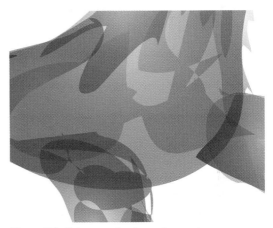

Figure 2.8 Peter uses freeform shapes, transparencies, and Multiply blending mode to create texture and dimension in the monkey's fur.

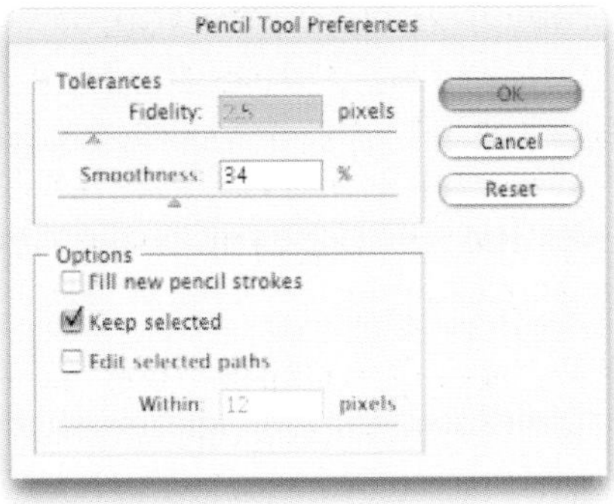

Figure 2.9 Double-click the Pencil tool to set your preferences for how tightly it follows your cursor.

NOTE: Double-click the Pencil tool to set your preferences for how it will work. "Edit selected paths" is something I uncheck so that as I draw shapes, the one I drew previously isn't edited by mistake. Leaving "Keep selected" checked is also handy since you can immediately delete a line you don't like without having to select it again (Figure 2.9).

4. Once the basic body parts are penciled in, go to town with random freeform shapes. For now, fill them with the same shade of brown you used for the body.

5. Select everything but the basic body parts.

   You can do this easily by targeting the object in your Layers palette: click the triangle next to the "draw monkey" layer, and Shift-click to select the objects (Figure 2.10).

   Or, select all (Command/Ctrl A) and then shift-click on the basic body parts to deselect them.

6. Open the Transparency palette. Choose Multiply from the mode pop-up menu (Figure 2.11).

There are a lot of blending options to choose from and each works differently to affect the colors that a blended object overlaps. We'll be looking at some of these options later, but you'll find that Multiply blending mode is a favorite in both Illustrator and Photoshop.

7. Select some shapes and assign them a radial or linear blend from one shade of brown to another, using the Gradient palette.

Peter makes great use of gradients, and one of his favorite tricks is to move the midpoint of the blend to one extreme or another.

Click the eye to hide a layer.

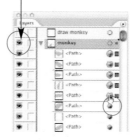

Figure 2.10 You can select individual parts of an image by clicking on the circle in the Layers palette. Shift-click to add to your selection.

Figure 2.11 Choose Multiply from the blend mode pop-up menu.

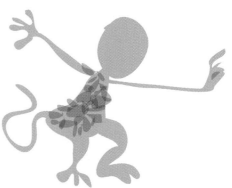

Figure 2.12 Setting shapes to Multiply is like turning them into tissue paper, with overlapping parts becoming darker.

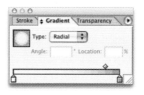

Figure 2.13 Peter exaggerates his gradients by pushing the midpoint to either end.

8. Keep going until you're pleased with the fur, on all parts of the body. Don't worry about his face at this point, but don't forget the hair! Refer back to Figure 2.6 for reference.

While not a part of this DIY, if you want to work on the tree and rock, go right ahead. The more you practice, the better you'll be.

At this point, your monkey should only be lacking his smile and his eyes. We'll work on his smile next. (Save your file before continuing.)

Study Figure 2.14. Note that the lips are made up of several shapes, many of them set to Multiply mode.

9. Add a new layer for your mouth (click the "new layer" icon at the bottom of the Layers palette), and lock your "draw monkey" layer. Click the box in the second column (next to the eye icon) to lock (or unlock) a layer.

10. Create the bottom and top lip as separate filled shapes. (Use the mouth shape on the "monkey" layer as a guide.) Set the Opacity of these shapes to about 50% in the Transparency palette.

Drag a copy (hold your Option/Alt key as you drag) of the bottom lip up a few centimeters, and then down a few centimeters. Make at least three copies, each slightly offset from the original.

Select the original and all the copies, and set their blending mode to Multiply.

11. Repeat this for the top lip. Feel free to add some additional shapes for definition, but don't forget to set their mode to Multiply as well, or they will block out what's happening underneath.

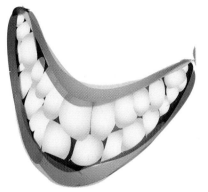

Figure 2.14 The lips are composed of overlapping shapes set to Multiply blending mode.

Figure 2.15 Create the mouth from several transparent shapes that are copied, moved, and set to Multiply.

12. Draw a shape that fills the space between both lips—go ahead and overlap them.

Select this shape and cut it (Command/ Ctrl X) and then paste it behind everything (Command/Ctrl B).

Fill it with a brown to pale yellow radial gradient (Figure 2.16). Make sure nothing else is selected or the gradient will be applied to them as well.

Now for the teeth!

Peter filled the teeth shapes with another radial gradient with a peachy-brown fill at the outside and a pale yellow center. He moved the midpoint all the way to the brown (right) side so that the teeth would be primarily white, with the appearance of shadows around their edges (Figure 2.17).

13. Create the gradient and drag it to your Swatches palette so you don't loose it.

14. Draw some teeth, and fill them with the gradient.

Terrific! A nice toothy grin.

Save your file (Command/Ctrl S). We'll be going back to it.

First, let's take a look at another of Peter's images that uses several of the same techniques.

Figure 2.16 Send the interior mouth shape to the back (Command/Ctrl X, Command/Ctrl B).

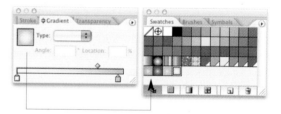

Figure 2.17 Drag the preview box from your Gradient palette to the Swatches palette. If the Swatches palette isn't open, select it from the Window menu.

DIGITAL DECONSTRUCTION: FOCUS

While Illustrator initially intimidated Peter, he realized he "didn't have to understand how it worked, just how to use it." He's found that Illustrator lets him work in ways that other software doesn't. Once he discovered he could draw "freehand," he started learning how to complement and enhance his work.

In this illustration for Tinge, he wanted to portray the benefits of one of their herbal products.

He started with basic shapes: the hair, and face. He filled the face with a circular gradient.

One thing you'll notice about Peter's work is that he doesn't worry about filling every nook and cranny of his images with color. These negative spaces enhance his whimsical approach.

A star shape with (count them!) 88 points and filled with another radial gradient adds some dimension to the face.

The addition of two semitransparent spirals (hand drawn) with radial fills focus the attention on the woman's bright eyes.

And oh, those eyes! They're one of Peter's trademark techniques, and demonstrate his knowledge of drawing, light, and anatomy.

DIY:
BIG EYEBALLS

This feature of many of Peter's images is a small detail that has a huge impact.

1. Open your monkey image if it isn't still available (check File ➡ Open Recent as a shortcut to browsing for it). Lock all the layers and add a new one to draw on above them.

2. Draw a circle where you'd like one of the eyes. Hold the Shift key to make it perfectly round.

3. Fill the circle with a radial gradient from white to dark pink, and shift the midway point almost all the way to the right, toward the pink color stop. Set the stroke to none.

Figure 2.18 Focus: this image was created to demonstrate the benefits of an herbal product.

Figure 2.19 Using a pressure-sensitive tablet and pen, Peter starts with freeform shapes using the Pencil tool, which he then tweaks until it suits him.

Figure 2.20 These freeform spirals have translucent radial fills. One also has a light-blue stroke for detail.

4. Copy and paste your circle in front (Command/Ctrl C, Command/Ctrl F). Delete the fill and set the stroke to a pale red.

   Set the stroke width to .18 point.

5. While this stroked circle is still active, select the Scale tool and Option/Alt click in the middle of the circle.

   Enter 65% and make sure Scale Strokes & Effects is checked. Click Copy (*not* OK) to create another, smaller circle with a thinner stroke.

6. Double-click the Blend tool in the Toolbar, and select Specified Steps from the pop-up menu in the Blend Options dialog box. Specify 10 steps and click OK (Figure 2.21).

   With the Blend tool still selected, click on the top point of the outer circle, and then click on the top point of the inner circle (Figure 2.22).

7. Draw the iris as a perfect circle and fill it with a dark-blue to light-blue gradient, again, moving the gradient's midpoint off to the far right.

8. Select the Star tool (behind the Circle tool) and click in the middle of your eye.

   Type .068" for your outer radius and .03" for your inner radius. Radius 1 is your outside dimension, and Radius 2 is your inside dimension. These numbers are just a rough estimate since there was no dimension specified for your circle (Figure 2.23).

   Set the number of points to thirty-six and click OK.

   Use the Scale tool to adjust the size.

Shift the gradient's midpoint to the right.

Figure 2.21 Specifying a number of steps for a stroked object will create multiple circles that decrease in stroke weight.

Figure 2.22 Concentric circles created with the Blend tool add some depth to the eye.

Figure 2.23 Add the iris as a circle and a star filled with radial gradients.

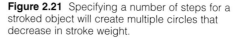

9. Fill the star with a radial gradient that goes from blue in the middle to white, again moving its midpoint to the right.

10. Create and center a black filled circle for the pupil on top of the star.

11. While the Circle tool is still selected, create three white circles toward the top right of the eye (Figure 2.24).

Voila! You have a Peter Sinclair eyeball.

12. Select all your eyeball parts and drag a copy for the other eye.

Notice Peter's monkey also has some upper and lower eyelids. These are created the same way you made the mouth: create one shape and drag-copy it a few times (hold the Option/Alt key), setting each instance of the shape to Multiply.

Add this detail, and save your file. Nice job.

FYI:
BLENDING OPTIONS

There are several ways you can blend objects and paths. The Transparency palette, as you've discovered, has several Blending modes that affect colors beneath an object.

The Blend tool, however, is used to create intermediary steps between two objects or two paths. These steps create a transition from the color and shape of one object to the color and shape of the second one. Use Object ➡ Blend ➡ Blend Options (or simply double-click on the Blend tool in the Toolbar) to decide if you want to blend using smooth color, a specified number of steps, or a specified distance. You can also use this dialog box to orient the blend to the page, or to a path.

A blend always begins with two shapes or two paths. (You can blend between a shape and a

Figure 2.24 Three white circles added to the basic eye create the "pop" that makes these eyes stand out.

Figure 2.25 Add some eyelids on top of your eyeballs, using the same technique you used for the mouth.

Figure 2.26 Peter uses blended shapes and lines in this image to create detail in the hair and face.

path, but the results are often unpredictable.) While a blend will work better if both objects have the same number of points, you can achieve some interesting effects even when they don't.

After determining the type of blend you want, use the Blend tool to click on one point in the first object, and another point in the second object. It's that simple. With some experimentation, you can achieve some spectacular results.

DIY:
THE BLEND TOOL

Blending and creating a gradient are two different things. Let's take a look at the Blend tool specifically to see how you can create more sophisticated morphed shapes and gradients.

1. In a new Illustrator document, create a basic geometric shape.

2. While it's still selected, hold Command Option/ Ctrl Alt and drag a copy some distance away (holding the Command/ Ctrl key here simply toggles the Shape tool to the Direct Selection tool). Hold the Shift key down to constrain the drag horizontally or vertically.

3. Use the Scale tool to squish your copied shape so that it's almost a straight horizontal line, then click and drag from the bottom edge up to the top edge (Figure 2.28, left).

4. Double-click your Blend tool and establish that you want three steps between your objects with a "page" Orientation (the icon to the left), then close the options dialog box (Figure 2.27).

5. With the Blend tool still active, click on a point in your original object, then click on

Figure 2.27 Double-click the Blend tool to set your options: specified steps, distance, or smooth color.

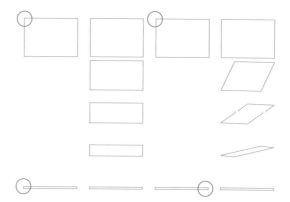

Figure 2.28 When creating a blend, click on the same relative point in each object to ensure a smooth transition.

Figure 2.29 You can blend strokes of different weights and colors.

Figure 2.30 Use the Smooth Color option to create unusual gradients.

the same relative point in the squished object. For instance, if you click the top left corner of one object, click on the top left corner point of the second object.

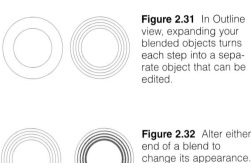

Figure 2.31 In Outline view, expanding your blended objects turns each step into a separate object that can be edited.

Easy enough. Try the same thing with shapes filled with different colors. Then try it with strokes of different widths and no fills (which you've already done in the eyeball DIY).

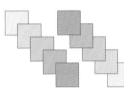

Figure 2.32 Alter either end of a blend to change its appearance.

Now double-click the Blend tool to open its options again. Set the Spacing to "Smooth Color" and blend two shapes or paths of different colors to see what that does.

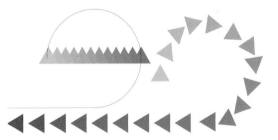

Figure 2.33 Reverse Front to Back switches the stacking order of your blend objects.

If you don't like the blend you've created you can modify it in a couple of ways:

Object ➡ Blend ➡ Release will eliminate your blend, leaving you with your original shapes/lines.

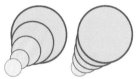

Figure 2.34 Reverse Spine switches the front and back objects.

Object ➡ Blend ➡ Expand will turn the blend into multiple objects, as if you had created each one individually. You can then modify each of these shapes or paths using the Direct Selection tool.

Click on either end shape and modify it—change the color, shape, or stroke weight—and the blend will be altered to reflect the changes.

Double-click the Blend tool to change the type of blend and/or the number of steps.

Figure 2.35 Create your blend and a new path. Select both objects and choose Replace Spine to have your blended objects follow the new path.

Figure 2.36 The orange slice and the watermelon slice (far right) were created separately. Each piece of fruit has the same number of objects (background color, seeds/sections, and a shape for the outer stroke). Blends were created individually between corresponding shapes.

Other options in the Blend menu include Reverse Front to Back, Reverse Spine, and Replace Spine. The spine is the path connecting two blended objects.

Reverse Front to Back will switch overlapping objects to overlap from the other way.

Reverse Spine trades the start and end shapes/paths.

By default, the spine is straight. If you want to blend an object along a curved path, you could use the Direct Selection tool to modify it. You could also use the Replace Spine command.

Create your blended object, then draw the path you want these objects to follow. Select both the blended object and the path and choose Object → Blend → Replace Spine to place the objects along the new path, rather than the default straight line. You could also add anchor points and adjust the default path if you want, but sometimes drawing the path from scratch is a lot easier.

As you can see, with a little imagination, you can do some elegant things with blends. Any blend can be masked to create an entirely different shape, making it a great way to escape from standard linear and radial gradients.

KEY POINTS

- Double-click the Pencil tool to adjust how tightly it follows your cursor to create a line.

- Use Multiply blending mode to create transparent shapes that affect colors beneath it.

- Create blended paths using Specified Steps with the Blend tool.

- Click on the same relative point in each object to generate a better blend.

- Use Smooth Color with the Blend tool to create unusual gradients

- Modify blended objects by reversing the spine, or replacing it with a path (Object ➡ Blend).

ON YOUR OWN:
GO TO THE ZOO!

Design a billboard that encourages people to visit the zoo or aquarium.

The dimensions of a layout of a typical billboard are 15.7" x 7.55" (horizontal format).

Use lots of colors, and try to re-create Peter's freeform technique of layering transparent shapes to create texture, as well as his blending techniques.

If you want color to bleed off the edges of your billboard, create a mask to clean them up when you're done.

3 JACK TOM

GREETINGS

Compound Paths • Divide Objects Below • Perfect Spirals

Transferring his graphic illustration style from Pantone film and technical pen work to Illustrator was a seamless transition for Jack Tom.

Growing up in San Francisco, Jack Tom thought he might be a herpetologist. With a bedroom full of lizards, frogs, turtles, and other reptiles, it seemed a natural fit.

"But when I flunked math, I realized maybe science was not the field for me," he admits.

After seeing some of the first psychedelic posters and handbills for rock groups playing at the legendary Avalon Theater, he realized that making art and design might be a possible career path.

"I started taking more art classes in high school, and had an amazing teacher. She was teaching design, including typography, at that level. I loved it."

Jack is passionate about his growing up experience and the role his ancestors played in creating a unique California culture.

"We were paper immigrants," he says. "My last name was Wong for the first eleven years of my life."

Just after World War II, the United States put a stop to the immigration of the Chinese. Anyone already in the country was automatically a naturalized citizen with the papers to prove it. As those people died, their papers were sold to others still in China so that they could enter the country legally.

"I think it was in 1963 that the government decided they wanted an accurate count of the number of Chinese people who were here, and

Figure 3.1 This stylized piece is reminiscent of Jack's original work, utilizing mechanically rendered black lines and colorful fills.

an amnesty was arranged. We finally got our family name back: Tom.

"I remember half the class changed their names overnight. It made the teacher crazy."

And while he admits to being part of what he calls a "project gang," and wearing the requisite black jacket, he moved away from the group when he began college.

He studied what was then called "commercial art," a combination of advertising design, graphic design, and illustration, and graduated in three and a half years from City College of San Francisco.

Hired by the professor who almost flunked him, Jack's first job was designing slides for

Figure 3.2 This cover for NYU is a great example of Jack's highly graphic approach.

Figure 3.3 Jack's education included all aspects of visual communication, allowing him to work at a variety of places, from magazines to TV corporate offices to ad agencies.

Figure 3.4 Jack's work for Gartner is a natural fit, utilizing detailed images to communicate the company's services.

multimedia presentations, and freelancing at various agencies and design studios.

"I realized I'd never forgive myself if I didn't at least check out New York City as a place to live and work."

After a vacation to Manhattan, he realized he'd found a home and moved there in the late 70s.

He'd interviewed at several places when the art director of *Psychology Today* suggested he apply for an opening at *McCall's* magazine. He worked there for three years before moving to CBS, where he worked as senior designer with the legendary Lou Dorfsman for four years. He also did a stint as the graphics art director at *Business Week* magazine before opening his own studio in 1985.

He shared his SoHo studio space with Daniel Pelavin (see Chapter 12) for many years.

"Danny was one of the first people to get a Mac. He was amazing. He'd just read the manual and figure things out. He was a natural."

Jack, on the other hand, didn't think the computer would dramatically change the industry.

"I held out until about 1991, and then got a small business loan so I could buy a computer, a scanner that I actually still use, and a laser printer."

His original illustration and design techniques utilized highly stylized, mechanically rendered black line on acetate, laid over meticulously cut Pantone and Zipatone film for the colors.

"My illustration style hasn't changed at all. It's so graphic you can't tell which pieces I did by hand, and which ones I did in Illustrator."

In the early 90s, Jack relocated his growing family to Connecticut where he's lived and worked for the past dozen years.

He teaches as an adjunct professor at the University of Hartford, and is a visiting professor with Syracuse University's Independent Study Degree Master's program in Illustration. His work has garnered numerous awards from the *Print Regional Design Annual, How* magazine, and The New York Art Director's Club, among others.

DIGITAL DECONSTRUCTION: MP3 COVER

This playful image (Figure 3.6) was created to illustrate the economics involved with downloading music illegally from the Internet. While Jack's strong graphic edges are still evident, he's incorporated blends and gradients to create depth and softer boundaries.

The symmetrical aspects are balanced by details with subtle changes from left to right.

To create the bug, Jack drew half of it, and then reflected and joined the two halves together. Instead of a black line, he used purple, which keeps the image from being too dark.

The blend in the background actually extended past the bottom of the grass, so Jack used Object ➡ Path ➡ Divide Objects Below to eliminate that part.

Figure 3.5 Jack drew the designs at the top of this image, rather than using a pattern. "I want things to be original, and I don't like to use the patterns that come with Illustrator."

Figure 3.6 Jack makes great use of symmetry, gradients, and compound paths in this image about downloading music from the Web.

Jack prefers to use a mouse when he's developing an image. Careful examination of the objects reveals his expertise with the Pen tool.

He's also made use of a compound path within the monitor to frame the musical notes.

DIY:
COMPOUND PATHS

A compound path is an object with a window. Letters like O, P, and D all make use of this feature: it's how to have something show through a hole in another element. The value of compound paths is that you don't have to re-create background elements in the shapes of the interior space where you want it to appear.

1. Open "door.tif" in the "tom" folder on your DVD. We'll use this as the background.

2. Lock the door layer and add a new one.

3. Using the Rectangle tool, draw a paned window (Figure 3.8).

    Start with the larger rectangle, then add the smaller ones on top. Remember you can draw just one pane, and then drag three copies using the Option/Alt key.

    If you can't see any change, add a fill color to your objects.

NOTE: The topmost object(s) in the stacking order will become the transparent areas in a compound path.

---

4. Shift-click each of the smaller rectangles to select them. Group them using Command/Ctrl G, or Object ➡ Group.

5. Select everything (double check to make sure your door layer is locked!) using Command/Ctrl A.

Figure 3.7 Objects that have transparent spaces, or windows, are created using Object ➡ Compound Path ➡ Make (Command/Ctrl 8).

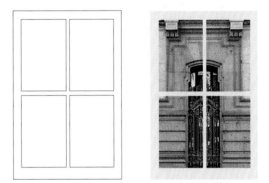

Figure 3.8 The rectangles used to create a window shape (left). After the inner panes are grouped, all the window objects are used to create the compound path (Command/Ctrl 8) (right).

6. Create the compound path using Command/Ctrl 8 or Object ➡ Compound Path ➡ Make.

NOTE: When you want multiple shapes to create the holes, you don't necessarily have to group them first. However, if you do group them, the entire group must be selected before you can create a compound path. A compound path becomes a grouped object by default.

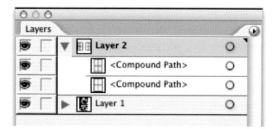

Figure 3.9 Unlike a group, you can't see the individual pieces of a compound path in the Layers palette.

7. Delete the two bottom panes in your window; use the Direct Selection tool and click on the very edge of the rectangles, then hit Delete twice.

8. Select the bottom edge of one pane with the Direct Selection and drag the edge down to make it taller. Use the Shift key to ensure you drag it straight down. Repeat the transformation on the other pane (select the bottom edge and use Command/Ctrl D!).

9. Use the Group Selection tool (hollow arrow +) to move one of your "windows" outside the frame (Figure 3.10).

Notice how the area that was once transparent becomes opaque when it's moved outside the background of the compound path. This is handy when trying to create positive/negative kinds of graphics like logos.

NOTE: To release a compound path, select all its parts and choose Object ➡ Compound Path ➡ Release.

Figure 3.10 Use the Group Selection tool to move one of the panes outside the basic shape.

Figure 3.11 Compound paths can be used to create interesting positive/negative effects.

Figure 3.12 Jack's background makes use of both gradient fills and blended objects.

DIY:
DIVIDE OBJECTS BELOW

This little feature is quite handy (I use it so frequently, I've saved it as an Action. See Chapter 9 for how to do that). It's used to slice elements so that you can delete the area(s) you don't need. It can also be used to create pattern tiles.

We'll begin by creating a blend similar to the one Jack used in the background of the MP3 image (Figure 3.12).

1. Start with a new Illustrator document.

2. Select the Star tool (in the shape tools fly-out pane) and just click in the middle of your page.

   In the Star Options dialog box, set the number of points to 45, with an outer radius of 3.75" and the inner one 3".

   Assign it a stroke of pale pink with no fill.

3. Copy and paste this star in back (Command/Ctrl C, Command/Ctrl B), and use the Scale tool to reduce the copy by 85%. Change the stroke color to a darker pink.

4. Select both stars completely (make sure all the anchor points are solid) and use the Align palette to center them to each other both vertically and horizontally.

5. Use the Scale tool to squish both stars a bit from top to bottom.

6. Double-click the Blend tool, select "smooth color" as the Blend option and click OK.

7. Click the top point of the outer star and then the top point of the inner star to create your blend.

Figure 3.13 Create a star shape using the Star Options dialog box: Option/Alt and click once with the Star tool to access it.

Figure 3.14 Use the Align palette to center the stars to each other.

Figure 3.15 Draw a path across the bottom of your star shapes. While the line is still selected, choose Object ➡ Path ➡ Divide Objects Below.

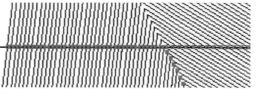

Figure 3.16 Drag the Direct Selection tool below the line to select those parts and delete them. Hit Delete twice to make sure you get rid of all the anchor points.

8. While it's still selected, choose Object ➡ Blend ➡ Expand to turn the blend into a series of individual lines.

NOTE: Divide Objects Below will work on a blend that hasn't been expanded, but the results can be unpredictable.

---

9. Use the Group Selection tool to select the inner star. Copy it, and paste it in front (Command/Ctrl C, Command/Ctrl F).

Fill this with a pale yellow color.

10. Use either the Line Segment tool or the Pen tool to create a path about an inch from the bottom of the star shape (Figure 3.15).

Select just the line.

11. Go to Object ➡ Path ➡ Divide Objects Below.

Your shapes will be sliced along the line you drew.

12. Select the bottom portion of the star shape with the Direct Selection tool and delete it (Figure 3.16).

Using Divide Objects Below is a nice, clean way to slice objects with any path you create.

13. Draw a wavy line at the top of your star and divide it again, deleting the upper portion when you're done.

Alternatively, you can use the Knife tool, which is hidden behind the Scissors. Just click and drag the tool in the shape you want, and it will slice through everything it crosses. You'll note that this isn't quite as precise as using a path.

Figure 3.17 Using a path to slice an object into a new shape is more precise than using the Knife tool.

Figure 3.18 Jack created this image to illustrate the quick processing of insurance claims.

Figure 3.19 Jack took the time to create his spirals using a trick that yields a shape quite a bit different from using the Spiral shape tool.

DIGITAL DECONSTRUCTION: MERCURY

In this illustration (Figure 3.18), Jack used the mythological character of Mercury (Roman God of swiftness and trade). Instead of the traditional caduceus, he's carrying money and insurance forms to illustrate speedy claims processing.

Jack's interest in his own Chinese heritage and with other cultures often provide opportunities for him to combine decorative design elements from many resources. Here he's used a classic Asian cloud form to add to the theme of flying and speed, along with a European influenced Art Deco background.

The repetition of spiral shapes in the clouds and the wings on Mercury's sandals and hat is a nice touch, and Jack used the Spiral tool (hidden behind the Line Segment tool) to create some of them.

Because he was educated before we had the ease of Bézier curves and vector drawing using the computer, Jack created some of his spirals using a traditional construction method. This technique creates spirals that are more perfect than those created using the Spiral tool. And if you're all about being mechanically correct, it's a great trick.

DIY: MECHANICALLY PERFECT SPIRALS

To do this right requires patience and some skill with the Scissors tool. You might want to watch the demonstration in the "tom" folder on your DVD called "spirals.mov" before continuing.

1. In a new Illustrator document, show your rulers (Command/Ctrl R).

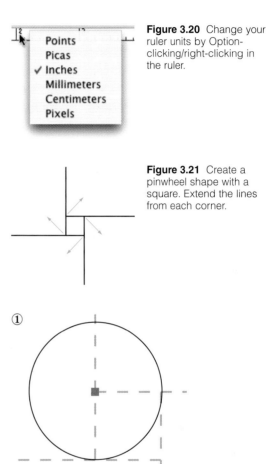

Figure 3.20 Change your ruler units by Option-clicking/right-clicking in the ruler.

Figure 3.21 Create a pinwheel shape with a square. Extend the lines from each corner.

Figure 3.22 Draw a perfect circle with the center point positioned exactly on the top left corner of your guides.

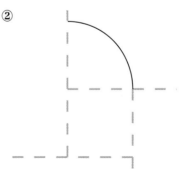

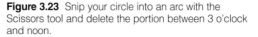

Figure 3.23 Snip your circle into an arc with the Scissors tool and delete the portion between 3 o'clock and noon.

2. Draw a square that's about .25".

   You can do this easily by just clicking with the Rectangle tool and entering the dimensions.

NOTE: You can use any unit of measure in the options dialog box. Illustrator will automatically translate it into the measurement system specified in the preferences.

If you want to change measurement units within a document, simply Option-click /right-click in the ruler and drag to the one you prefer (Figure 3.20).

---

3. Use the Pen tool to draw lines that extend like a pinwheel from the corners of your square. Make them about 4 inches long (Figure 3.21).

   The arrows in Figure 3.21 indicate the quadrants where you'll be creating the arcs that make your spiral.

4. Turn your rectangle and lines into guides by selecting them and typing Command / Ctrl 5 (View ➡ Guides ➡ Make Guides).

5. Grab the Circle tool and draw a perfect circle with its center positioned over the top left corner ① (Figure 3.22).

6. With your scissors, snip the circle into an arc by clicking at noon and then at 3 o'clock. Delete the lower left portion of your circle ② (Figure 3.23).

7. Draw another circle, this time with the center in the *lower left corner*. Remember, you can draw a shape from the center by holding the Option/Alt key as you click and drag. Make your shape a perfect circle by holding the Shift key as well.

   Make sure it's large enough to intersect with the first circle at the top ③ (Figure 3.24).

③

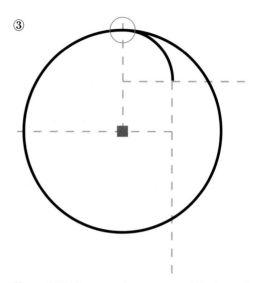

Figure 3.24 As you make subsequent circles, make sure the new path meets the end of the previous one.

④

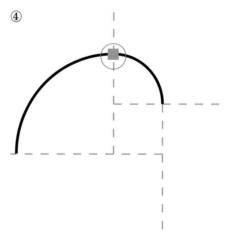

Figure 3.25 After you snip the second circle, select the overlapping points and then avereraging and joining them (Command Option Shift J/Ctrl Alt Shift J).

8. This time, snip the circle at noon and 9 o'clock with the Scissors and delete the lower right portion ④ (Figure 3.25).

   Connect the two arcs by selecting their overlapping points, and averaging and joining them (Object ➡ Path ➡ Average, then Object ➡ Path ➡ Join, or simply Command Option Shift J/Ctrl Alt Shift J).

NOTE: Command Option Shift J/Ctrl Alt Shift J is a little known secret and very, very handy, especially when you're creating a symmetrical object by drawing half and then reflecting it—use this keystroke shortcut to connect one half to the other.

Instead of drawing a straight line between two selected points, which is what Object ➡ Path ➡ Join does, this keystroke averages both points and joins them in one step. Otherwise, you'd have to average them first (Command Option J / Ctrl Alt J), then join them (Command / Ctrl J).

---

9. Draw a third circle centered from the *lower right corner*, again making sure it's large enough to meet the end of the previous arc.

   Snip it at 9 o'clock and 6 o'clock, deleting the upper right portion ⑤ (Figure 3.26).

   Join and average the overlapping points.

10. Repeat your circle shape with its center positioned in the last, upper right, corner ⑥ (Figure 3.26).

    Join and average the overlapping points.

    You're now back at the beginning!

Keep going around like this (Steps 5-10) until you have two or three rotations.

If you analyze what you've done, you'll realize that the size of the initial square (in this case, .25" x .25") determines the size of your spiral.

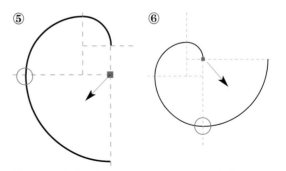

Figure 3.26 Continue to create ever-larger circles using the corner points of your guides to center them. Snip them into arcs, and join each new one to the previous one.

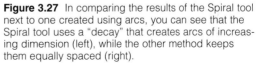

Figure 3.27 In comparing the results of the Spiral tool next to one created using arcs, you can see that the Spiral tool uses a "decay" that creates arcs of increasing dimension (left), while the other method keeps them equally spaced (right).

A smaller box results in a tighter spiral.

Compare the difference between a mechanically created spiral (Figure 3.27, right) and one created with the Spiral tool (Figure 3.27, left).

Now that you know how to make a spiral using this trick, you can choose between which kind you need for any particular purpose. It's always good to have choices!

KEY POINTS

- The topmost object becomes the "hole" or window in a compound path.

- You can have several "holes" within a single object. All selected shapes above the bottom-most object will become transparent when you create a compound path.

- Use compound paths to create interesting positive/negative elements.

- Divide Objects Below only works on closed paths, not open ones. If you want to use it to divide an open path, outline the path first (Object ➡ Path ➡ Outline Stroke.)

- When dividing objects, make sure only the path you want to use as the "knife," or "cookie cutter" is selected.

- To avoid dividing objects that you want to keep whole, select and hide them when using Divide Objects Below (Command/ Ctrl 3, or Object ➡ Hide ➡ Selection).

- For more reliable results, expand any blends you want to divide (Object ➡ Expand, or Object ➡ Blend ➡ Expand).

- The space between whorls in a mechanically created spiral depends on the size of the box you start with.

- To average and join two end points in one step, use Command Option Shift J/Ctrl Alt Shift J.

ON YOUR OWN:
T-SHIRT DESIGN

Jack's use of compound paths can be utilized in a variety of instances. It's a great way to create interesting combinations of shapes and images. In addition, knowing how to construct spirals with arcs that are equidistant, rather than "decayed," is a trick that could prove valuable, especially when you need to create something technically perfect.

In this assignment, use the "tshirttemplate.eps" file in the "tom" folder on your DVD to design your own T-shirt.

See if you can use a compound path (or several) and, so as not to let your spiral go to waste, try to include a spiral shape or two.

4 COLLEEN O'HARA

Custom Calligraphic Brushes • Custom Scatter, Pattern, and Art Brushes • Envelope Distort

Colleen O'Hara's nontraditional career path has provided her with interesting opportunities and experiences as both an illustrator and a designer.

Colleen O'Hara's first and second grade teachers were convinced she'd be an artist. "I was the kid in class who was always doodling in the margins of my notebooks. I remember copying the pictures from the Sears catalogs, dozens at a time. I'd staple the pages together to make little books and then I'd write stories to go with them."

Although she loved to write and draw, her high school guidance counselor suggested going to teacher's college. Luckily, Colleen took her time deciding. She took courses in English, fine arts, art history, illustration, and design at both MacMaster University and the Ontario College of Art & Design.

"My first real job was with a small agency that was all women, which I really liked. I was surprised they hired me, with my motley portfolio, but I think the owner, who was originally an art history major, saw some potential."

Colleen purchased her first Mac in the late 80s, even though the agency where she was working at the time was a PC shop. She took a few weekend workshops to get a handle on what she calls the "sacred triad" of programs: Adobe Photoshop, Illustrator, and QuarkXPress.

"I knew how to use Corel Draw at that point, and Pagemaker, and Aldus Persuasion (slide show presentation software), but it seemed to me that the results from Illustrator were always more polished."

It was the satisfaction she drew from creating illustrations and designing ads and collateral

Figure 4.1 One steady client, the *Hamilton Spectator*, would provide a theme for the cover of their magazine and let Colleen loose to develop a final image.

pieces that led her from working full time at the ad agency to freelancing.

Networking with friends led to her first freelance job, and her first "professional" illustration using Adobe Illustrator.

"There was a jazz group that was putting on an Ella Fitzgerald retrospective, and they wanted me to do a poster for it. I even got paid!"

That led to more posters for a local theater and CD covers for several groups. She also established a relationship with the art director at the *Hamilton Spectator*, which led to many special projects where she had free reign in developing concepts and illustrations for covers of their magazine insert called *Alt Spec*.

"That was great. I didn't even usually have to provide a sketch, which was probably a good

Figure 4.2 This Illustrator image was created for the Easter edition of *Alt Spec*.

Figure 4.3 For this Corolla brochure cover, the client wanted a fun style in an urban setting with no people.

Figure 4.4 Colleen mixes more structured objects, like the hat in this case, with looser, less refined bits for contrast and dimension.

thing since my sketches are kind of wispy and never bear any resemblance to the final image."

The art director provided the theme for the cover and let Colleen loose to explore a visual solution.

"I just started with the theme for that issue, spring. So I drew some flowers. Then I added some bugs. Ultimately it was the idea that spring is a major event here (after our long, cold, snowy winters) that the final element just sort of evolved: a woman the size of a bug on a ladder watering the flowers."

Colleen's done illustrations for advertising as well, and has developed several different styles to suit the needs of her clients. Some of her images make use of a lot of line work, and some don't. She prefers a looser, fresher look and will often go back to the first version of

something she created, abandoning efforts to refine a line. She uses a pressure-sensitive tablet for all her work.

Colleen, and illustrator/husband Rocco Baviera (see Chapter 7), recently adopted a little girl, Bianca Lun, from China.

"I can't keep up with the most current versions of software anymore! Bianca keeps us so busy. We take turns working and caring for her, but mostly end up working late at night while she's asleep."

Colleen urges aspiring illustrators to pursue their dreams. "If you love it, read everything you can, work at learning everything you can. Jump in with both feet. And be persistent!"

DIGITAL DECONSTRUCTION: SKATING FUN

Colleen has included some interesting techniques in this image, including creating her own brush shapes and saving them to a special Brush Library. The snowflakes are actually dingbats from a font that were outlined and enlarged.

This image is a great example of the interplay between tightly manipulated shapes and free-flowing black lines that tie the image together.

While this image is rich in content, it looks deceptively simple. A quick look at Outline View, however, provides a better clue as to the complexity that was involved in creating it.

Another aspect worth noting is Colleen's use of the Color palette.

"I see color combinations while I'm out and about and jot them down. I have a file called 'color ideas,' where I create little boxes and fill them with these colors. They could be from anywhere: a beach bag, a book cover, a tea cup."

Custom brush shapes are also a major passion with Colleen.

"I used to just use whatever came with the program, but ended up finding that they were often too clunky. I started making my own, and saving them to use again."

Figure 4.5 Colleen used a pressure-sensitive tablet and custom brush shapes to create the lively black outlines in this piece.

Figure 4.6
This seemingly simple image is actually quite involved, and includes custom Brush shapes that Colleen has saved to a library.

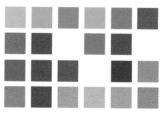

Figure 4.7
These are some of the color combinations Colleen has collected in her "color ideas" file.

One of the other tricks Colleen employs with her brush lines is to expand them from paths to shapes. That way, should she decide to flip the image from left to right, the angle of the brush shape doesn't shift (Object ➡ Expand).

Illustrator's Brushes are an interesting feature. There are several different kinds, many libraries to choose from, and of course the opportunity to create your own.

DIY:
ILLUSTRATOR BRUSHES

Let's do some exploratory brush work on that penguin in the lower left corner of "Skating Fun."

1. Open the "penguin.eps" file from the "o'hara" folder on your DVD. You'll notice it has several layers: a background color, the penguin in his full glory, the brush strokes Colleen used to add black details, and one with the white brush strokes. The top two layers are where you'll experiment with the brushes.

2. If the Brushes palette isn't open, select it from the Window menu so you can play with it.

3. Select the Paintbrush tool from the Toolbar, and make sure you're working on the "practice/black" layer.

4. Click on each brush in turn and draw a few lines. Select one with the Direct Selection tool and notice that it's actually a path. Type Command/Ctrl Y to see the Outline view of the brush stroke. They look like pen or pencil paths, not shapes.

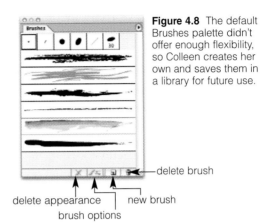

Figure 4.8 The default Brushes palette didn't offer enough flexibility, so Colleen creates her own and saves them in a library for future use.

delete brush

delete appearance   new brush

brush options

Figure 4.9 Open some of the Brush Libraries from the Brushes palette submenu to get an idea of the myriad choices.

Figure 4.10 Any path you create with the Pen or Pencil tool can be assigned a brush stroke attribute.

Brush strokes are, in fact, artwork that has been applied to a path. You can change any path you've drawn with the Pen or Pencil tool into a brush stroke. Select it and then click on the brush style you want in the Brushes palette.

By default, the Brushes palette contains calligraphic brushes along the top, and art brushes in a list. You can open other Brush Libraries using the Brushes palette submenu. Choose from bugs, florals, geometrics, and household items, to name a few. The possibilities are vast. There are even places on the Web where you can download brushes created by third parties.

To eliminate a brush stroke from a path, select it and open the Appearance palette from the Window menu. Click and drag "Stroke" to the trash. When you do this, your path will loose any stroke attributes it might have had, including color, but will retain the fill if it had one to begin with (Figure 4.10).

5. Select all (Command/Ctrl A) and delete everything from your document.

6. If you haven't turned on the "black brush strokes" layer so you can see it, do that now. Keep it locked, however, so you don't inadvertently draw on it or otherwise change anything.

    Leave the other layers hidden for now. Make sure to work on the "practice/black" layer.

Colleen used two custom Brushes to create the lines that enhance her penguin. They have thick and thin strokes, indicating they're calligraphic styles, rather than art style brushes.

7. Choose List View from the Brushes palette submenu so you can see the names of each.

Figure 4.11 Delete a brush stroke you've applied by dragging it to the trash in the Appearance palette.

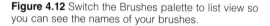

Figure 4.12 Switch the Brushes palette to list view so you can see the names of your brushes.

Figure 4.13 Try drawing the penguin's bow tie with the 6 pt flat brush.

There's one called "6 pt flat" about six styles down. Select the Paintbrush tool and then click on that style to use it (Figure 4.12).

8. Trace over the bow tie guide with a contrasting stroke color. The Paintbrush works like the Pencil. Just click and drag the shape you want. Illustrator automatically adds anchor points as needed to define the path.

The angle isn't quite right on the bow tie path, and it's a bit too thick. Let's adjust it and save our adjustments.

9. Double-click the 6 pt flat brush in the Brushes palette to open a dialog box.

   a) Change the Diameter to 4 pt.

   b) Change the Angle to -140°.

   c) Rename the Brush to "4 pt flat," and click OK (Figure 4.14). If you get a warning whether to leave existing brush strokes or apply the change, choose to leave them as is.

10. Delete the bow tie you drew and draw it again with the new Brush.

Much better!

Chances are the placement of the brush stroke isn't identical to Colleen's. You can fix that with the Direct Selection tool. Deselect the stroke, and then adjust the anchor points one at a time until you're pleased.

Experiment with this new Brush to see if there are any other parts of the penguin that use it.

Let's create another custom brush to use for the steam coming up from the teacup.

11. Click on the "new brush" icon at the bottom of the Brushes palette (to the left of the trash can).

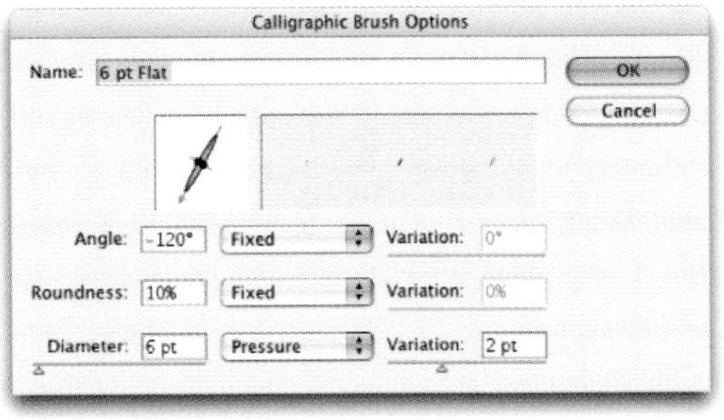

Figure 4.14 Open the Brush Options dialog box and change the diameter to 4 points and the angle to -140°.

Figure 4.15 You can use the Direct Selection tool to adjust brush paths. You can also add or delete points with the Add and Delete Anchor Point Pen tools.

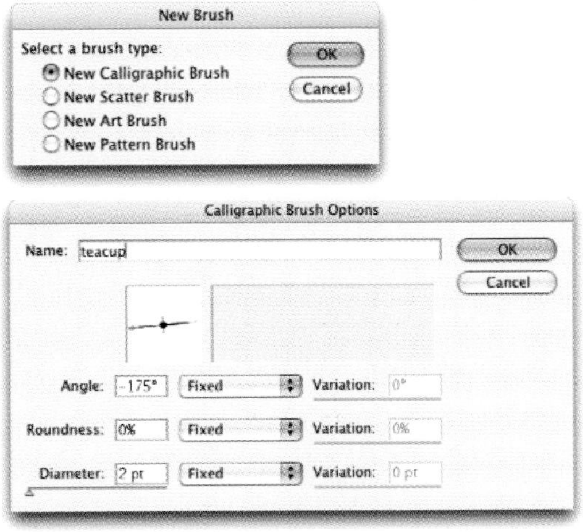

Figure 4.16 Create a new Brush for the teacup.

Leave New Calligraphic Brush selected and click OK.

12. In the Brush Options dialog box, name your brush "teacup."

a) Change the Angle to -175°.

b) Change the Roundness to 0%.

c) Change the Diameter to 2 pt, then click OK (Figure 4.16).

13. Select your new brush and trace the steam.

What do you think?

14. Either double-click the teacup Brush in the Brushes palette or click the "brush options" icon at the bottom of the palette to access the Options dialog box again. Adjust the Angle to about -165°.

This time when you're asked whether to apply to or ignore existing stokes, click "apply."

See if this version works for any other strokes in the penguin.

You should have almost all the purple guides re-created at this point. (If you haven't been using a black stroke, select everything and change the stroke color to black.)

15. Hide the "black brush strokes" layer and turn on the "white brush strokes" layer. You'll be working on the "practice/white" layer now, creating more custom brushes. Let's start with the feet.

16. Use an existing calligraphic brush to get an idea of the weight of the stroke, and the angle. Make adjustments using the Brush Options. See if you can create the Brush you need for these strokes on your own.

Work in a contrasting color—you can change them to white when you're finished.

Figure 4.17 These are the strokes you should be able to create with your two new Brushes (4 pt flat, and teacup).

Figure 4.18 You should be able to finish the rest of the strokes with the Brush you create for the feet.

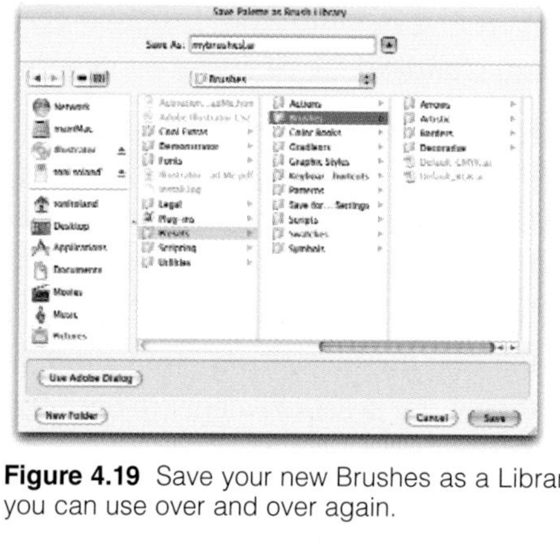

Figure 4.19 Save your new Brushes as a Library that you can use over and over again.

Don't forget to check if you can create the tray with this new brush (make sure it's black!). Unhide the "practice/black" layer to work on it.

17. Select all the strokes you created using the "white brush strokes" layer as a guide and change the stroke color to white.

   Hide the "white brush strokes" layer, and turn on the penguin and background layers. How does it all look?

Almost there! You've spent a bit of time creating new brushes and customizing existing ones. Let's not allow that to go to waste.

18. From the Brushes palette submenu, choose Select All Unused and then click the trash icon to delete them. (Click OK when asked if you're sure you want to do this.)

19. Select Save Brush Library at the bottom of the Brushes palette submenu. Name your Library and make sure it's being saved to Illustrator's Brushes folder (Illustrator ➡ Presets ➡ Brushes).

Done! While trying to copy someone else's custom brushes is a bit difficult, it's easy to see how creating your own and saving them can enhance your own illustrative style.

DIY: SCATTER, PATTERN, AND ART BRUSHES

Although Illustrator has multiple Brush Libraries to choose from, it's always nice to have total control over your image, and that includes knowing how to create custom Brushes for scattered icons, patterns, and artwork. In each case, you need to create the objects you want to turn into a Brush style before you can define it. In the case of a pat-

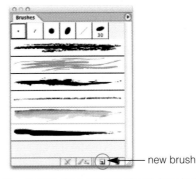

new brush

Figure 4.20 Click the New Brush icon in the Brushes palette to create a new Scatter Brush.

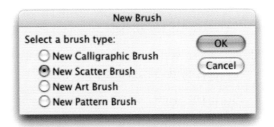

Figure 4.21 Select "New Scatter Brush" from the New Brush dialog box.

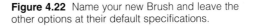

Figure 4.22 Name your new Brush and leave the other options at their default specifications.

tern brush, you need to create pattern swatches that will define the sides and corners of a brush path.

1. Open a new CMYK Illustrator document, and make sure the Brushes palette is available.

2. Create a simple shape, either with a shape tool, or draw one. You can use multiple pieces for the scatter shape—for instance, all the bits that would make up a butterfly.

    There are limitations, however, to the elements you can use. Gradients, blended objects, brush strokes, graphs, masks, placed files, and bitmaps are all off-limits.

3. Once you have your shape(s), select everything and click the New Brush icon at the bottom of the Brushes palette (Figure 4.20).

4. Select New Scatter Brush from the list of options and click OK.

5. In the Scatter Brush Options dialog box, name your new brush. You'll note there are several options here to determine how this brush will work as it places your image along a path. For now, leave them set to the defaults and click OK.

6. As mentioned earlier, you can create a path with the Pen or Pencil tool and assign a brush attribute to it, or you can use the Brush tool itself. Use the Pen tool to create a path, and while it's still selected, choose your new Scatter Brush from the Brushes palette (Figure 4.23).

Pretty slick!

7. Use the Paintbrush tool to create more random lines with your new Scatter Brush.

Figure 4.23 Use the Pen tool to create some paths. While they are selected, choose your new Scatter Brush from the Brushes palette to change their appearance.

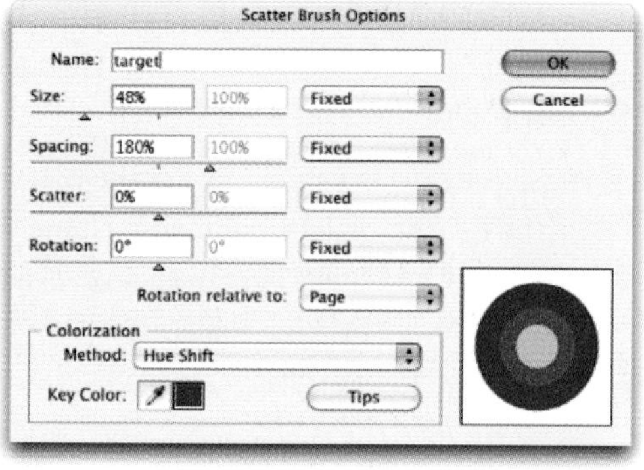

Figure 4.24 Create a multicolored object for a new Scatter Brush. In the Scatter Brush Options dialog box, choose Hue Shift as the method for how changing a stroke color will affect your new brush.

NOTE: Using Scatter Brushes is not the same as using the Symbol Sprayer tool. Brushes create paths that have artwork applied to them. Symbols are groups of images created with the Symbol Sprayer tool and symbols from the Symbols palette.

8. If you didn't use multiple shapes and colors in your brush design, create a new one. A simple target with three different color circles will work.

9. Select all the pieces and drag them to the Brushes palette—this is the same as clicking the New Brush icon at the bottom of the palette.

10. Choose New Scatter Brush, and when the Scatter Brush Options dialog box opens, name your Brush. At the bottom of the dialog box, choose Hue Shift from the Colorization Method pop-up menu (Figure 4.24).

    By default, Illustrator decides which color will be the primary one, as represented by the box of color next to the Eyedropper icon. If you want to change that, click the Eyedropper to select it, then click within the graphic representation of your Brush to select another color. This color will dictate how the other colors change when you change the stroke color of a Scatter Brush path.

    Click OK.

11. Draw a few paths with your new Brush.

12. Select one, and change the stroke color to see what happens.

Creating an Art Brush follows the same steps. Create the artwork using any drawing or shape tool(s), add color(s), and then either drag your art to the Brushes palette, or click the New

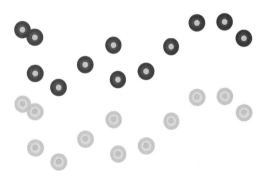

Figure 4.25 Assigning a Hue Shift mode allows you to change the stroke color of the Brush to create different color combinations.

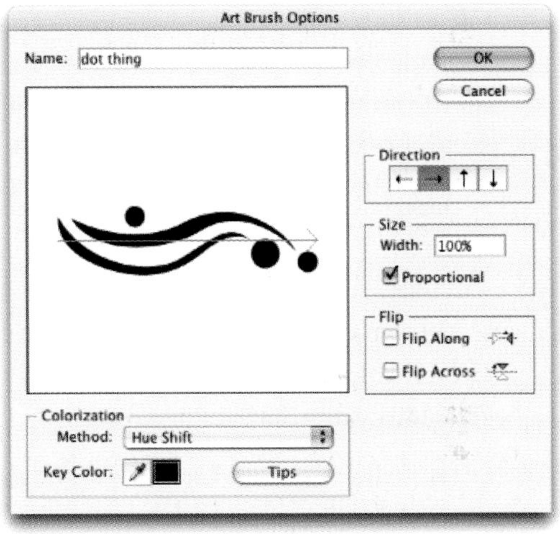

Figure 4.26 Creating an Art Brush is almost the same as creating a Scatter Brush. Create your art, select it, and in the New Brush dialog box, choose Art Brush to access the Options.

Brush icon at the bottom of the palette. Select Art Brush as the type. You'll notice in this options dialog box that you can specify the direction of the art as it's mapped along the path. Play with these choices. Select one, paint a few lines, then double-click the brush icon in the Brushes palette to modify it.

DIGITAL DECONSTRUCTION: ICE CREAM PACKAGING

Colleen's clients rely on her for design as well as illustration. She's done several package designs, including some for Lacteeze. These include both a "flat" rendering for design and client approval purposes, and the pre-press art that the printer uses to print and die-cut the actual cartons.

For these packages, Colleen wanted a realistic look to the fruit and nut images, but didn't want to resort to photography. She elected to create them using, in some cases, the gradient mesh tool in order to reproduce the subtle color shifts within the actual objects.

"I went to the supermarket and bought some nuts and fruit. I just sat and stared at, say, a walnut, and really studied how it looked."

Once she's visually dissected the object, she begins to draw directly in Illustrator, without creating a sketch to use as a template.

Some of the other features in this packaging are the use of a dotted pattern in the background, type on a path, and of course, dealing with wrapping the graphics around the curved shape required to print the actual cartons.

Figure 4.27 Colleen opted to use Illustrator for these packages rather than photography to save money.

Figure 4.28 Colleen studies objects in real life in order to re-create them with the Mesh tool.

DIY:
ENVELOPE DISTORT

Wrapping a label around a bottle, for instance, or curving it to fit the shape required for an ice cream carton isn't as difficult as it might seem. Illustrator's Envelop Distort function can do both in one simple step.

Let's create some graphics that could be used for a paper cup design.

1. There's a "cuptemplate.eps" file in the "o'hara" folder on your DVD. Open that in Illustrator.

You'll note that there are three layers. The bottom one is the shape that we'll need to make the graphics actually wrap into a cup shape. The middle layer is the cup shape as a two-dimensional graphic, appropriate for client presentation, and the top layer is where you'll design your cup.

You can create any graphics you might want for your cup. This one was created as follows:

2. The two-dimensional shape was copied and pasted on a new layer for reference.

   A background shape was created for color.

3. The wavy line was drawn with the Pen tool and duplicated to use as a path for the type.

4. The upper wavy line was selected and used to divide the cup shape into two parts using Object ➡ Path ➡ Divide Objects Below, and then each half was filled.

5. A rectangle filled with purple was created at the top of the cup, with a copy placed at the bottom.

6. A perfect orange square was rotated 45° and duplicated several times. Option/Alt drag to

Figure 4.29 Creating the pre-press art for an ice cream carton involves wrapping art and text around a curved shape.

Figure 4.30 Design a coffee cup using the "cuptemplate.eps" file on your DVD.

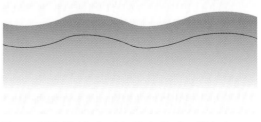

Figure 4.31 Divide the label in half using Object ➡ Path ➡ Divide Objects Below using a wavy line.

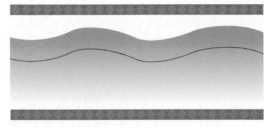

Figure 4.32 Add other graphic elements.

make one copy, then use Command Ctrl D several times to create multiple objects the same distance apart.

These diamond shapes were then selected and grouped (Command/Ctrl G). A duplicate of the group was drag-copied onto the other purple rectangle.

7. The second wavy line was used as a text path with the Type on a Path tool to type and format different slang words for coffee.

8. The cup shape was copied again from the bottom layer and pasted in front (Command/Ctrl F) of everything on the top layer.

9. With the bottom layer locked, everything was selected and a mask was made to block out the graphics and type that extended beyond the cup's shape.

Since most of the graphics for this design are straight, converting them to the curved shape needed for actually printing the cup is easy. The difficult part will be matching the two areas where the wavy line and wavy type meet up at the seam in the cup, once it's bent into shape.

First we need to create a layer for the artwork that a printer will need for production.

If you used any wavy bits in your design, you'll need to adjust the ends so they start and stop at the same place at the left and right edges.

10. Add a new layer and copy and paste all the graphics from your cup design onto it. While everything is still selected, release the mask (Object ➡ Clipping Mask ➡ Release), and delete the 2D cup shape.

   Lock this layer—we'll just use it as a guide.

   Hide your 2D cup design layer.

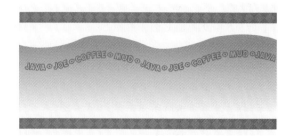

Figure 4.33 Type was created along a copy of the path used to slice the cup's background.

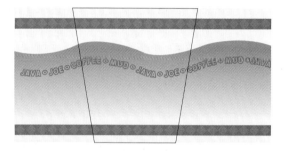

Figure 4.34 The flat coffee cup guide was used as a mask to block out the graphics to either side.

Figure 4.35 Use the coffee cup shape to create a Clipping Mask to block out the extra pieces around your design.

11. Re-create your cup background, but this time pay attention to how things will meet.

12. Make sure any straight graphics extend from one edge to another and that any shapes, like the diamonds in this example, are divided in half, or start and end, at each edge.

13. If you have any wavy lines, you'll need to re-create them using your original design as a guide. In order to make sure their start and end points are the same, drag a guide from your ruler to align them (Figure 4.36). It's also not a bad idea to drag a copy of your wavy line to one side or another to see how they look when the two ends meet up.

14. Create any text you might have used. If you have text in your design, turn it into outlines (Command Shift O/Ctrl Shift O).

15. Select everything that you need to include in your final design and group them (Command/Ctrl G).

    Use the Scale tool to reduce the width of the graphic group by about 35%. Do this using Option/Alt and clicking with the Scale tool to specify a horizontal scale of 65% and a vertical scale of 100%, using the Non-Uniform scale fields) (Figure 4.37).

16. Unlock the Template layer and copy the arc shape, then lock that layer again. Paste the arc shape in front of your grouped graphics (Command/Ctrl F). Make sure they are aligned along the center vertical axis using the Align palette (Figure 4.38).

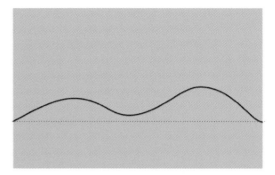

Figure 4.36 Use a guide dragged from the ruler to make sure any wavy pieces of your design start and stop at the same place so they'll meet when the cup is bent into shape.

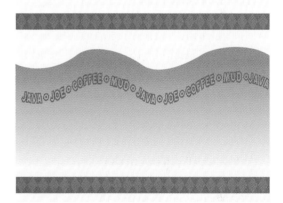

Figure 4.37 Distort your cup design so that it's not as wide and still the same height using the Non-Uniform scaling option.

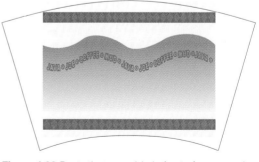

Figure 4.38 Paste the arc guide in front of your graphics; use the Align palette to make sure they're centered from side to side, and line up the top of the graphic with the top of the arc.

17. At this point you're ready to create the final art that a printer would use to print the coffee cup.

    Select the arc shape and your grouped graphics and use Object ➡ Envelope Distort ➡ Make with Warp.

The reason we aren't using Make with Top Object is because doing that would make the text and graphics appear to recede at the edges, and what we really want is flat graphics that are bent.

18. Select Arc as the Warp style and set it to about 16%. Leave both the horizontal and vertical distortion set to 0%. Check the Preview button to see how it looks compared to the template.

    Make adjustments, if needed—it won't be perfect, but you should be close to matching the template (Figure 4.39).

19. Click OK. Now you can use the Direct Selection tool to adjust the corners and anchor points so that the outer shape matches the template shape.

20. Delete your template shape and save your file!

If you want to you can print this, trim it, and bend it into a cup shape to see how it looks.

Truthfully, this artwork is not quite ready to go to the printer. It still needs bleed areas, for where the paper will overlap when the cup is glued together and at the top and bottom, along with trim marks and other technical data (look again at figure 4.29). This is a great way, however, to prepare a three-dimensional comprehensive layout for portfolio presentation or client approval.

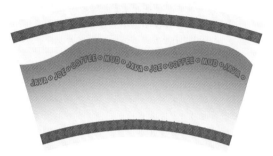

Figure 4.39 Object ➡ Envelope Distort ➡ Make with Warp and choosing the Arc style will bend your graphics to match the template shape.

While you didn't get a chance to create the life-like mango image Colleen used, you can watch the short "how-to" video on your DVD to see how it was done. Try to re-create it yourself, or create another piece of fruit, like a banana or apple, from scratch by observing a real one. We'll be playing with the Mesh tool in Chapter 8.

KEY POINTS

- The Paintbrush tool creates paths that have artwork applied to them.

- Open default Brush Libraries from the Brush palette submenu.

- Double-click an existing Brush in the Brushes palette to modify it.

- Click the New Brush icon at the bottom of the Brushes palette to create a new Calligraphic brush style.

- Create artwork, select it, and use the New Brush icon in the Brushes palette to create custom Scatter, Pattern, and Art Brushes. Remember that these brush styles can't include gradients, blended objects, other brush strokes, graphs, masks, placed files, or bitmap images.

- Art Brushes are not the same as using the Symbol Sprayer tool.

ON YOUR OWN:
PARTY INVITATION

Who doesn't need a reason to celebrate once in a while? Colleen's brushes, and those you've learned how to make, are a great way to spice up an invitation to something—anything!

Design and illustrate a 5" x 7" party invitation (either vertically or horizontally). Create some brushes of all types to use for edges and other graphic elements (confetti and streamers!).

See if you can include some Envelope Distort features as well.

5 KENNY KIERNAN

Graphic Edges • Warped Type • Die-Cuts

Kenny Kiernan has developed a style and method of working that lends itself to all forms of visual communication, from stickers to games, to point of purchase promotion, and animation.

Kenny Kiernan has a fan club. His work has gotten a lot of attention from amateur graphic designers. It's been featured on hundreds of web sites devoted to creating digital signatures.

"I've gotten over a thousand e-mails about my work. It's this huge thing. It's great."

A far cry from his original career plan as an industrial organizational psychologist.

Even though Kenny was practically born with a pencil in his hand and has been drawing since he was two, he ended up with his bachelor's degree in psychology with a business minor.

"It never occurred to me to pursue art as a career. That always seemed unrealistic to me— like planning to be a movie star or something."

Kenny was born and raised in the Bronx, and attended Hunter College High School in Manhattan. He yearned for a college experience like the one he saw in "Animal House." He applied to Penn State, and was accepted into their art program.

"I ran into a few art snobs; I couldn't relate. I felt really outclassed, even though I could draw better than most of them. I switched to liberal arts after my freshman year."

It took two years of graduate school and $40,000 in loans to put him back on the artist track.

"I was living in Hoboken, New Jersey, just across the river from Manhattan, playing music and generally trying to pretend I was

Figure 5.1 A lot of Kenny's work ends up in Flash for pharmaceutical presentations. He exports his Illustrator images as .swf files.

Figure 5.2 This image is one from a series for a Flash movie for Garmin GPS devices.

still in college when I realized I needed to find a career that I was passionate about."

He spent the next year working at Pearl Paint on 23rd Street and drawing seriously for the first time in six years.

While at work one day, a kid he knew in high school wandered in to buy some gouache.

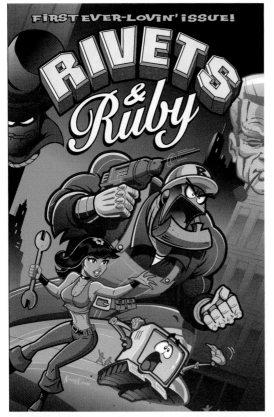

Figure 5.3 This cover was originally done by hand. Kenny re-created it in Illustrator for an anthology of the Rivets and Ruby series.

Figure 5.4 Kenny does a lot of work for educational publishers. Not surprisingly, kids really relate to his style.

"It was Kyle Baker, who is now an acclaimed Eisner Award-winning cartoonist. At the time, his professional comics career was just taking off.

"In high school he had always been totally absorbed in doing his artwork, even drawing during class. And now here he was making money drawing comics. It truly inspired me to get serious."

After a year at Pearl, Kenny answered a want ad in the *Village Voice*. A small design studio was looking for help. Someone with Mac experience.

"I didn't even know what one looked like."

After a quick tutorial from a colleague of his father's, Kenny got the job: answering phones, taking out the garbage, and making coffee. Over the next three years, he spent much of his spare time teaching himself Photoshop, Illustrator, and QuarkXPress.

"I tried using a Wacom tablet but, it just didn't feel right. I use a mouse and the Pen tool. At the beginning, I was having a hard time drawing anything that looked like what I could do by hand. That's when I discovered scanning my own drawings to use as a template. What an epiphany!"

When he discovered the studio he worked for was paying freelancers $25 an hour, he decided it was time to change jobs.

In 1994 he started freelancing at night at a large, international pharmaceutical agency (Foote Cone Belding) doing mostly Photoshop work.

"They'd tell me they wanted an old lady in a car at the top of a mountain with the sun setting, so I'd grab a bunch of stock and put it together. When the comp was approved, they'd go out and do a real shoot."

The studio and agency work taught Kenny a lot about being organized. After losing some digital work due to system crashes, he learned to back up his files on a regular basis. That discipline is the reason behind the structures of his Illustrator files. Every layer has a specific purpose, and each layer is named.

His first big independent freelance gig was designing T-shirts for Hooters.

"The guys were kind of shady, but in the end they handed me a check for $15,000 and that was the exact balance on my school loans. I just turned it over to the bank, and I was debt-free."

In his first year freelancing, Kenny tripled his previous annual income. No surprise there. His love of the graphic comic book style and his proficiency with Illustrator, along with his funky, hip imagery, make his work very popular.

Since 2000, Kenny has been freelancing for various clients from his home studio in Manhattan, and is also working on merchandising some of his stickers and other characters. You can see his work at *http://www.kennyk.com*

DIGITAL DECONSTRUCTION: ROBOPS

Kenny created this image for Taco Bell as an in-store toy giveaway display. Because he worked as an assistant to art directors, he's very conversant with the production process and includes layers in all his pieces that contain crop marks, die-cuts (as in "Download Diva," Figure 5.5), and other print requirements.

Figure 5.5 Kenny's current project is a series of stickers that appeal to young teenagers.

Figure 5.6 "Robops" was created as part of a point-of-purchase display for Taco Bell.

He's also very meticulous about organizing his visual information.

"I start with a layer for my scan. I dim it to 33%. Then I draw on another layer using a really thin stroke, about .1 point, so I can stay true to my pencil sketch."

He labels every layer with a descriptive name. In "Robops," each character in the band has about five layers dedicated to its makeup.

Once he's got his edges drawn, he assigns different stroke weights, depending on where he wants something to pop, or where it's a detail. He also manipulates some lines for a more calligraphic look by outlining them and tweaking the points. In other places, he adds a shape that blends into a line, as in the character MC Mike's shoulder (Figure 5.7).

Once he's got the line work in place (in this image, there are ten layers devoted entirely to line work, and thirty-seven layers in all!), he adds layers for color and shading. He creates multiple layers for colors for each character and area of his image, naming them according to whom or what they represent: highlights, shadows, and color.

His organization extends to his Swatches palette as well. He saves each color he uses in his palette, and frequently will open another image, delete everything, and Save As (Command Shift S/Ctrl Shift S) to start a new piece with the same swatches.

One of his favorite tricks is to hide and show his paths as he works.

"At first it was hard to remember what was selected once it was hidden. But now I use Command/Ctrl H to hide and show anchor points and paths all the time as I tweak things.

Figure 5.7 MC Mike, one of the characters in Kenny's "Robops" image is rich with a variety of line styles and techniques.

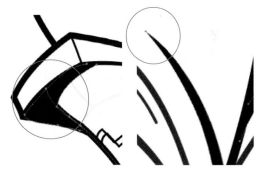

Figure 5.8 In order to create a true pen and ink look, Kenny will either add shapes to continue a line (left), or outline a stroke and manipulate its end points (right).

It's easier to see what you're doing with the anchor points hidden."

One hand on the keyboard, and one hand on the mouse makes Kenny's efforts very efficient.

DIY:
GRAPHIC EDGES

There is a scan called "animehead.psd" in the "kiernan" folder on your DVD. Feel free to use it for this exercise, or one of your own scans. The objective is to re-create the paths that define the image, change stroke weights, and use Kenny's techniques to make some lines thick and thin.

1. Open a new Illustrator document and select Place from the File menu (Figure 5.9). Locate the scan you want to use. (For this DIY, I'm assuming you'll use "anime-head.psd.")

    In the dialog box, you'll notice that you can choose to link a file, place it as a template, or replace a selected placed image.

    Check the Template option and leave the other two unchecked, then click Place.

    Double-click on the name "Layer 1" in your Layers palette and rename it "thin line."

NOTE: Leaving the Link option unchecked embeds the scanned image in your Illustrator file. It makes the file size larger, but also prevents "missing links" errors if the original scan is moved from its original location, or deleted from your computer.

If you forget to Link a scanned image, or any image you place in Illustrator, and that file is subsequently moved (or, heaven forbid, delet-ed!), Illustrator will ask you whether you want to locate it or ignore it. If it's a scan that you're

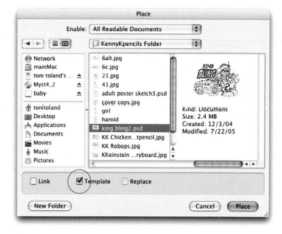

Figure 5.9 Use the Place command to add an image to your file to use as a template.

Figure 5.10 Use a stroke weight of about .2 to make sure your lines meet perfectly as you trace the scan.

finished with, choosing "Ignore" will open your image without the scan attached. If it's an image that's integral to the image—a small photograph, for instance—then you really need to find it or re-create it, or it won't appear in your image ever again.

2. Set the stroke to black and the fill to none. Your stroke weight should be quite thin—.2 point is good (Figure 5.10).

   Use the Pen tool to re-create the scan. It actually would work better if you created the outline of Animeboi's head and shoulders as one complete shape.

The reason you want to use such a thin line is so that where one line meets another, you can make them as accurate as possible. You don't want any white space between them.

3. Select the paths that you want to be thicker. In this image, I'd suggest everything except the studs in the wristband and holster, the lightning bolt graphic, and the irises in his eyes.

4. Change the stroke weight of these paths to about 4 points (Figure 5.11).

Now we need to adjust the endpoints of some of these paths. Let's focus on the eyes to give you an idea of the effect we're after.

5. Select all the paths you used to create the eyes, except the iris and the pupil. Use Object ➡ Path ➡ Outline Stroke to turn these lines into shapes.

6. Select the two outer endpoints of the left eye's cheek and average them. With the Direct Selection tool, click on one point, then shift-click the other to select them both. Then use Object ➡ Path ➡ Average

Figure 5.11 Select the lines that you want to be fatter and assign them a weight of 4 points.

Figure 5.12 Use Object ➡ Path ➡ Outline Stroke so you can adjust the endpoints.

(Command Option J/Ctrl Alt J). Click OK to average them using both axes.

Do this for the outer eyelid, too (Figure 5.12).

For the inner eyelid, instead of averaging both points, just move one of them closer to the other. We don't want a severe point here, just a change in the weight.

Take a look at the rest of the image and decide where else you'd like to use this type of line— for instance, in the hair there are some blunt ends that would look better if they were pointy. Select the paths, outline them, and then average the two points where you want a point.

Now it's time for color.

7. Create a new layer and drag it beneath the one you've been working on. Name it "color." You might want to lock the "thin line" layer so you don't inadvertently move or alter something.

    Use the Pen tool to create the shapes you need to add color to your animehead image (Figure 5.13).

The final piece in the way Kenny works is to create the thick black line around his characters and other shapes. Here's how he does that:

8. Once all the color has been created, unlock the "thin line" layer and select everything on both layers—the black lines and shapes along with your colored objects.

    Copy them (Command/Ctrl C).

9. Create another layer and name it "fat line." Drag it below the first two (above your Template layer).

    Select your new layer and paste what you copied in front (Command/Ctrl F).

Figure 5.13 Add your color using a new layer, dragged beneath the line layer.

10. Hide your first two layers—"thin line" and "color."

11. Select everything on the "fat line" layer, and use the Pathfinder palette (Window ➡ Pathfinder) to combine all these shapes into one. Click the "Add to shape area" icon while holding the Option/Alt key—it's the left one in the top row.

You may lose all your colors and strokes. While everything is still selected, change your stroke color to black.

12. You probably have a lot of shapes inside the outline you just created. You don't need them, so select and delete them until you're left with a nice black shape that essentially outlines your entire image (Figure 5.14).

13. Make the "thin line" and "color" layers visible again, and lock them so you don't mess them up.

14. Select your new solid shape on the "fat line" layer and adjust the stroke weight to about 10 points. Use the Strokes palette to change the endcaps and joins to round (Figure 5.15).

Save your file!

These simple techniques can turn an ordinary drawing into a nice graphic. If you have the time, add new layers and create fill colors, additional shadows, and any other details you want.

Remember to name each layer and to lock the ones you aren't drawing on. You might also play with Kenny's trick of hiding and showing edges using Command/Ctrl H (or View Hide/Show Edges).

Save your file when you're done: we'll be using it again later.

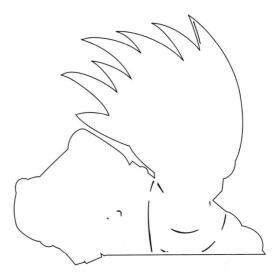
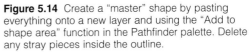

Figure 5.14 Create a "master" shape by pasting everything onto a new layer and using the "Add to shape area" function in the Pathfinder palette. Delete any stray pieces inside the outline.

Figure 5.15 Assign your outline shape a stroke weight of about 10 points, and choose rounded end caps and joins.

DIGITAL DECONSTRUCTION: NANOTECH NINJA

Kenny is working on marketing and licensing some of his images. He's already done several sets of stickers that have wide appeal for both boys and girls. In "Nanotech Ninja" he's created a high-tech rollerblading warrior, complete with ray guns and other sci-fi contraptions.

One of the reasons Kenny's illustrations are so rich is the attention he pays to his original pencil drawings.

"I start rough, then trace and redraw it several times to refine it."

That takes time and talent. You'll also note that he uses a variety of grays to indicate which areas will be the black "holding" lines, and which shadow areas will be a gray or dark blue (Figure 5.17).

He used his line techniques to define the basic image then added solid and gradient fills on separate layers.

What's fun about this image is his use of type.

"I'm always downloading funky fonts to use. As long as they're free!"

He doesn't settle for what comes "out of the box" where type is concerned, however. He pays a lot of attention to letterspacing (kerning). Then he turns his type into outlines (Command Shift O/Ctrl Shift O). He'll alter the shape and size of some of the characters' counters, and otherwise adjust them until they looks the way he wants. He also uses Object ➡ Envelope Distort to bend and warp them to his liking. In this case, the type's shape and perspective adds real movement to the image (Figure 5.18).

There are a couple of ways to achieve this effect. Let's play with them.

Figure 5.16 Nanotech Ninja employs a die-cut shape and warped text.

Figure 5.17 Kenny always begins with a meticulously drawn pencil sketch.

Figure 5.18 Kenny uses the Envelope Distort function to alter his type.

DIY:
WARPED TYPE

Altering type from its typical straightforward appearance is easy, and there are several ways to approach it, depending on the desired effect.

1. Open a new Illustrator document, select the Type tool, and type your first name. Click the Type tool in the Toolbar again, and then type your last name on a new line. This way, you'll have both words as separate elements (Figure 5.19).

    Make a copy of both names by selecting them and holding the Option/Alt key while you drag them off to the side.

2. With your copy still selected, use the Character palette (Command/Ctrl T), to choose a font you like and set the point size to at least 72. (I've used a font called "Skater Dudes" designed by Jakob Fischer, a.k.a. Pizzadude.)

3. Adjust the letterspacing for each name.

    Add space between letters (kerning) by putting your cursor between them and using Option/Alt and the right arrow key.

    Delete extra space using Option/Alt and the left arrow key.

While you don't have to turn your type into outlines to warp and distort it, you do if you want to adjust the shape of a letter, or a counter.

4. Select the baselines of your type with the Direct Selection tool and type Command Shift O/Ctrl Shift O to turn your type into outlines (Type ➡ Create Outlines). Play around with your letterforms to change them (Figure 5.20).

Figure 5.19 Type your name on two separate lines.

Figure 5.20 Make a copy and turn it into outlines (Command Shift O/Ctrl Shift O) and alter the letters in some way.

NOTE: When you turn type into outlines, all the letters are grouped by default. If you have trouble isolating a piece, use Object ➡ Ungroup to separate one letter from another.

5. Select one of your names and then use Object ➡ Envelope Distort ➡ Make with Warp.

The Warp Options dialog box has several areas to experiment with. The pop-up Style menu offers a variety of options to distort your type, from the popular Arc, to the more bizarre Fisheye, Inflate, and Squeeze. To see what you're getting, make sure to check the Preview option (Figure 5.21).

Once you've chosen your style, you can use the Bend slider to determine the amount of warp you want.

Below that are the directions (vertical and horizontal) in which you want the distortion to bend. As long as you have Preview checked, you can play with these options until you see something you like. Then click OK.

6. Select your second name and distort it as well. Choose a different style and adjust the Bend and Distortion settings. Make sure Preview is checked so you can see what you're doing (Figure 5.22).

That's all there is to it.

Let's do it another way, using "Top Object." Use the copy you made previously.

1. Use the Ellipse tool to create an oval shape. It doesn't have to be directly on top of the type, but it does have to be at the top of the stacking order.

2. Select one name and the oval (click on one, then shift-click on the other).

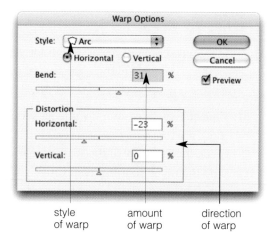

style   amount   direction
of warp   of warp   of warp

Figure 5.21 Make sure you check the Preview option so you can see what you're getting as you warp your type.

Figure 5.22 Use the Arc style and shift the Bend and Distortion options to warp each name separately.

NOTE: You don't have to turn this into outlines unless you want to distort the characters in some way first.

3. Use Object ➡ Envelope Distort ➡ Make with Top Object. This option takes the shape you created and distorts the type to fit within it (Figure 5.23).

4. Create another shape for your last name using the Pen tool and warp it (Figure 5.24).

Take another look at the Envelope Distort submenu. You'll see that there are a few other options there.

The Make with Mesh option brings up a dialog box where you can specify a number of columns and rows. This grid alters your object where the columns and rows intersect. Use the Direct Selection tool or the Mesh tool to move these anchor points around (Figure 5.26).

Use the Release function to reset your type to its original form. If you used an object to warp it, you can just delete it after it's been released.

Envelope Options control the quality of the distortion and how it will interact with other elements in your image.

You may have noticed the blue bounding box and anchor points around your warped text. Warping objects essentially groups them. Use Object ➡ Ungroup (Command Shift G/Ctrl Shift G) to ungroup them.

The Envelope Distort feature can be used on any object, not just type.

Figure 5.23 Create a circle and use "Make with Top Object" to distort the type to fit the shape.

Figure 5.24 Create a custom shape with the Pen tool and warp your second name.

Figure 5.25 The Envelope Distort function has several other options for warping things.

Figure 5.26 Using Make with Mesh creates a grid where you manipulate the anchor points that warp the type.

DIGITAL DECONSTRUCTION: DIE-CUT SHAPES

One other aspect of Kenny's work, the stickers in particular, is the unusual shapes he uses to surround the images, and which dictate their final printed shape. He does this by creating a compound path. His process is a bit complex, and worth looking at.

Once he has all the drawing done, including the background colors and shapes, he unlocks all his layers except the background, selects everything in the entire image, and copies it.

He then locks all his layers and adds a new one, where he pastes the entire image.

While everything is still selected, Kenny outlines everything (Object ➡ Path ➡ Outline Stroke) and then uses the Add to shape area pathfinder so that all the shapes combine into a single object. If there are small bits that create spaces within this shape, he uses the Direct Selection tool to select and eliminate them (① and ②).

He sets the fill of this object to none, and the stroke to black, and then moves the layer underneath his main elements, but above the background layer in the Layers palette. This way, he can see his character while he's creating the die-cut shape.

He adjusts the weight of the stroke so that the outer edge is some distance from his image. He also selects rounded caps and joins in the Stroke palette, which simplifies the shape (③).

With the path selected, he uses Object ➡ Path ➡ Outline Stroke to turn his shape into a compound path. He then deletes the inner path and any stray points that may show up (④).

Figure 5.27 Kenny's stickers start as square images. He uses a compound path to create the die-cut shape (below).

① combine all shapes

② clean up

③ outline stroked path

④ delete inner path

He creates a rectangle that covers the entire image, and sends it behind the mask shape (Command/Ctrl X, Command/Ctrl B). Finally, he selects the rectangle and the mask shape and makes them a compound path (Command/Ctrl 8, or Object ➡ Compound Path ➡ Make), setting its stroke to none, and fill to white. This creates a window in the rectangle in the shape of the mask (⑤).

Now he can move the layer back to the top of the Layers palette. His image shows through the mask shape within the compound path (⑥).

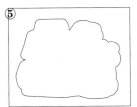

create compound path | move compound path to top of Layers palette

DIY: DIE-CUT

The reason Kenny creates a compound path for his image is because he wants to make sure the background colors and objects are included in the final shape of a sticker. Rather than fussing with adjusting where these objects end to define the shape, he lets the compound path create that edge. He also includes a mask layer that the printer uses to create the die needed to trim the printed piece into its final shape.

1. Open the "anime" file you created in the first DIY and add a layer for your background. Drag it underneath your line and color layers.

2. Create an interesting background. It could be as simple as a rectangle with a color or gradient fill, or, as Kenny does, you might want to add some details that further illustrate just where animeboi is (Figure 5.28).

Lock this layer when you're finished.

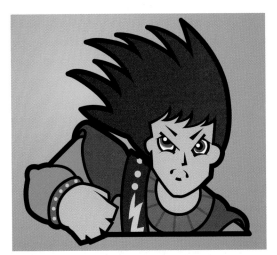

Figure 5.28 Add a background to Animeboi.

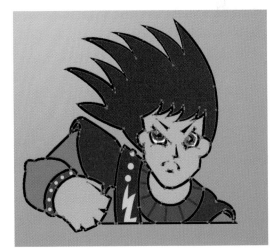

Figure 5.29 Select everything and paste a copy to a new layer, then outline all your strokes.

3. Unlock the color and line layers and select everything (Command/Ctrl A), and copy it (Command /Ctrl C).

    Lock the color and line layers.

4. Add a new layer and paste what you've copied in place (Command/Ctrl F or Command /Ctrl B) (Figure 5.29).

5. While everything is still selected, use Object ➡ Path ➡ Outline Stroke to make sure all the paths are turned into shapes (Figure 5.30).

6. Combine all these elements into a single shape using the "Add to shape area" option in the Pathfinder palette (the far left icon in the top row).

7. Hide the color, line, and template layers and toggle to Outline View (Command/Ctrl Y, or View ➡ Outlines). If there are any stray bits inside the outline, delete them, then toggle back to Preview mode (Command/Ctrl Y). Show the color and line layers again; you'll need to see how your die-cut shape will look surrounding your image.

8. Select your shape and set the fill to none and the stroke to at least 100 points or more. Also select rounded ends and joins in the Stroke palette to soften the edge a bit.

9. When you've established a nice shape, some distance away from Animeboi, out-line it (Object ➡ Path ➡ Outline Stroke). Delete the inner shape this will create, and again, check for any stray bits inside the shape and delete them, too.

10. On the same layer, draw a rectangle that's larger than your background object(s) and send it to the back.

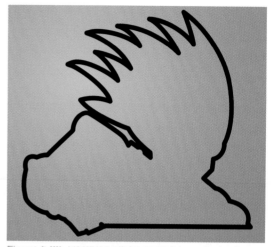

Figure 5.30 Combine all the parts into a single shape and delete any interior elements.

Figure 5.31 With your image visible, make the stroke around it about 100 points thick and outline it.

Figure 5.32 Create a compound path using the outer edge of your outlined path and a large rectangle. Set the fill color to white (not black) when you're done.

NOTE: To make a compound path, the shape of the "window" needs to be on top.

11. Select both the die-cut shape and the rectangle and make a compound path (Object ➡ Compound Path ➡ Make, or Command/Ctrl 8) (Figure 5.32).

NOTE: If you don't get a clear window in the shape of your path—that is, if the resulting object is all one color—open the Attributes palette and switch the path direction (Figure 5.33).

12. Set the fill color for the compound path to white with no stroke and drag this layer to the top. Show all your layers, if any are hidden.

Save your file!

Using a compound path this way lets you see what the final image will look like after it's been trimmed into the shape you created. While we just used the basic outline of Animeboi to dictate that shape, you could just as easily create an object from scratch with the Shape tools or Pen tool to use as your "window."

KEY POINTS

- Use a very thin stroke weight when you create your initial line with the Pen tool to ensure there are no gaps where one line meets another.

- Use layers to organize your objects.

- Leaving the "Linked" option unchecked when placing a template image embeds it in your image.

- Use Object ➡ Path ➡ Average (Command Option J/Ctrl Alt J) to modify the ends of an outlined path.

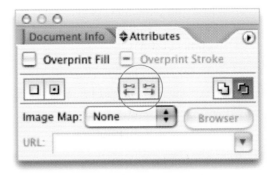

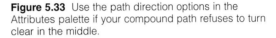

Figure 5.33 Use the path direction options in the Attributes palette if your compound path refuses to turn clear in the middle.

Figure 5.34 Move the compound path's layer to the top to see your final product.

- Create thicker outer edges for your image by using the "Add to shape area" Pathfinder on a copy of your objects.

- Turn type into outlines (Command Shift O/Ctrl Shift O) to modify the letterforms.

- The Envelope Distort feature can be used on type as well as objects.

ON YOUR OWN:
CANDY PACKAGE

Kenny's style and techniques are a hit with the middle school crowd in particular. And while I am not condoning inappropriate eating habits, it would be a perfect visual approach to the packaging for a candy or snack product.

Design and illustrate a package for an invented treat and see how many of Kenny's techniques you can incorporate: the graphic edges, the warped type, and even the idea of a die-cut shape.

HEIDI SCHMIDT

Custom Patterns • Spot Color

Heidi Schmidt didn't bill herself as a professional illustrator until she realized her favorite gouache technique was a perfect match with Illustrator's vector-based graphic approach.

Heidi was born and raised in the San Francisco area. She is an avid bike rider, logging more than 8,500 miles to raise funds and awareness for the San Francisco Aids Foundation.

While she is incredibly busy with her freelance illustration and web site design, she admits to playing hooky once in a while, indulging in trips to the Napa Valley a short distance away, as well as Full Belly Farm, where she gets her organically grown produce.

Another favorite pastime is visiting the art supply store, just down the block.

"I'm always interested in trying new things, so I'm probably over there about three times a day," she jokes.

Trying new things includes working with egg tempera, a time-honored medium that requires egg yolks to bind powdered pigments. It's a complicated process, and painting this way is exacting.

"My egg tempera pieces are all pretty small," Heidi says. "They're easier to manage that way."

She's enjoying the challenge of working with the media because, she says, it suits her style: tight and very graphic.

She also takes printmaking courses at a local community college.

"I spend a lot of time in my studio, isolated from other artists. It's good to go over to the school to be with other people, get a new perspective on things, and just talk about making art."

Figure 6.1 Heidi's illustration style grew out of her graphic design education, where she learned to let small shapes of solid color create an overall image. This poster was one she created for a local theater group she was involved with. It's one of her first printed digital illustrations.

Heidi attended the California College of Arts and Crafts, which has two campuses. One across the bay from San Francisco, in Oakland, offers the fine art courses. The other campus in San Francisco houses their design programs, where Heidi studied. She earned her B. F. A. in Graphic Design.

One of Heidi's first jobs was with a company that provided schematics for high-powered microscopes. They had a Macintosh computer and she instantly recognized its value as both a design and illustration tool.

Figure 6.2 Heidi doesn't scan a sketch into the computer before developing an image. She rarely sketches anything first, except when some piece of anatomy might be creating issues.

After moving to New York City where she worked as a designer and illustrator for *Games* and *Games Jr.* magazines, she began to play around with the Mac as a way to make illustration.

"Back then, it was almost impossible to get someone to take a digital file. I'd have to create all the films and separations and hand that in as my finished image. Not to mention making the colors on your monitor match the actual printed piece."

Now, of course, it's almost the exact opposite.

That fact also had an impact on Heidi's career in terms of working with artist's representatives. She's been with Mendola Artists for almost ten years at this point. When she thought she should get another rep for the west coast, she quickly discovered that a rep's job is no longer regional. With the advent of the Internet, Heidi's rep can garner work for her from all corners of the world.

So Heidi is back in California at this point, and her rep is in Manhattan. They've yet to meet in person. "I've been incredibly busy this year. It's crazy, but it's good. You never know what next year will bring. I love working with Mendola."

Figure 6.3 Heidi's interpretation of real objects is very graphic and stylized. This image uses the gradual absence of detail to imply depth.

Figure 6.4 While Heidi uses flat colors in most areas of her illustration, she is an expert at adding just the right touches of gradients and transparencies to something to make it pop. She's even created a "recipe" for drawing chocolate covered cherries (see the chapter title page).

Even though Heidi's formal education didn't include working with the computer, her professional work in illustration has always been totally digital.

"I'd done some assignments with gouache in school, and I liked the flat, graphic way I could

Figure 6.5 Heidi credits the art director she worked with on this assignment to get the detail just right on her strawberries.

Figure 6.6 This is one of the few of Heidi's illustrations where she's used duplicates of an object (the leaves). Traditionally, she draws each element individually to ensure there's visual diversity. The only exception to this is in her pattern designs.

represent things. The computer was an easier, cleaner way to achieve the same results."

She's been using the computer as her illustration medium so long that she was one of the beta testers for Aldus FreeHand, before Macromedia took it over. In return, they used some of her artwork as the opening splash screen for the program.

Heidi's advice to students is great: "Be flexible!" She cautions illustrators who are just starting out to be open to new ideas for how to do things, to take art direction seriously, and to be willing to make changes. She credits this attitude for her continued success.

"When people hire me, they know what they're going to get in terms of style, they know I'll be on time with the assignment, even if it's an emergency, and that I am always willing to make corrections or changes."

Heidi's clients include package design and illustration for Fisher Price Toys, Hasbro Toys (she

recently created a jigsaw puzzle image of desserts for them), Sunsweet, Budweiser, and MGM studios, among others.

Because she uses so many colors in each piece, Heidi is meticulous in saving her swatches as Libraries. If she forgets, she's developed a way to retrieve a lost palette.

"If I want to use the same Color palette again, I'll open the illustration that used it, copy everything, and paste it into a new document. Then I delete everything, but the colors I want are now in my Swatches palette."

One area of work that Heidi enjoys a lot is creating patterns. She's been responsible for a lot of the patterns used on Fisher Price packaging.

DIGITAL DECONSTRUCTION: FABRIC PATTERNS

Illustrator comes with several libraries of patterns to use as fills, and it's always a good idea to know how to make your own. In Heidi's case, she has no choice. Her clients require original artwork.

She also follows the time-honored procedure of creating a single "tile" that can be developed into an overall pattern. Her biggest concern is that the overall design flows, and that the edges of her tiles are invisible.

That usually demands very large images in order to develop complex designs with no apparent repeats.

In this floral pattern, Heidi has created two layers of shapes, and used three different design motifs.

After she created the paisley-shaped design, she grouped it (Command/Ctrl G) so she could more easily select all the elements involved. She rotated and reflected it to begin the pattern, and then continued to make copies across a large area.

The second layer of the design is created by the top objects—flowers and leaves. As with the paisley, once Heidi had an element complete with all the shapes and colors assigned, she grouped it to simplify making the repeats.

The most challenging aspect of creating a pattern, after you've developed your concept and designed the parts, is to create the tile that allows the pattern to be printed in an all-over fashion, whether the final use is for wallpaper, wrapping paper, fabric, or in Heidi's case, package design.

Figure 6.7 Heidi's work for Fisher Price sometimes includes creating patterns for their packaging. These assignments are one of the few times Heidi will use an element multiple times.

Figure 6.8 After creating an element, Heidi groups the individual parts so she can select the entire thing with her selection tool.

Heidi manages this by creating a mask, rather than dividing overlapping parts and deleting them to create a pattern tile. If she were interested in making her patterns into swatches, she would have to create a perfect rectangle, and delete any portions of the pattern that fell outside its borders. Since she isn't, it simplifies her job quite a bit. And while this particular pattern tile is rectangular in shape (and could therefore be made into a swatch), tiles for surface pattern design can range from T shapes, to triangles, to polygons. Working this way provides more design freedom for Heidi than Illustrator's Swatches palette can deliver.

Creating a pattern to use as a swatch requires the same care that Heidi takes, and can create problems if the tile isn't perfect.

Even though it's nice to play with the pattern libraries that come with Illustrator, knowing how to make one of your own provides you with a lot more freedom as a designer and illustrator. Let's take a look at how it's done.

DIY:
CREATE A PATTERN SWATCH

Since Illustrator can't work with shapes for pattern tiles other than rectangles, that's where we'll start.

1. In a new Illustrator document, use the Rectangle tool to create a perfect square (either click and type in the dimensions, or hold the Shift key as you drag) (Figure 6.10).

This will be the shape of your pattern tile. If you want a background color, you can add it now. Ultimately, you're going to want to eliminate the stroke color for this rectangle so you don't get a checkered effect in your pattern.

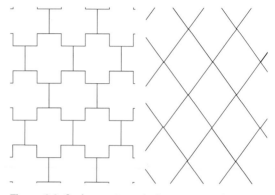

Figure 6.9 Surface pattern designs are not always based on rectangles. They can be just about any geometrical shape, as long as the individual tiles can be laid side by side, top to bottom.

Figure 6.10 Illustrator can only make pattern swatches with rectangular tiles, so start with a perfect square as your foundation.

Figure 6.11 Center a nice circle in the middle of your square. By the way, you can't use a pattern fill in something you intend to make into a pattern swatch, so don't go there!

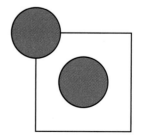

Figure 6.12 Drag a copy of the circle to the corner of your square, making sure the center of the circle is exactly on the corner point. Turning on Snap to Point in the View menu will help.

2. Draw a circle with a different fill color in the middle of your square. Use the Align palette to make sure both objects are centered to each other (Figure 6.11).

3. Grab the circle and drag a copy to the upper left corner of your square, making sure to place the center of your circle exactly on the corner of the square (Figure 6.12). Use Command/Ctrl Y to toggle to Outline View and zoom in to guarantee it's perfectly positioned.

4. Select both the corner circle and the square and drag a copy of both of them to the right so the left edge of the new square lines up exactly with the right edge of the original square. Hold the Shift key to ensure a constrained movement (Figure 6.13).

5. Now select the two top circles and the original square and drag a copy straight down, again holding the Shift key (Figure 6.14).

You now have the basis for a simple polka dot pattern.

6. Delete the two copied rectangles (Figure 6.15).

   You're ready to create the actual tile, so it's time to change the stroke around your square to none.

7. Select your square and cut it (if you don't want a background color) or copy it (if you do want a background color).

   If you decide to copy it, make sure to deselect it before moving to the next step.

8. Paste the square in front (Figure 6.16).

9. There are two ways you can proceed from here. Either use Object ➡ Path ➡ Divide

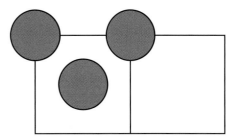

Figure 6.13 Drag a copy of the square and the corner circle to the other side of the original.

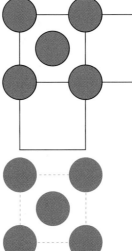

Figure 6.14 Drag another copy of the top two circles and the original square down below the original.

Figure 6.15 Delete the two squares you copied and eliminate any strokes assigned to your objects.

Figure 6.16 Cut or copy your rectangle and paste it in front (Command/Ctrl X or C, Command/ Ctrl F).

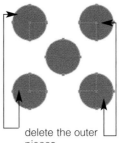

delete the outer pieces

Figure 6.17 Your finished tile should be a square with quarter circles in each corner.

Objects Below, or the Crop option in the Pathfinder palette.

10. If you choose to Divide Objects Below, you'll be left with some remnants that need to be eliminated before you can make your swatch.

Select the outer three-quarters of the four corner circles and delete them (Figure 6.17).

11. Drag your pattern tile into the Swatches palette.

12. Create a shape and fill it with your new pattern (Figure 6.18).

If your pattern is too large or too small, you can scale it without affecting the size of the object.

13. Select the shape you filled and either:

Select the Scale tool and Option/Alt click on the object. In the dialog box that pops up, uncheck "Scale Strokes & Effects," and "Objects." Then type in the percent of enlargement or reduction you want.

or

Use Object ➡ Transform ➡ Scale to access the same dialog box. Make sure "Patterns" is the only thing checked. Then type in the percentage of enlargement or reduction you want. Check the Preview button to see what you're getting (Figure 6.19).

That was a very simple example. Let's take it a step further and make a pattern that isn't quite so ordinary or symmetrical.

The key to being successful here is to remember that whatever you cut off one edge of your tile has to be at the opposite edge (Figure 6.20).

Figure 6.18 Draw a new shape and fill it with your new pattern!

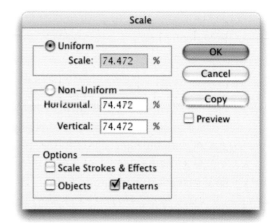

Figure 6.19 To adjust the size of the pattern without affecting the the size of the object, uncheck "Scale Strokes & Effects," and "Objects."

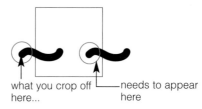

what you crop off here...   needs to appear here

Figure 6.20 If something falls outside your pattern tile at one edge, then that piece needs to be placed to the inside at the opposite edge of your tile.

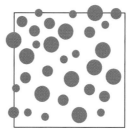

Figure 6.21 Fill your square with randomly sized circles. Have some of them overlap the edge at the top and left. Don't put any circles overlapping the corners.

14. Create a new square. If you choose to stroke it at this time, remember you'll have to eliminate the stroke color before you make your swatch.

15. Let's continue with the dot theme, but make it more random.

16. Draw several circles of varying sizes (and colors, if you want), but make sure you keep them all within the boundaries of your square.

17. Selectively add circles at the left and top edges, so they are partially "out of bounds" (Figure 6.21).

18. Repeat Steps 4 and 5, only make sure you are selecting and copying the square and *all* the circles that overlap the edges. (You can copy the square and all the dots, if that's easier.)

19. Delete the extra squares. If you copied all the circles as well, delete any that are totally outside your original square.

20. Delete the stroke on your square, if you have one, then cut or copy it, and paste it in front.

21. Use either method from Step 9 to crop your tile so you can make a swatch, and drag the results to your Swatches palette.

When you use this pattern to fill an object, you'll still have polka dots, but in a much more random pattern. It should be difficult to see where the tiles begin and end.

If you follow the simple premise that what gets cut off on one side must be within the tile at the opposite side, you can create very sophisticated patterns, like the ones Heidi creates for Fisher Price.

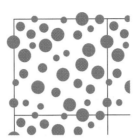

Figure 6.22 Drag copy all the circles and the square to the left and down to make sure the overlapping circles are repeated at the right and bottom edges.

Figure 6.23 Use the Divide Objects Below or Crop Pathfinder using the original square (see Step 9). Then drag your tile to the Swatches palette.

Figure 6.24 It's still polka dots, but much less symmetrical and boring.

DIGITAL DECONSTRUCTION: CHRISTMAS ORNAMENTS

Heidi's done a lot of food illustrations, and has truly perfected the technique for capturing the highlights on anything from strawberries to candy apples and chocolate. She's used those techniques for a series of Christmas tree ornaments, demonstrating that a good technique is broadly applicable.

In this particular illustration, each ornament was composed of small shapes, sometimes overlapping with transparencies. It's very complex, using literally hundreds of paths.

The key to Heidi's success with this image is her ability to re-create the distortions and reflections inherent in glass objects. That takes a lot of study and experimentation.

Heidi elected to use spot colors when she created this image, resulting in a Swatch Library with dozens of colors. Every time you use a spot color for strokes and fills, Illustrator automatically creates a swatch for it in your Swatches palette. We'll look at spot colors specifically in a minute.

While the Pantone, TOYO, and other Color Libraries make it very easy to select colors, it's important to remember that using more than three spot colors becomes redundant. The minute you need four colors, you should seriously consider printing the job in process color (CMYK).

That doesn't mean you can't use these great colors in your work, though. It just means that they'll need to be changed to process colors later.

Luckily, Heidi worked for a commercial printer at one point, and knows how to deal with converting these colors before she sends a job like this to a client, or to press.

Figure 6.25 Heidi's Christmas ornaments (above).

You can see the number of shapes she created for the grape ornament in order to visually define the contours and highlights (left).

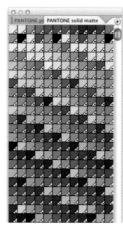

Figure 6.26 The Pantone Library offers literally hundreds of colors (left).

Each time you use one, Illustrator automatically places it in your Swatches palette so you can use it again (above).

FYI:
ABOUT SPOT COLOR

It's every designer and illustrator's dream to be awarded the budget that can afford full-color printing. Unfortunately, that's not always the case. When process color isn't an option, it pays to understand flat color, also referred to as "spot" color.

A spot color is premixed ink. Each time you specify a spot color, you incur the need for creating a separate negative and printing plate. Since most commercial presses are one-, two-, or four-color, it stands to reason that creating an image that utilizes one, two, or four colors will be the most economical.

There are also six-color presses, which essentially let you print a process color job with a couple of spot colors—like a metallic ink or a varnish to make something shine.

Illustrator comes with several Spot Color Libraries, each with an overwhelming number of colors. It's very tempting to use them instead of mixing colors using CMYK values.

If you succumb to that temptation, you could easily wind up using dozens of spot colors in an image. This isn't an issue unless you also use transparencies and need to save your file in EPS format to use in a page layout program, like QuarkXPress.

Illustrator can only export up to twenty-seven spot colors with transparencies in an EPS file, and will let you know when you exceed that number.

Let's experiment with the Spot Color Libraries and the issues that occur when they're used inappropriately. (You'll explore how to create your own in Chapter 9).

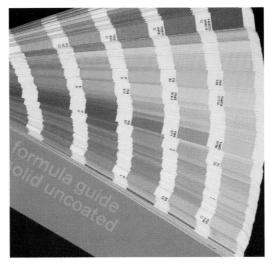

Figure 6.27 Pantone, a manufacturer of spot color inks, also publishes guides to converting spot colors into CMYK values.

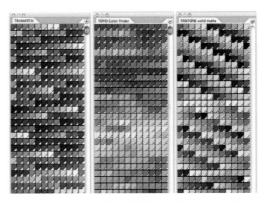

Figure 6.28 TRUMACH, TOYO,and Pantone are all examples of spot color systems, each made by a different manufacturer.

DIY:
USING SPOT COLOR LIBRARIES

1. In a new Illustrator document, create a 1" x 1" square in the upper left corner. Drag a copy of it to the right (hold your Shift key to keep it in line) and then duplicate it several times (Command/Ctrl D) (Figure 6.29).

   Create a grid of these boxes by selecting the row or column of boxes you created and dragging a copy, and duplicating that a couple of times.

2. Open the Pantone solid matte Library from the Window menu (Window ➡ Swatch Libraries ➡ PANTONE solid matte) (Figure 6.30).

3. Fill your squares with spot colors. Select a square, then click on a color in the Swatch Library.

4. If the Swatches palette isn't open it, open it from the Window menu.

NOTE: Opening a Swatch Library doesn't replace your Swatches palette—they're two different things. A library is a resource you can use. As you select colors from a Swatch Library, they are placed in your Swatches palette (Figure 6.31).

---

5. From the Swatches palette's submenu, choose "Select All Unused" and then click the trash icon at the bottom of the palette. Click OK when it asks you if you're sure.

   This removes any colors that you haven't used in your grid.

6. You'll notice that each of these swatches has a little dot in it, indicating it's a spot color.

   Switch your Swatches palette view to "List View" from the submenu. You'll see both a

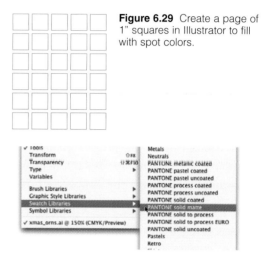

Figure 6.29 Create a page of 1" squares in Illustrator to fill with spot colors.

Figure 6.30 Open the Pantone solid matte Library from the Window menu.

Figure 6.31 The PANTONE solid matte Library and the Swatches palette look alike, but they are two separate entities.

dot as well as a CMYK icon next to the swatch and its name (Figure 6.32).

7. Select one of your squares and take a look at your Color palette.

The color ramp at the bottom, and the CMYK sliders, have been replaced by a ramp of the spot color. Clicking anywhere in this space changes the spot color to a lighter value, or tint (Figure 6.33).

NOTE: Using a tint of your process color won't add another swatch to your library. Also note that a tint is not the same as creating a transparency.

A tint is produced by screening a spot color so that it's broken into dots. The smaller the dots, the lighter the appearance of the spot color (Figure 6.35). You won't see the dots on your monitor, or on a soft proof, but when the image goes to a commercial printer, they'll be created for the printing plates.

8. Save this file, making sure you choose the EPS file format in the Save dialog box.

9. Duplicate one or two of your squares, and assign them a transparency of 50% (not a tint) using the Transparency palette (Figure 6.36).

10. Save your file again.

Did you get an error message? Illustrator doesn't like spot colors and transparencies together. Since it's assumed that you're using spot colors, Illustrator also assumes that if you need a lighter value of a color, you'd create a tint, not a transparency.

You can only create transparencies with process colors, because, in fact, they really aren't transparent—they're a mix of cyan,

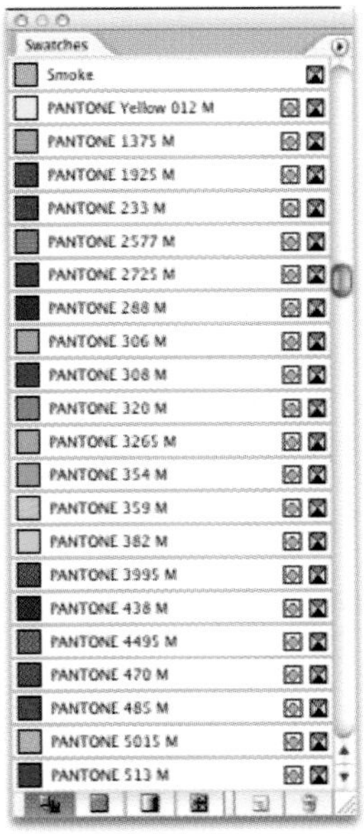

Figure 6.32 No matter how you view the Swatches palette, each swatch is marked as either a spot or process color.

Figure 6.33 Note how a spot color is displayed in the Color palette.

Figure 6.34 Use the tint ramp in the Color palette to create a lighter version of a spot color.

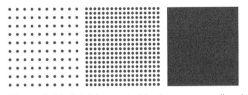

Figure 6.35 A tint is created by larger or smaller dots of a spot color. Smaller dots create the illusion of a lighter color.

Figure 6.36 Duplicate some squares and make them transparent.

magenta, yellow, and black that make the color *appear* transparent, whether on its own, or overlapping another color.

In order to continue working on and saving this file, we need to either delete the transparent objects, delete some of our spot colors, or convert the spot colors to CMYK values.

11. To convert a spot color to a process color is easy: select one of your squares, then click on the dot in your Color palette (Figure 6.37).

12. Repeat this for each of the squares in your document, and save it.

Unless you use more than twenty-seven spot colors, along with transparencies, you're fine. The minute you step over that limit, Illustrator will balk.

Don't let this scare you into not using your spot color libraries, though! Many artists prefer working this way. There are so many colors, and having a palette that diverse can be liberating.

Just remember that for a full CMYK color job, you need to either convert any objects that use spot colors into CMYK values, or delete some of them from your Swatches palette before you go to print.

NOTE: You can safely delete as many swatches as you want without damaging your image; Illustrator simply converts those colors to CMYK values automatically.

Figure 6.37
Convert a spot color to a CMYK color by clicking the dot in the Color palette.

Figure 6.38 Heidi uses spot color libraries frequently, both to simplify mixing colors, and to generate tints and transparencies for the subtle shadows and other details in her work.

KEY POINTS

- Pattern tiles can be square or rectangular.

- To ensure your pattern tiles meet at the edges, any objects cropped off one edge must be placed within the tile at the opposite edge.

- Avoid using a black stroke around your pattern tile unless you want a checkered effect.

- Avoid using a colored background for your pattern if you think you might want to change it later. Use a duplicate of the shape pasted behind the pattern-filled shape and fill that with a solid color.

- Use Object ➡ Transform, or Option/Alt click with the Scale tool to enlarge or reduce the size of your pattern within a shape.

- Open Spot Color Libraries from the Window menu (Window ➡ Swatch Libraries).

- Spot Color Libraries are resources for you to use which are separate from the Swatches palette.

- Spot colors are automatically added to your Swatches palette when you use them.

- Create lighter values of spot colors using the tint ramp in your Color palette.

- Illustrator will balk at saving a file with too many spot colors and transparencies. Convert your spot colors to CMYK.

ON YOUR OWN:
FOOD IMAGE

Heidi's amazing talent with creating food or glass ornaments that include intricate details and accurate reflections, highlights, and shadows is enviable. Her faculty with creating patterns is also a very marketable skill.

Try your hand at using both techniques. Design and illustrate a cookbook cover, or a cooking magazine cover. Use one of the Pantone libraries for your colors, and include at least one pattern.

ROCCO BAVIERA

Defining Negative Spaces • Using Bitmaps

Rocco Baviera's use of negative space to create his images is a fascinating approach that yields illustrations suitable for a variety of clients.

In spite of his parent's lack of enthusiasm regarding a career as an artist, Rocco Baviera attended Sheridan College and the Ontario College of Art & Design in Toronto, both prestigious art schools. He studied drawing, painting, and graphic design. His first professional job was an oil painting depicting the winning goal of the Canadian hockey team against the Soviets during the 1972 Olympics.

Since then, Rocco has reinvented himself as an artist and designer many times. Always open to a new technique, his work shifted from oils to watercolors in a fairly realistic style (Bernie Fuchs was one of Rocco's early inspirations).

Before he bought his first computer, Rocco used a variety of media to create his images. Although he may be best known for his translucent paintings with oils, he's been known to work with oil crayons, charcoal, watercolors, and even mixed media on plaster. His work using these media is more representational than what he does on the computer. It was during this phase of his career that he began illustrating children's books.

When he made the transition from traditional media to using the Macintosh, his style of illustration changed completely. He does still get assignments now and then from clients looking for his oil or watercolor technique, but not often. While he started with Photoshop collages, his work using Illustrator is alternately rich and vibrant or light and airy, and always playful.

Why the shift from Photoshop to Illustrator? "I didn't want to keep worrying about finding or

Figure 7.1 This painting, from the book *The First Painter*, uses a variety of media on plaster tablets that Rocco created to imitate the quality of painting on cave walls.

creating the perfect photographs for the Photoshop work, plus you're working with existing images, rather than something from your imagination. Illustrator is a more graphic program, so I can refer to a photo and then reinterpret it."

He's enjoying his current work a lot. "I like being able to distort and exaggerate elements. I never thought I'd be a cartoonist, but my work is taking on a more graphic look."

He's currently balancing his freelance work, which is about half illustration and half design, with being a new dad to Bianca Lun.

"She's amazing. She changed our lives. We had no idea what we were missing."

Rocco and his wife, Colleen O'Hara (also an accomplished Illustrator; see Chapter 4) flew from Toronto, Canada to Beijing, China, and from there to the Hunan province farther south to pick her up. A week-long journey for a lifetime of joy.

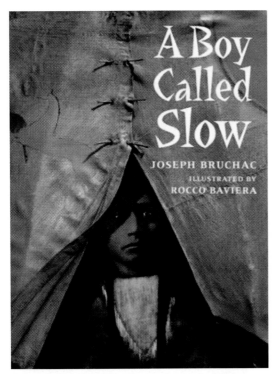

Figure 7.2 *A Boy Called Slow* is the story of Sitting Bull. It won the 1996 Mountain and Plains Book Award, and an Award of Excellence from *Communication Arts* magazine.

Figure 7.3 Bianca Lun is running the Baviera/O'Hara household, in spite of not speaking in complete sentences yet. "She can shake her head 'no' with great vehemence."

The years leading up to his recent parenthood were equally eventful.

"I learned how to do pre-press production the old-fashioned way, before there were computers. I do not miss spec'ing type!" But that training has served him well, as evidenced by the strong graphic style of his current work and his sensitivity to type.

"I get my fonts from all over...and will frequently create a graphic element to replace a character. I love Illustrator's glyphs palette."

He began his career by freelancing as both a designer and an illustrator for ad agencies and magazines. In the past twenty years as a professional, Rocco has worked for such clients as the World Wildlife Fund, Westinghouse, the Grammy Awards, Molson's Brewery, Penguin Books (he's illustrated many children's books), and Harcourt Publishing.

He's also won numerous awards, including those from The New York Society of Illustrators, *Communication Arts* magazine, and the Art Director's Club of Metropolitan Washington.

Early experiences with artist's reps left a sour taste, so Rocco prefers to represent himself. He maintains online portfolios on *theispot.com*, *childrens–illustrators.com*, and *folioplanet.com* web sites along with his own site, *roccobaviera.com*. He and Colleen have a joint web site, "but we haven't done anything with it yet."

His advice to students: learn how to draw well with a pencil. "Just knowing how to use a com-

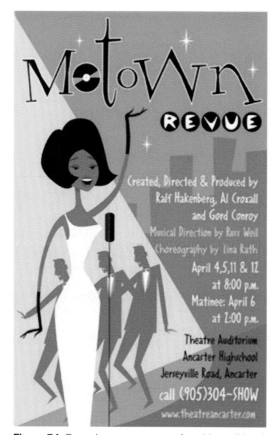

Figure 7.4 Rocco's success comes from his traditional training in typography and design. This poster was featured in an article about color palettes in *Dynamic Graphics* magazine.

Figure 7.5 This bear is one of several images that Rocco was commissioned to create for the World Wildlife Fund.

Figure 7.6 Rocco starts with a colored rectangle for his background, which he then masks using a free-form shape created with the Pencil tool and a pressure-sensitive tablet.

puter is sort of like using a calculator. You're not relying on a concept, you're just pushing the right buttons."

He always starts with tight 3" x 5" pencil drawings that he either photographs with a digital camera, or scans in to use as templates in Illustrator.

"I've started taking digital images of my thumbnails instead of scanning them. They're just as good to send out for approval, and to use as templates. And, when you have ten or twelve thumbnails, scanning them all takes too much time."

DIGITAL DECONSTRUCTION: TIGER

This tiger image, one of a series of animals he produced for the World Wildlife Fund, uses an interesting approach to the line quality defining the tiger's head and features.

Rocco doesn't establish the layer where he places his scanned sketch as a Template layer. Instead, he sets the sketch's transparency to about 60%, locks it, and keeps it at the top of the Layers palette. This allows him to see his plan at all times, while he's actually drawing on layers he adds below.

Rocco started with a black background and drew his colored shapes on top. What wasn't covered became the black edges and other negative spaces of his composition (Figure 7.7). He maintains that "what you leave out is as important as what you put in." And the colors are more vibrant when placed over black. He draws a black rectangle, and then with the Pen tool and a pressure-sensitive tablet, he draws a freeform shape that is used as a mask to create the edge of his image (select both the rectangle and the mask shape and type Command/Ctrl 7, or Object ➡ Clipping Mask ➡ Make). Rocco's black is a mix of cyan, yellow, magenta, and black, so it's dense and rich.

While Rocco prefers a pressure-sensitive tablet and pen for drawing, he's no stranger to the Pen tool. In this image, he created the large areas of color using that tool, rather than the pencil to ensure smoother curves with a minimum of anchor points.

He also tries to keep his color palette fairly simple and is in the process of creating custom Swatch Libraries so he can use the same palette

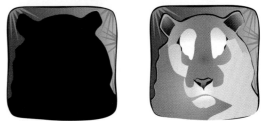

Figure 7.7 He adds his shapes using the Pen tool. Where there is no color, the black background creates the illusion of a black outline.

Figure 7.8 Rocco uses found images as reference, but is not married to the amount of detail they provide, preferring to exercise his vision of the final image in deciding what details to include.

in more than one image (see Chapter 9, David Brooks, for how to create a Custom Swatch Library).

Once the basic shapes are in place, Rocco adds the details. He generally uses photos for reference in deciding how complex or basic these features will be (Figure 7.8).

The eyes, which are simple linear gradients, and the subtle drop shadows under the whiskers add dimension and texture to the image.

DIY:
WORKING WITH THE NEGATIVES

In the "baviera" folder on your DVD, you'll find a scanned sketch of another image Rocco created for the World Wildlife Fund called "whalescan.pict." Open this file in Illustrator. Don't check the Template option this time.

1. Set the sketch's transparency to about 50% and lock the layer so you don't inadvertently move it. While you're working, make sure this layer stays on top so you can always see it.

2. Add another layer for your background and drag it below the layer with the scan.

3. Set your fill to black with no stroke color and trace the surrounding box with the Pen or Pencil tool (Figure 7.11). If you're comfortable with a pressure-sensitive tablet, you could use that to achieve a more fluid line when using the Pencil tool.

4. Set the Transparency of your black background to 40 or 50% so you can see the scan. Lock the layer, name it, and add a new one.

Figure 7.9 The black areas of this whale are actually negative spaces in the illustration.

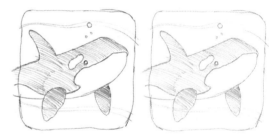

Figure 7.10 After opening the scanned sketch, set its transparency to 50% and lock the layer.

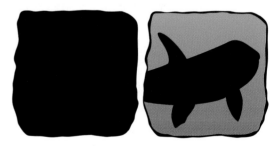

Figure 7.11 After you create your black background, the water shape should follow the outer edge while leaving some black showing, and surround the whale's silhouette.

5. With either the Pen or Pencil, create your "water" shape. Be careful to echo the contour of the black edge, and the outline of the whale (Figure 7.11). The fill for this shape is a linear gradient from turquoise to light purple. Use the Gradient tool to establish the direction of the blend from top to bottom.

   Lock this layer, name it, and add a new one.

Remember as you add layers to keep the scanned sketch layer on top so you can see it.

6. On the new layer, use the sketch to create the whale's belly. As you're drawing, make sure to leave some space between the belly shape and the water background; this will create the black outline around the whale.

   Fill this shape with a white to black gradient.

   Create the subtle highlights above the whale's mouth, at the top of its head, the white spot, the eye, and the front fin. Set the transparency of the highlights to about 50%.

   Lock this layer, name it, and add a new one.

7. This final layer will hold the eye, wavy water lines and the bubbles. Use the Pen or Pencil tool to create the water shapes.

   The top shape is the same turquoise as the top of the water gradient. Once you've drawn this, use the Transparency palette to set its blending mode to Multiply.

   The bottom shape is pale blue, with a transparency of about 35% (Figure 7.13).

8. Finally, you can add your bubbles and eye. The top bubbles have a fill of white with a transparency of 60% and solid white highlights. The bottom bubbles are stroked with white and have no fill.

Figure 7.12 The belly, fin, eye, and highlights are filled with a gradient. The highlights should have a transparency of about 50%.

Figure 7.13 The top wavy shape is set to Multiply, darkening the turquoise behind it. The bottom shape is a pale blue with a transparency of 35%. Add the bubble details and voila!

Don't forget to reset the black background's transparency back to to 100% and hide your scan to get the full effect!

Save your file when you're finished.

DIGITAL DECONSTRUCTION: BEAR

Rocco recently created a series of animal images for *Scholastic* magazine. They represent a significant stylistic change from the piece we just looked at, but rely on many of the same techniques.

The color palettes are softer, and the backgrounds aren't black, but his use of negative space to define the positive elements is still evident. Rocco used the Pencil tool with his pressure-sensitive tablet exclusively in these images to create more naive shapes.

He began with a blue-to-white gradient for the basic background shape, which also defined the sky. Then Rocco sketched in a rough bear shape. He did this first so he could create the ground as a shape that surrounded the bear, rather than going behind it.

The trees came next, and actually extend to the bottom of the image.

With the exception of the ability to set transparencies and blending modes, Illustrator is a lot like using silk screen, or cut paper, where shapes can overlap, covering up what's underneath.

The ground shape was added next. Note the two different shades of blue that create the bear's shadow. Rocco used the Multiply blend mode for the top shape, so the blue underneath it would be intensified.

Because the trees are a large solid shape, Rocco added an additional larger and looser bear shape with a white fill Figure 7.15). He moved this

Figure 7.14 Rocco's style in this series of images for *Scholastic* magazine is looser and lighter.

Figure 7.15 A loosely drawn transparent shape echoes the bear to create the outline.

Figure 7.16 You can see that Rocco is as deliberate in choosing what he leaves out of an image as he is of what he includes.

shape behind the brown bear and set it's transparency to 50%. This effect imitates the black outline technique he used in the tiger image.

Finally, Rocco used the Pencil to create the black shapes that further define the bear: the feet, ears, eyes, and nose. He used Object ➡ Path ➡ Outline Stroke so that all the line work is actually composed of black shapes, rather than strokes.

The final details like the clouds, snow, and tree branches were all added later.

DIGITAL DECONSTRUCTION: THE WOMEN

All illustrators are constantly creating images, even when they aren't working on a specific assignment. Rocco is no exception, and he created this series of women to experiment with a unique technique that includes a bitmapped image from Photoshop.

As usual, Rocco began with a sketch of his image. He either scans it, or takes a digital picture to use as his tracing image.

Since these images incorporate his "negative" edge technique, he began with a black background and set the transparency to about 40% so he could see his scan as well as the image he was creating.

The sky was created as a gradient, and it's shape created a negative space that echoes the shape of the girl's head and shoulders.

In the "Fro" image, Rocco created another black shape that was the same size as the hair shape. He cut this shape and then pasted it as pixels into a new Photoshop file. He added additional space around the shape in which to work (Image ➡ Canvas Size).

Figure 7.17 Rocco used a bitmapped image for the hair in this illustration.

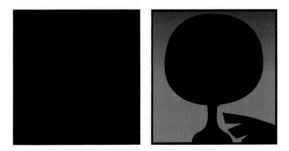

Figure 7.18 After creating the background, Rocco drew the sky he needed to define the woman's head and shoulders.

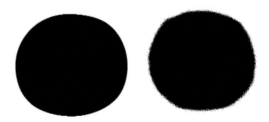

Figure 7.19 Rocco used a soft brush with the mode set to Dissolve to create the fuzzy hair. This image was set to Bitmap mode and saved as a TIFF.

Using a fairly large and very soft brush, and the painting mode set to Dissolve, Rocco painted around the edges to create the fuzzy edge he wanted for the hair (Figure 7.19).

He then changed the mode of this Photoshop file from CMYK to Grayscale, and then to Bitmap so that it was pure black and white with no shades of gray (Image ➡ Mode ➡ Grayscale, then Image ➡ Mode ➡ Bitmap). Doing this allows him to change the color of the shape (if need be) once it's placed it back into Illustrator.

Even though this image was a bitmap, he saved the file as a TIFF to place back into Illustrator. This little trick creates a black-and-white file with the white areas being transparent (Figure 7.20).

Once back in Illustrator, Rocco used File ➡ Place to import the TIFF file, and positioned it where he wanted it.

He also used this technique to create the two golden circles to the right of the figure. In this case, once he imported the circles (one file, used twice), he changed the color from black to a golden orange, and set the transparency to 75% (Figure 7.21).

He added yellow circles on top of these and then another circle filled with a complex gradient of reds.

With the red gradient circles selected, he used the Flair tool (found with the Shape tools) to create a gentle sparkle over the glowing orbs. Even though this gradient is harsh to begin with, the flair effect turns it a soft pink when placed over the lavender background (Figure 7.22).

Once these bits were complete, Rocco created the body and face details, and added his leaf shapes.

Figure 7.20 This bitmapped TIFF file has a transparent background.

Figure 7.21 He added an additional bitmap TIFF file and duplicated it to create the glowing lights in the background.

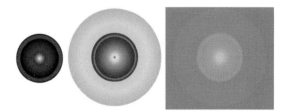

Figure 7.22 Rocco simplified the flair options so the results would be subtle.

Figure 7.23 The other figures in this series use negative space as well. The "Beehive" image also includes a bitmapped image in the background.

He used a similar approach to the beehive woman, changing the bitmap image color from black to a pale lavender gradient that gradually blends into the background color (Figure 7.23).

DIY:
BITMAPS IN ILLUSTRATOR

Let's create a similar effect by creating Rocco's simple bee and adding a bitmap "halo" around it.

1. In Illustrator, open the "bee.pict" file, found in the "baviera" folder on your DVD. Set its transparency to 50% or so, and lock the layer. As before, make sure this layer stays on top of the layers you'll be adding. Don't make it a Template layer.

2. Add a new layer underneath this one.

3. Using the Pen or Pencil tool, draw your bee's body as a solid black object with no stroke.

4. Select the body (make sure all the anchor points are solid) and copy it.

5. Launch Photoshop and create a new document (Command/Ctrl N, or File ➡ New).

If you don't have Photoshop available, jump to Step 12 and use the "beebody.tif" file located in the "baviera" folder on your DVD.

When you have something in your clipboard, Photoshop assumes you want a new document that's the same size, color mode, and resolution of what you cut or copied (Figure 7.25).

6. Click OK to accept the defaults Photoshop presents in the New dialog box, and paste the bee's body as pixels into your new file (Command/Ctrl V). Hit Enter or Return to rasterize the shape.

Figure 7.24 Open the "bee.pict" file in Illustrator.

Figure 7.25 Photoshop assumes you want your new file to be the same size, resolution, and color mode as what's in your clipboard.

This creates a new layer, above the Background layer. You can flatten the image now or later.

7. From the Image menu, choose Canvas Size, and enlarge the canvas by ¹/₂" on all sides.

8. Select the Brush tool, and from the Control bar, set the Brush mode to Dissolve and choose a fairly large, very soft brush.

9. With the foreground color set to black, gently paint around the edge of your bee's body to create a speckly sort of texture (Figure 7.26).

10. When you're satisfied, change the mode from CMYK to Grayscale (Image ➡ Mode ➡ Grayscale). If you didn't flatten your image earlier, Photoshop asks if it's OK to do that. Click Flatten. Click OK again if you're asked if it's all right to delete all the color information.

    Then change the mode again from Grayscale to Bitmap (Image ➡ Mode ➡ Bitmap). Accept the default resolution of 150 pixels per inch and Diffusion Dither.

11. Save your file as "beebody.tif" and you're ready to move back to Illustrator.

12. Once back in Illustrator, use File ➡ Place to put the bee's fuzzy body where it belongs. Make sure it's behind the original body you drew. Command/Ctrl X, Command/Ctrl B will cut it and paste it behind everything else on that layer (Figure7.27).

13. Now you can begin to draw the rest of your bee. Use whatever drawing tool is comfortable, and follow these specifications:

    The bee's body is a gradient from yellow to orange—either linear or radial.

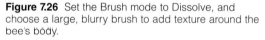

Figure 7.26 Set the Brush mode to Dissolve, and choose a large, blurry brush to add texture around the bee's body.

Figure 7.27 After placing the fuzzy bee's body in Illustrator, make sure to arrange it behind everything.

The wings are white, with a transparency setting of 60%.

The eyes are four circles: black in back, yellow, black, then white for the highlight (Figure 7.28).

The antennae are created by outlining a 3-point stroke (Object ➡ Path ➡ Outline Stroke) then filling them with black and a stroke of white.

You're finished with your tracing image now, so you can either delete that layer or hide it.

14. To make the glow really glow, you're going to want to change its color from black to yellow. Click on the placed TIFF image to select it, then choose a yellow fill color.

The only issue now is adding a background color so we can see the wings.

15. Add a new layer below the one you're working on and create a background. Either use a Shape tool, or draw a freehand shape with the Pen or Pencil, and fill it with a solid color or gradient.

Experiment with the transparency and color of the glow by selecting your placed TIFF and modifying it the same way you would with an object you drew directly in Illustrator. Play with its blending mode. Change the background color.

Your mind is probably racing with all the possibilities for using this technique. If you have time, create a glow behind the bee's eyes (just follow Steps 4 through 11 using the large black eye shape instead of the body to create your Photoshop TIFF file).

One caveat: placing these TIFF files in an Illustrator image increases the file size significantly! Make sure you crop your Photoshop

Figure 7.28 The eye is made up of four shapes.

Figure 7.29 Add some stripes, then delete or hide the tracing image layer.

Figure 7.30 A background color will make the transparent wings more obvious.

files so you aren't placing more image than you really need.

KEY POINTS

- Instead of using a Template layer, you can set the transparency of a placed image to 50%, lock the layer, and draw on layers placed underneath it.

- You can use digital photos of artwork in place of scanned images for tracing.

- When using negative space to define edges, it's important to create closed shapes.

- To create a bitmapped image, set its mode to Bitmap in Photoshop, and save it as a Photoshop or TIFF file.

- Adding bitmapped images to Illustrator significantly increases file size.

ON YOUR OWN:
HALLOWEEN CELEBRATION

Rocco's style is well suited to creating bold, graphic images. His black backgrounds are a natural for spooky Halloween illustrations.

Design and illustrate a poster for a costume shop, or a Halloween event of some sort. A typical poster size is 18" x 24".

See what you can do to use a black, or very dark, background as the edges or lines that define the positive areas in the image. You might also consider adding a bitmapped image, as well.

Don't forget to check out "droplets.mov" in the "baviera" folder on your DVD to learn how to make cool water drop details!

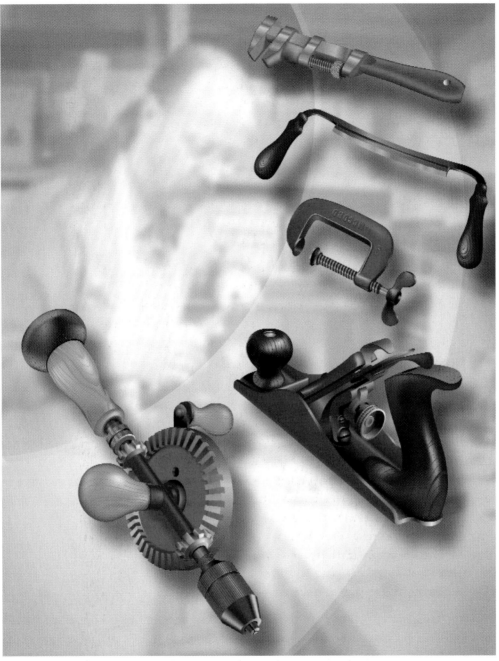

 DAVID MCCORD

Woodgrain Texture • Gradient Mesh

David McCord's interests in mechanics, architecture, and technology have led him to become a highly skilled technical illustrator—a niche in the professional arena that very few illustrators can fill.

Figure 8.1 "I'm a real R. Buckminster Fuller fan." David did this piece to illustrate a blend of the several versions of Fuller's Dymaxion car, an innovative automotive idea developed during the 1930s.

Technical Illustration is one aspect of the illustration field that appeals to those with strong mechanical interests. David McCord, who was drawn to mechanical drafting at an early age, pursued higher education courses in technical documentation at a local community college—until he ran out of money and had to find "a real job."

His portfolio was good enough to land him a series of jobs with engineering firms and manufacturers, and he eventually settled in at Lear-Siegler (now part of Smiths Industries Aerospace) in the engineering department. There, he discovered his aptitude for understanding a lot of the product design and engineering aspects of the projects he worked on. Before long, with the development of CAD (computer-aided design) systems, he found himself as the liaison between the CAD users and the software programmers. In that position, he was instrumental in assisting with the advancement of CAD applications, especially in terms of bridging the gap between the software and its users.

"I have a pretty good balance between my right and left brain...I was able to communicate with both the software and hardware guys to define user interfaces that would work better, and therefore increase productivity."

After a decade of working in this highly technical environment, David realized that he was "a creative person working in an engineering world. In short: I was bored."

While looking for a more fulfilling vocation, he was fortunate to remain at Smiths Industries Aerospace in the position of Art Director for their North American operations. He quickly converted the creative department to using Macs. "I've been a happy Mac user since 1984, and still believe it to be the best platform for professional graphics."

When a corporate decision left no alternatives, David took the opportunity to start his own graphic design firm. He invested his retirement fund into hardware and software, and went from a one-man show to a staff of five within three years.

The business thrived, but David didn't. "I realized that I just wasn't 'boss' material. Even my employees could see that I was more suited to solving design challenges—and my creativity was suffering."

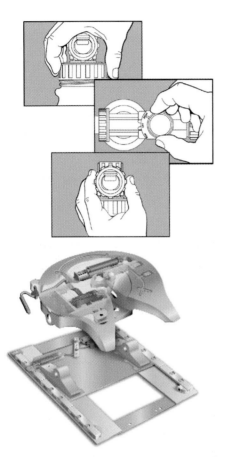

Figure 8.2 David's technical illustrations range from simple step-by-step instructions to extremely complex cutaway images.

Figure 8.3 This illustration of the Airbus A-380 airliner (the largest commercial airliner to date) was done for *Air Transport World* magazine to illustrate an article about the plane's advanced hi-tech "nervous system."

His team moved on to positions elsewhere, and after a year flying solo, David accepted a position as Creative Director at eMedia Solutions. His work now involves development of a wide range of marketing materials, including print, Web, multimedia, and trade show displays—as well as technical illustration (still his favorite work).

Over the years (mostly thanks to Internet marketing), David has done work for clients around the globe, including agencies, industries, and publishers. One of these was *The New York Times*.

"That *New York Times* project was a funny thing. I got a call out of the blue from someone who sounded like he was in a bar or coffee house." It turned out to be legitimate, though, and David enjoyed creating a series of images to illustrate an article about high-tech products that celebrities would love to own. These included the "cap of silence," which allows the wearer to filter out the voices of boring companions, and the "tennisbot" that would replace tennis refs and ensure accurate line calls on the courts.

When David isn't earning his living, he fills his time with a host of activities and interests. He's very involved in his community, including serving

Figure 8.4 David is an avid woodworker and musician when he's not begging at a Medieval Faire, or creating his highly technical images.

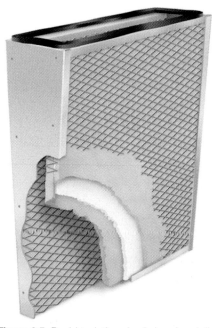

Figure 8.5 David took tin snips in hand and dissected a prototype of this filter in order to illustrate it accurately.

as a Scout Master for a local BSA troop. He also composes original music, plays in a local acoustic trio, and has a digital recording setup in his home. And on the occasional weekend, he plays the part of a beggar at Medieval Faires. He's a long-time member of the SCA (The Society for Creative Anachronism: *http://www.sca.org/*). As he says of a recent weekend of jousts, feasts, and revelry, "This is my great escape. I leave the day-to-day technology behind for a while. I sometimes wish it was for a longer while."

David's advice to aspiring illustrators is to be diverse in your interests. A wide range of experience brings a larger world view, and more range to your creative work as well. But always keep the objectives of your client in mind, and help them achieve it through your illustration.

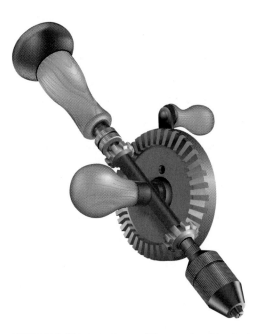

Figure 8.6 This is just one of the woodworking tools David developed for the poster featured on this Chapters introduction page.

DIGITAL DECONSTRUCTION: CRAVIOLA GUITAR POSTER

This poster of David's favorite guitar looks deceptively simple. His innovative use of blends lends a super-realism to the woodgrain in the neck and sides of the body, and his attention to detail in other areas, like the strings and frets, combine to create the illusion of a stylized photograph, rather than an Illustrator image.

"I developed the woodgrain technique almost by accident," he says, while working on a project for Audio Advisor who manufactures high-end audio equipment. Time spent with his dad, an avid woodworker, helped a lot in knowing when he was on the right track.

He began by drawing the grain with the Pen tool, creating a line and then tweaking it with the Direct Selection tool to make it just right. He created a copy of the line, changed it a bit, and then used the Blend tool to create intermediary steps (Figure 8.8). "Sometimes I'll expand the blend and tweak the individual lines in between."

The strings on this guitar are composed of several lines of varying thicknesses and colors, to create a 3D effect (Figure 8.9).

He then created black strokes as shadows diagonally underneath the strings for additional dimension. He set the opacity of these strokes to 30% and Multiply mode so they would become less apparent as lines by blending with the woodgrain beneath them.

The frets on the neck are rectangles with a linear gradient fill of yellows and golds and a single thin stroke of white for the highlight.

David spent an equal amount of attention to detail when constructing the bridge for the guitar. He created the primary shape and added

Figure 8.7 David created this poster of his favorite guitar as a self-promotion piece.

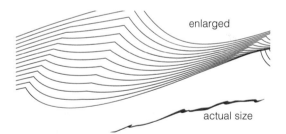

Figure 8.8 David creates the detail in his woodgrain by blending and tweaking paths.

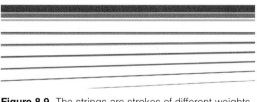

Figure 8.9 The strings are strokes of different weights and colors to create a 3D effect.

his woodgrain blends to start. The pins are simple circles with a radial fill. He added a drop shadow using the same technique as the strings: a shape filled with black, set to a transparency of 67% and Multiply blending mode.

The thoughtfully created details here are the shapes that define the contour of the bridge. David created two shapes that defined the indents on either side. He filled one with a black-to-white linear gradient, and the other with a radial gradient from yellow to brown.

The black-and-white gradient shape was set to Multiply, which darkened the area beneath it. The shape with the radial gradient was set to Overlay mode, which lightened the area beneath it, creating the highlight. Both shapes where assigned transparencies to soften the effect (Figure 8.10).

The sound hole also has wonderful detail. It was created using the Offset Path command (Figure 8.11). After David created the center black shape, he filled each successive shape with a different color to create the illusion of inlaid wood. The elegant brown boxes are simply a dashed stroke.

An Art Nouveau border, typographic treatment, and subtle drop shadows complete this elegant image.

Technical illustration is an area of the profession that has great appeal for people who are devoted to detail. Developing techniques that make those details easy to achieve is one of Illustrator's fortes. Let's play with some woodgrains using David's blending trick.

The most important aspect of technical illustration is research.

Radial blend set to Overlay to create a highlighted area.

Linear blend set to Multiply to create a shadowed area.

Figure 8.10 David's attention to the smallest details are what give this piece its dimension and texture.

Figure 8.11 The sound hole is a simple series of shapes made using the Offset Path command (Object ➡ Path ➡ Offset Path).

Figure 8.12 This woodgrain is fairly open and should be easy to re-create using David's blended paths technique.

Figure 8.13 Start with a brown rectangle which will serve as the background color.

In the case of creating a woodgrain, it's important to analyze the patterns in the grain so you can re-create them more realistically.

DIY:
WOODGRAIN TEXTURE

Figure 8.12 is a photo of a bit of an armoire made of oak. The grain is obvious, and rather coarse, so it should be fairly easy to re-create. The detail in this piece is also ideal for experimenting with the highlight and shadow details David used in the bridge of his guitar.

1. Open a new CMYK Illustrator document and create a 8" x 6" rectangle. Use the Color palette to assign it a stroke of none and a fill of brown (C=40, M=50, Y=65, K=30).

2. Use File ➡ Place to locate and add the "armoirewood.tif" file to this document. Once it's in your document and selected, move it so it doesn't overlap the placed image for now. Lock it so you don't inadvertently move it (Object ➡ Lock ➡ Selection, or Command/Ctrl 2).

3. Using either the Pen or Pencil tool, start re-creating the grain by tracing along the right and left edges of each grain area.

   Your stroke should be set to 1 point black at this point, with no fill color (Figure 8.14).

4. Select every other grain path and change the stroke color to the same brown as the background rectangle (Figure 8.15).

NOTE: Shortcut the Colors palette by using the Eyedropper and click on the background rectangle. Switch the brown from fill to stroke in the Toolbar by clicking on the double arrow at the top right (Figure 8.16).

Figure 8.14 Using the "armoire.tif" as a guide, re-create the left and right edges of the grain with the Pen or Pencil tool.

Figure 8.15 Select every other path and change the color to the same brown you used for the background.

Figure 8.16 Click the arrow to switch the fill and stroke colors.

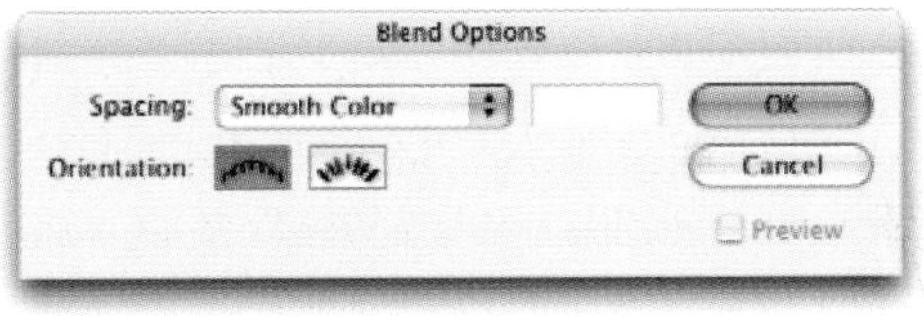

Figure 8.17 Make sure The Spacing option is set to Smooth Color by double-clicking the Blend tool.

①   ②

Figure 8.18 Use the Blend tool and click once on the top point of a black path ①, and then click again at the top of a brown path ②.

At this point, every other stroke should be brown, while the others will remain black.

5. Double-click the Blend tool and make sure it's set to Smooth Color (Figure 8.17).

6. With the Blend tool still active, click on the top point of the left-most path ①, and then on the top point of the path directly to the right ② (Figure 8.18).

    When the blend appears, deselect these two lines by holding the Command/Ctrl key and clicking outside your drawing area.

Toggling to the Direct Selection tool using the Command/Ctrl key saves you from selecting it, deselecting things, and then reselecting your blend tool each time.

7. Continue to create the blends between two strokes (black at the left, brown at the right) all the way across, remembering to deselect each pair in between.

If you don't deselect the pairs before creating the next blend, you'll actually create another blend between the second stroke and the third (Figure 8.19), which is nice, but not what we want right now.

8. Since you've locked the photo of the woodgrain, you can now select all your blends and drag them over on top of your background rectangle without moving the reference image as well.

    Hold the Command Option/Ctrl Alt keys and drag across the blends to select them all, then release the Option/Alt key when you begin your drag. If you continue to hold the Option/Alt key as you drag, you'll create a copy of these objects, rather than moving the originals.

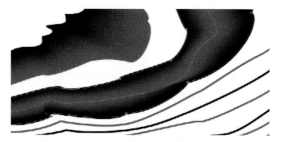

Figure 8.19 If you forget to deselect a pair of blended paths, you'll create a blend from path 1 to path 2 to path 3, which we don't want to do.

Figure 8.20 Your finished woodgrain blends should look something like this.

Figure 8.21 Drag your finished blends on top of your background rectangle.

9. While the blends are still selected, use the Transparency palette to set their opacity to about 70%.

Now we're getting somewhere! While it's probably not identical to the reference photo, it's a pretty decent imitation of woodgrain.

Let's add some highlights and shadows.

10. Draw a rectangle that's about ¼" tall and a bit wider than your background rectangle. Place it directly on top of your woodgrain.

NOTE: Instead of approximating the size, click once with the Rectangle tool and type in the dimensions (8.5" wide and .25" high) in the dialog box.

---

11. While this is selected, use the Gradient palette to fill it with a linear gradient from black to white to black (Figure 8.22). Start with the default black to white and drag the white color stop to the middle of the bar, then click below the bar at the right to add another stop. Set this one to black.

Select the Gradient tool and redirect the blend to top to bottom, instead of the default left to right (Figure 8.22).

12. Set the blending mode to Multiply in the Transparency palette.

13. Option/Alt drag a copy of this below the first (Figure 8.23).

Now we'll add a highlighted section between these two "bumps."

14. Draw a rectangle that fills the space between the two narrow bands. It should have the same linear gradient fill.

15. Use the Transparency palette to set the blend mode to Overlay, with an opacity of about 40% (Figure 8.24).

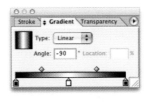

Figure 8.22 Fill the rectangle with a linear blend that goes from black to white to black. Use the Gradient tool to have it blend from top to bottom.

Figure 8.23 After setting the blending mode to Multiply, drag a copy of this rectangle about ½" below the first.

Figure 8.24 Add a third rectangle between the first two with a blend mode of Overlay and a transparency of 40%.

Finally, just to clean things up, create a mask.

16. Create a rectangle just slightly smaller than your background rectangle. Position it over your woodgrain so the edges are just inside the background rectangle.

17. Select everything, and use Object ➡ Clipping Mask ➡ Make (Command/Ctrl 7) to eliminate any raggedy edges.

While this exercise may have taken longer than you expected, the extra time spent on details like these make all the difference between a haphazard image and a truly finished technical piece.

DIGITAL DECONSTRUCTION: CAP OF SILENCE

The New York Times asked David to develop images illustrating celebrities' desires for future technology. This cap is intended to filter out unwanted sounds (note the small microphone on the visor). In this illustration, David used an entirely different set of techniques to highlight the technology, while making the other areas of the image less intrusive (Figure 8.25).

He used the Mesh tool for the hat and hand, along with blended paths for the microphone, the coiled wire leading to the earplug, and the controls. He intentionally kept the other areas of the image flat by making the shaded areas more graphic and enhancing everything with a richly undulating black edge.

He started with a sketch that illustrated his concept for client approval. Once he had that, he took a photo of his daughter pretending to operate the hat's control button (Figure 8.26). With this as reference, he created a tighter sketch, which he then scanned to use as a template in Illustrator.

Figure 8.25 The "cap of silence" features blends, mesh objects, and expressive lines using a variety of techniques.

Figure 8.26 David started with a rough sketch of his idea for client approval (top), then took a photo of his daughter to use as reference for the final image (bottom).

Since the hat and controls are the focal point of the image, David used the Mesh tool to make the cap as realistic as possible.

The Mesh tool divides a shape into a grid defined by mesh points. Each point and its handles can be modified using the Direct Selection tool, much like anchor points (Figure 8.27). And, each mesh point can have a different fill color assigned to it.

Because David was looking for something more complex than the default mesh (which is usually two columns by two rows) he used Object ➡ Create Gradient Mesh to specify a more complex grid of 7 rows and 8 columns.

Once the mesh was in place, he created the highlight areas by selecting mesh points with the Mesh tool and clicking on a lighter blue in the Color palette. He created the areas in shadow the same way, using a darker blue.

David used the Direct Selection tool to move mesh points and adjust their handles to modify the grid. Adjusting points and handles within the mesh alters the shape and size of the shaded and highlighted areas (Figure 8.28).

The coiled wire leading from the controls to the earpiece is a series of simple path blends. He created the bottom loop of the coil with two paths. The first was a thin line with a white stroke, and the other was about four times thicker, with a stroke of gray-brown. By clicking on the end point of each, he created a blend between the thickness of the strokes, as well as the colors. The rest were just copies he dragged from the bottom up (to make sure each copy was on top of the one below). Additional blends were added to create the top

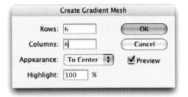

Figure 8.27 Use the Object menu to specify the grid you want for your mesh. To specify highlight colors and positions, choose "flat" for Appearance.

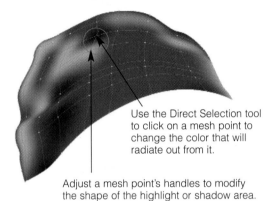

Use the Direct Selection tool to click on a mesh point to change the color that will radiate out from it.

Adjust a mesh point's handles to modify the shape of the highlight or shadow area.

Figure 8.28 You can use either the Mesh tool or the Direct Selection tool to modify the color and the handles of a mesh point.

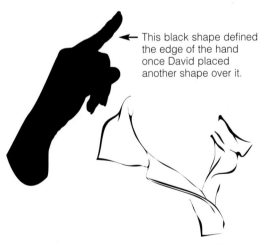

This black shape defined the edge of the hand once David placed another shape over it.

Figure 8.29 David used black shapes under filled objects to define the edge of something, and shapes that created an expressive pen and ink quality stroke.

and bottom, the shadowed area behind the top loop, and a rear loop to connect everything. Again, a very simple technique creates a remarkably realistic look.

David kept the rest of the illustration fairly flat in order to emphasize the technology in the hat. There are a few blends and meshes in the other parts, but they're small and quite subtle.

The final touch is his use of a descriptive black edge to define each element in the image. These are a combination of black shapes placed behind a colored object, and black shapes that actually describe the shape of the edge, as if he'd used a brush and ink to create it (Figure 8.30).

Figure 0.30 We'll use a template to experiment with the Mesh tool and create a hand like David's.

DIY:
GRADIENT MESH
AND OUTLINE TECHNIQUE

1. You'll find a file called "hand.tif" in the "mccord" folder on your DVD. Either open that file in Illustrator (File ➡ Open), or place it into an already open Illustrator document (File ➡ Place).

2. Designate the layer with the photo as a template by choosing Template from the Layers palette submenu, then add a new layer to draw on.

3. Use the Pen tool to trace the contour of the hand. Make sure you complete your shape so it's one whole object and not a series of shorter paths (Figure 8.31).

4. Create a copy of this shape for the black edge.

   Select the hand so all the anchor points are solid and either copy and paste a duplicate, or Option/Alt drag a copy off to the side.

5. Fill the original hand with a color of your choice.

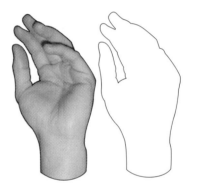

Figure 8.31 Outline the entire hand using the Pen or Pencil tool, then make a copy of it for later use.

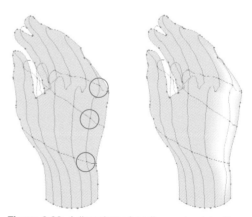

Figure 8.32 Adjust these handles and points, then select each point and fill it with a lighter color.

6. While the hand is still selected, use Object ➡ Create Gradient Mesh to create a grid that's 6 columns by 4 rows, with a Flat Appearance inside the hand.

   If you get an error message, use Object ➡ Path ➡ Simplify to modify the mesh, then add the mesh.

7. Use the Direct Selection tool to straighten out the handles on the anchor points at the right side of the hand and to move them slightly to the right.

8. Select each of the modified points and fill with white, or a paler version of your color (Figure 8.32).

Now we need to add another small highlight in the thumb area.

9. Select the top anchor point in the thumb area and fill it with white or a lighter shade of your hand color.

That's really all there is to it!

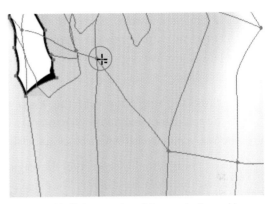

Figure 8.33 Delete mesh points you don't need by holding the Option/Alt key while the Mesh tool is selected. You can add points using the Mesh tool as well—just click anywhere along a path.

You can fine-tune the grid with the Delete Anchor Point Pen tool. When you select a gradient mesh object with the Direct Selection tool, you'll notice that the grid is actually composed of anchor points along with mesh points. Use the Delete Anchor Point Pen tool to eliminate any points you don't think you need.

To delete an actual gradient mesh point, use the Mesh tool, hold the Option/Alt key, and click on the point you want to eliminate (Figure 8.33).

The black outline in David's hand is actually a black shape behind this gradient mesh hand. We'll use the copy of the hand we made in Step 4 to create that effect.

10. Select the plain hand and increase the stroke width to about 5 points.

11. Use Object ➡ Path ➡ Outline Stroke to create a shape from this path.

By outlining the stroke, we've actually created a compound path: a transparent object within a black shape. We don't need this transparent inner shape.

12. Select the inner shape with the Direct Selection tool and hit the Delete key twice. You should be left with a black hand shape.

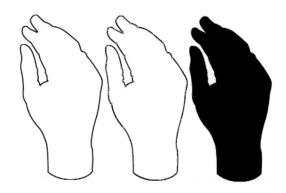

Figure 8.34 After you outline the stroke, delete the interior shape by selecting it right at the edge with the Direct Selection tool. Make sure you delete two times to eliminate all bits of it.

This shape is actually larger than the original because the stroke was thicker. That means when it's positioned behind our mesh hand object, its edges will show.

13. Select the black hand and align it with your mesh hand.

    If it's behind your mesh hand, great! That's where it needs to be. If it isn't, use Object ➡ Arrange ➡ Send to Back to put it there (or Command/Ctrl X, Command/Control B).

14. Use the Direct Selection tool to select random points along the black hand's edge and move them slightly to create a pen and ink effect.

Of course, you're not totally finished, but at this point, you should have a good grasp of both the Mesh tool and the edge technique David used in the "cap of silence" image.

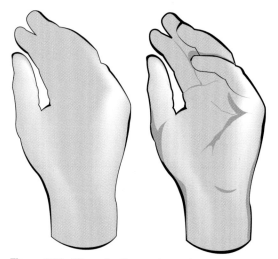

Figure 8.35 After adjusting anchor points to imitate the pen and ink stroke around your hand, feel free to add shading and detail as flat objects.

Add some detail by way of paths and shapes to create shadowed areas. Keeping these objects flat visually separates the hand from the more realistic hat and controls (Figure 8.35). Experiment with Multiply mode for these shadows.

KEY POINTS

- Research is key in developing an accurate technical drawing.

- Woodgrain can be realistically created using two blended paths.

- Refine a blended path by expanding it (Object ➡ Expand, or Object ➡ Blend ➡ Expand) and tweaking the individual paths with the Direct Selection tool.

- Use Multiply and Overlay blending modes to create molded areas.

- Create a mesh by clicking within a selected object with the Mesh tool, or using Object ➡ Create Gradient Mesh.

- Modify a mesh with the Mesh and Direct Selection tools.

- Clean up a gradient mesh object with the Delete Anchor Point Pen tool.

ON YOUR OWN: TECHNO GADGETS

Creating texture by using blended paths, and definition and contrast between elements in an image through a variety of techniques, works well in technical images; the detailed areas create focus, while the simpler areas provide context.

Practice your skills by creating a technical illustration using these techniques. Any piece of technology would lend itself to this project. If you prefer, you might want to create something of wood to work on perfecting that technique.

DAVID BROOKS

Custom Swatch Library • Outline Stroke • Custom Actions • Streamline & Live Trace

David Brooks made the move from designer to professional illustrator by developing a comprehensive business plan and then sticking to it.

David Brooks's illustration style is no accident. That's why his career in children's book publishing is so successful. His approach is methodical, well researched, and totally on target.

He began his career far from where he is now, both artistically and physically.

"I can remember drawing all the time; in the margins of my schoolbooks, on my mom's kitchen counters, sometimes on the garage floor."

Before attending college, he joined the U. S. Navy and did a tour on a small minesweeper. He was able to continue his artistic efforts by creating illustrations for various Navy publications.

When his stint in the service ended, he returned home to Pennsylvania. Thinking he was interested in architecture, he took courses at Bucks County Community College, earning his associates degree in Architectural Design and Structural Engineering.

"That's when I realized I was less interested in building things than in drawing them."

He moved to Maine where earned another associates degree in Graphic Arts and then became a corporate "big important guy" and hated it. After several unfulfilling years as the communications manager, he quit his position with Central Maine Power, the electric company where he was in charge of in-house communications, and moved to California.

There he began to develop an illustration style that would garner him jobs doing what he real-

Figure 9.1 David's original illustrative style involved using scratchboard techniques to create his blacks, then adding watercolors for color and texture.

Figure 9.2 In his work with the electric company in Maine, David created a lot of black-and-white images using his scratchboard technique.

ly wanted to do: illustrate books and articles for pre-schoolers through fourth graders.

He wanted the work to be bold, colorful and different. He developed thumbnail ideas for several images and then set about developing a style that could be easily translated into digital illustrations.

He also created a strategic marketing plan, something he strongly recommends for every

Figure 9.3 It took David about six months to translate his scratchboard technique into a digital one. He had two book contracts within a year.

Figure 9.4 This image is one of several for a book called *Clueless George*.

freelance artist or designer. His plan included finding a rep he could count on to share his business philosophies and help him develop his own picture books.

He is a proponent of putting one's work in front of art buyers at the "point of purchase." That is, when they're actually in the market for an illustrator. "I don't do direct mail because that just puts a lot of paper on someone's desk." Instead, he maintains online portfolios on *theispot.com*, *bookmakersltd.com*, and his own web site: *http://www.djbrooks.com*. He also maintains a presence in illustration directories including *PictureBook* and *American Showplace*.

It hasn't been all work and no play for David since he moved to the Los Angeles area, though. He loves to cook, claims to have a green thumb, and, at one point, even tried out for the San Francisco Giants!

He's also the proud dad of four-year-old Ben, whom he allows to help "paint" some of the images that appear in his books. Clients include Grollier, *Ranger Rick* magazine, and Houghton Mifflin, among others.

David begins each assignment with a lot of discussion with his editor and art director for a particular project. Then David produces a computer-generated file that establishes the content and composition of the image, but doesn't dwell on the specific style of the illustration. "It's more about the basic layout of the objects in a composition, not the aesthetics of the drawing." He e-mails these to his client for approval.

David and the publisher's art director have many conversations about how a project is developing. "I like to think out loud," he says, "and it's also a good way to make sure we're all on the same page."

Once his ideas have been approved, he begins his hand-drawn images.

One of the most important aspects of his images is the character of his black lines. He uses a Sharpie pen on coated, recycled paper to get a blurry effect. "I love my lines; they're big and fat." He draws small, because he discovered that he prefers the quality of tiny images rather than larger, more finished drawings.

Figure 9.5 David draws his characters in bits and pieces, then assembles the best parts in Photoshop.

Figure 9.6 Here are the yaks after David selected the parts he wanted to use and arranged them.

Figure 9.7 The dialog boxes for the Maximum and Minimum filters; Maximum thins the line, and Minimum makes it thicker.

He also creates his images in bits and pieces (Figure 9.5). "I'll draw an arm over here, two or three heads over there, some mustaches, and scan them all in. Then I can build the image in Photoshop with the elements that work best."

But wait, isn't this supposed to be about Illustrator? David's work may begin as an image in Photoshop, which he manipulates carefully in order to maintain the quality of his "big fat" lines, but everything is then turned into vector art using Adobe Streamline software. At that point, the real work begins using Illustrator.

Before we get into the Illustrator aspect of his work, however, it's worth taking a look at his process of turning his sketches into digital compositions in Photoshop.

He begins by scanning his various pieces as a grayscale image. That way, he can use Image ➡

Adjustments ➡ Levels (Command/Ctrl L) to control the intensity of black and white. He also uses the Maximum and Minimum filters (found under Other at the bottom of the Filters menu) to fine-tune his lines. These can thin a "black blob" into something more in keeping with his style. "I start with an increment of 1, then use Command/Ctrl F (to repeat the adjustment) until it's the way I want it." Depending on the intended audience, he may also use the Crystallize filter to give his line a bit of texture.

Once he's happy, he saves the scan as a PSD file.

David uses Adobe's Streamline software to turn the bitmapped image into a vector file (Figure 9.8). At this point, the most current version is not OS X compatible, so opening it launches the Classic system on David's G5. Illustrator CS2 has a new Live Trace feature that's replaced Streamline, making life that much easier.

David establishes the preferences for how his image is converted within Streamline, much the same way you would using Illustrator CS2's Live Trace function. He uses "preview" while making these adjustments to make sure the file Streamline will create is as true to his drawing as possible.

This conversion creates a shape using anchor points and Bézier curves, the same way using Illustrator's Pen or Pencil tool would, but in a fraction of the time. Because his tolerances are so tight, the character of the original pen line stays true. It also creates thousands of anchor points in each image. He saves this converted file as an EPS image.

Now he's ready to work in Illustrator!

DIGITAL DECONSTRUCTION: LET'S GO FISHING

This image for *Boy's Life* magazine, utilizes some of David's favorite techniques and tricks (Figure 9.9).

David's approach to color management is unique. He created a Swatch Library where the colors are always mixed using cyan, magenta, yellow and/or black in 5% increments (Figure 9.10). For example, the water in this image is a gradient from blue to white. The blue is made up of 65% blue and 25% magenta. Because the colors are created mathematically, it's a foolproof system to guarantee accurate color reproduction when an image is printed.

Working with a limited color palette, or by creating colors using precise percentages, as David does, is a favorite technique of many illustrators. It's easy to make one of your own.

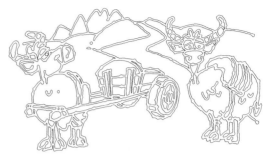

Figure 9.8 Streamline turns the black bitmapped stroke into vector objects using compound paths where necessary. At this point, David can use the Direct Selection tool in Illustrator to further fine-tune his edges.

Figure 9.9 This image was created for *Boys Life* and includes some of David's trademark techniques, such as a precise color matching system, gradients, and outlined strokes.

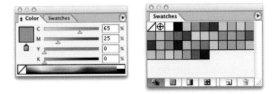

Figure 9.10 David customizes his palettes so that all the colors are created using 5% increments of the process colors.

DIY:
CREATE YOUR OWN
SWATCH LIBRARY

1. Open a new CMYK Illustrator document.

2. Open the Swatches palette from the Window menu. Drag it away from the attached Color palette so you can see both at the same time.

3. From the submenu of the Swatches palette, choose Select All Unused. Then choose Delete Swatch. Illustrator will ask you if you're sure you want to do this. Click Yes (Figure 9.11).

If there are any remaining swatches of color click on them and delete them as well (make sure to leave the black, white, none, and registration swatches intact).

Let's create a Swatches palette of blues.

4. Use the percent fields in the Color palette to type in a color consisting of 15% cyan (Figure 9.12).

5. You can either drag your new blue from the Color palette into the Swatches palette, or click the New Swatch icon at the bottom of the Swatches palette. It becomes a swatch you can now use as a fill or stroke color.

6. Repeat this process in increments of 10% or 15% until you have about seven or eight shades of blue. Create a swatch of 25% cyan, another that's 35% cyan, and so forth.

7. Reset your blue to 15%, and add 15% magenta by typing that percentage in the magenta percent field (Figure 9.13).

Keep creating new colors by adding magenta in increments of 10% or 15%. Reset your cyan to 15% and add 15% magenta, then 25%

Figure 9.11 Select all your swatches and delete them. Make sure you don't delete the basic "no color" swatch, the black and white swatches, and the registration swatch.

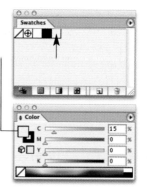

Figure 9.12 Drag your new color from the color box to the Swatches palette.

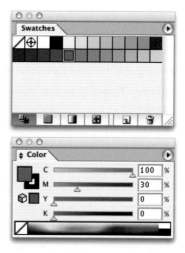

Figure 9.13 After you've done all the cyan options, start adding magenta in increments of 10% or 15%.

magenta, until your last swatch is 15% cyan and 100% magenta. Mix another set using 25% cyan, and varying percentages of magenta. Create at least 20 swatches this way.

8. Choose "Save Swatch Library" from the Swatches palette submenu.

Illustrator will point you to the swatches folder where you can name your palette and save it to use whenever you want it. If it doesn't, navigate your way to the Illustrator application folder, to the Presets folder inside that, and then the Swatches folder (Illustrator ➡ Presets ➡ Swatches) (Figure 9.14).

9. Quit Illustrator and then relaunch it. This will reset your swatches to the default CMYK palette.

10. From the Swatches palette's submenu, choose Open Swatch Library. You should be able to see your set of blues in the list to select and open it (Figure 9.15).

Opening a Swatch Library this way adds a new swatch-like palette to your workspace, but doesn't replace the default Swatches palette. You can add your library to the Swatches palette by selecting Add to Swatches from the library palette's submenu. David also selects Persistent from the library palette submenu so his custom library opens automatically every time he launches Illustrator.

DIGITAL DECONSTRUCTION: MORE OF THE FISH STORY

Obviously, the most interesting aspect of David's work is the black line that he creates in Streamline. Since that aspect of an illustration is created for him, David's only job is to make sure it's the blackest black he can get. He selects

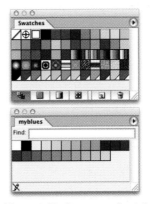

Figure 9.14 Save your swatches in Illustrator's Swatches folder so you can use them again.

Figure 9.15 Open your Swatches Library in a new palette using the Swatch palette's submenu.

Figure 9.16 David sets the fill color of his "strokes" to 60% of cyan, magenta, and yellow, and 100% black to ensure a dark, rich black.

the lines in his image and sets their fill color (since they are actually shapes, rather than strokes) to 60% cyan, 60% magenta, 60% yellow, and 100% black to guarantee a nice deep, rich, "inky" black (Figure 9.16). As you might guess, he has this special black formula saved as a swatch.

The outlines of the fish in the stream aren't this intense black, however. David changed these to a shade of gray to give the illusion that the fish were underwater (Figure 9.9).

The next step is creating objects that conform to the shapes inside his black outlines. His system is truly ingenious. He creates a rectangle larger than the image and sends it to the back (Object ➡ Arrange ➡ Send to Back, Command/Ctrl Shift [, or my favorite: Command/Ctrl X, Command/Ctrl B).

He selects everything on the layer (Command/Ctrl A) and then uses the Trim Pathfinder option. This uses the black edges as sort of a cookie cutter, dividing the white areas of the image into multiple shapes that he can then select individually to add color. Because the shapes are created using the black edges, there is no overlap, and no tedious drawing of each shape with the Pen or Pencil tool. (David uses the Pencil tool to add other color elements, but we'll get to that in a bit.)

DIY:
CREATING POSITIVE SPACE

Let's run through a little exercise so you can experience David's technique for yourself.

1. Locate the "myfish.eps" file in the "brooks" folder on your DVD and open it in Illustrator (open it using Illustrator's File menu, or drag the file from the DVD to the

Figure 9.17 Where the black line needs to look faded (if it's in the distance, or underwater in this case), David adjusts the CMYK values to create a less intense color.

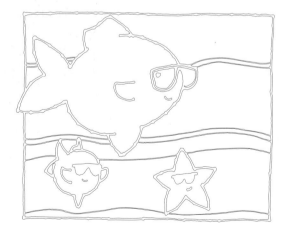

Figure 9.18 Take a look at how the black line was converted into vector shapes by typing Command/Ctrl Y (or View ➡ Outline).

Illustrator icon in your dock if you're using a Mac). Make sure Template is *not* checked in the Place dialog box since this image is the beginning of the actual illustration.

Name this layer "line."

Type Command/Ctrl Y to take a look at the "wire frame" view of this file—it was created from a scan that was converted using Streamline. Type Command/Ctrl Y again to get back to artwork view.

2. Draw a rectangle larger than the fish image and send it to the back, then select everything (Select ➡ All, or Command/Ctrl A).

3. Open the Pathfinder palette from the Window menu (Window ➡ Pathfinder).

4. Click the Trim Pathfinder button (it's the second from the left on the bottom row of the Pathfinder palette) (Figure 9.19).

Great! You've now divided your rectangle into shapes based on the black lines of the fish image.

5. Use the Direct Selection tool to select one of the white spaces in your image.

6. Use Select ➡ Same ➡ Fill Color to select all the white areas at once (Figure 9.20).

    While they're selected, change the fill color to a pale gray or blue—anything but black or white—so you can see these shapes against the white drawing surface (Figure 9.21).

NOTE: You can also use the Magic Wand to select everything with the same fill; just click within a colored area and all objects with that fill color (and stroke) will be selected as well.

---

7. Create a new layer by clicking on the pad icon at the bottom of the Layers palette. Name it "color."

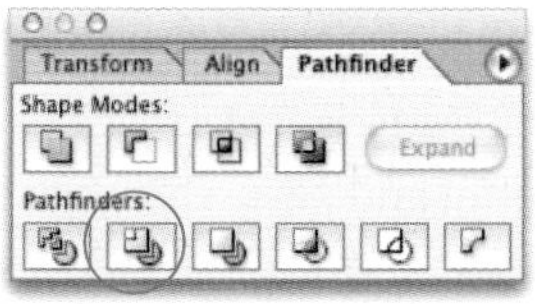

Figure 9.19 Use the Trim option to break your rectangle into separate bits that correspond to the spaces within the black outlines.

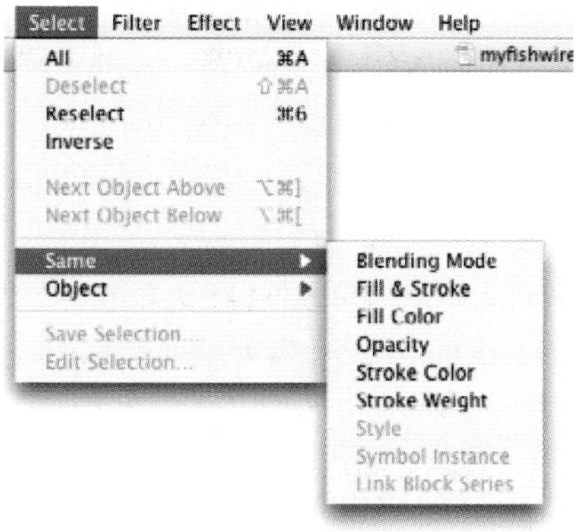

Figure 9.20 Select all the white bits using Select ➡ Same ➡ Fill Color.

Figure 9.21 Change all your white objects to a pale gray so you can see them against the artboard.

8. Cut your selected objects (Command/Ctrl X).

9. Then, highlight the new layer (click on it in the Layers palette) and paste the objects you just cut. Use Command/Ctrl F (Edit ➡ Paste in Front) to make sure these objects are pasted on your new layer, and not the one they came from.

   If Illustrator insists on pasting them on their original layer, lock the original layer so Illustrator can't paste anything on it. You can also check the Layer submenu to make sure Paste Remembers Layers is unchecked.

Figure 9.22 Hide the black layer so you can see what you're doing without having the lines interfere.

I prefer either Command/Ctrl B or Command/Ctrl F when pasting things, since it will place the cut or copied objects in the exact location where they were cut or copied from. If you just paste (Command/Ctrl V), the pieces will likely shift from their original position, and you'd have to mess around trying to realign things.

10. Now, drag the "color" layer underneath the "line" layer and hide the "line" layer so we don't disturb it while we're adding the colors (Figure 9.22). This will also let you see where the black lines intersected your white areas.

    You can also select and delete the outer areas of the box you created in Step 2.

Figure 9.23 When you're done, turn the black line layer back to visible, and voila!

At this point, you're on your own. Select the various parts of the image and start adding color. Use some of the blues you made in your Custom Swatches palette! Have fun creating an underwater world. When you're done, show the original line layer by clicking the eye icon and save your file (Figure 9.23). We'll be using it again.

In an upcoming DIY, you'll get to play with Illustrator CS2's Live Trace feature, which replaces the need for Streamline.

DIGITAL DECONSTRUCTION: COUNTING GECKOS

Part of David's business plan included creating and publishing his own books for children. He's done this with a series of four counting books that will be published by Northword Publishing. *You Can Count in the Desert* is a picture book for preschoolers.

When beginning a children's book project like this, it's very important to think the whole thing through before beginning the work of creating illustrations.

David began by writing the text, using desert animals as things to count along with a pleasant rhyming scheme that helps young children learn and remember.

Here's the text for this story:

One sun shines
Two tortoises meet. . .
Three roadrunners run
on hot hot feet
Four geckos hurry
scoot scoot scoot
Five owls hoot
hoot, hoot, hoot
Six sleepy snakes stay cool in the shade
Seven prairie dogs play in tunnels that they made
Eight vultures fly way up in the sky
Nine sheep climb
high high high
Ten coyotes howl at the rising moon
How many stars twinkle
come back soon.

Figure 9.24 The cover design for *You Can Count in the Desert* that David wrote and illustrated.

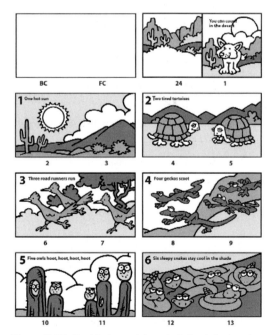

Figure 9.25 David planned the whole book in thumbnail size before beginning his final illustrations.

Once he determined which animals he was going to use, and how many of each, he began to design the book's pages in thumbnail form. He planned for twelve double-page spreads plus a back page, as well as the front and back covers (Figure 9.25).

Because David does his thumbnails as computer-generated images to determine content and composition, the animals in here are not drawn and scanned with the same meticulous process he uses for the final pieces.

Figure 9.26 The sketches David scanned in to create the gecko page.

He then began the process of drawing his animals in the same bits and pieces we saw in the yak image (Figures 9.5 and 9.26). As with all his work, he selected, copied, and pasted the various elements to compose the final black-and-white image in Photoshop.

Note that on pages 8 and 9 of his thumbnails (Figure 9.25) the geckos and the details in the background are not the same as those in the final image (Figure 9.27). Note, too, the lack of detail in the geckos. At this point, they're fairly plain little guys.

Figure 9.27 David's final black-and-white image, constructed from his scan.

Once he was pleased with his line work, he moved the file into Streamline to convert it to vector art. After the piece was converted, he opened it in Illustrator and created the objects he needed for color (as described in the DIY: Creating Positive Space).

This image and the others in his book use a technique that David is very fond of: outlining strokes. This small detail lends a nice glow to otherwise simple elements (Figure 9.28).

Notice the different shades of blue outlining the mountains and the gecko's head. If you look very closely, you'll also see an additional

Figure 9.28 David uses an outlined stroke to add a subtle glow around the elements in his illustrations.

outline inside the shape of the gecko as well. These outlines are actually shapes, so David can fill them with gradients. In the outline around the mountain, you can see the gradient shift from a pale-blue to white.

He's also taken some of the original black lines in the mountains and made them purple to increase the sense of space and distance between the geckos in the foreground and the scenery behind them.

Finally, these little guys and their surroundings are full of dimension with the addition of spots and stripes, shadows and highlights, all of which David adds using the Pencil tool and a pressure-sensitive drawing tablet (Figure 9.30).

DIY:
OUTLINING PATHS

If your fish isn't still available, find the file you saved and open it.

1. Begin by selecting one of the bands of (presumably blue) ocean. Make sure you select all the pieces in one stripe by holding the Shift key as you click on each piece (Figure 9.31).

You'll note by checking the Color palette or the color swatches in the Toolbar that these objects have no stroke color.

2. Add a darker blue stroke around these selected shapes, and set the stroke weight to 2 points.

3. Use Object ➡ Path ➡ Outline Stroke to turn this edge into its own element. The water shape is now back as it was, and we've actually added an additional object—a blue shape that surrounds the wave.

Figure 9.29 The finished "Four geckos scoot" double-page spread.

Figure 9.30 David uses a pressure-sensitive tablet and pen to draw the shapes that create the detail in each image.

Figure 9.31 Select all the areas in one of the ocean waves. Hold the Shift key to add noncontiguous pieces.

You could leave this as it is, or add a gradient to it the way David does (Figure 9.32). When you're done, save your file.

You may have discovered that Object ➡ Path ➡ Outline Stroke has no keystroke shortcut, nor is it a transformation you can repeat using the Command/Ctrl D shortcut (Object ➡ Transform Again). As luck would have it, Illustrator has a palette called Actions that allows you to auto-mate tasks you perform on a regular basis. It's a snap to add a function like "outline stroke" or any other menu item, or even a series of steps that you use frequently in your work.

Figure 9.32 After you outline your stroke, fill the new shape with a gradient.

DIY:
CREATING CUSTOM ACTIONS

You can use any file for this exercise, but you do need to have an open document for it to work.

1. Open the Actions palette from the Window menu.

You'll note that it has a folder with a set of default actions already programmed. We'll make our own set.

2. Click on the folder icon at the bottom of the palette to create a new set, or choose New Set from the palette's submenu.

    A dialog box pops up asking you to name your set. Name it something like "my favorites" and click OK.

3. Then click on the Create New Action icon at the bottom of the palette. You'll be asked to name your action, and in which set you want to put it. You can also assign a key-stroke shortcut for it here. Name this "out-line stroke" but don't assign it a keystroke shortcut at this point, then click Record (Figure 9.34).

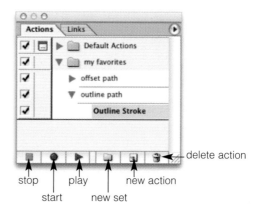

Figure 9.33 Use the Actions palette to record processes and menu items you use frequently.

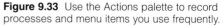

Figure 9.34 Name your action and assign it to a set. You can also set a keystroke shortcut (in this case, Shift F1).

At the bottom left of the palette, there are three buttons that control the recording. At this point, you could perform several operations and Illustrator would "memorize" them, adding each step to your new action. When you were finished, you'd click the Stop Playing/Recording icon and your new Action would appear in the Actions palette. Note in Figure 9.33 that sets can be opened to reveal their contents, and actions can also be opened to reveal the steps they contain.

4. Since we want to record a simple menu item—Outline Stroke—click the Stop Playing/Recording icon at the bottom of the palette instead (Figure 9.35).

5. From the Action palette's submenu, select Insert Menu Item.

6. A dialog box will open; go to Object ➡ Path ➡ Outline Stroke and select it. When it appears in the Menu Item field, click OK (Figure 9.36).

Brilliant! You now have a shortcut to one of the techniques David uses on just about every object in his illustrations.

To make it happen, select the object you want to outline, select the Outline Stroke Action, and click the Play Current Selection icon—it's the triangle at the bottom of the Actions palette.

Or, my favorite; from the palette's submenu, drag all the way to the bottom and choose Button Mode. This makes playing an Action a one-click activity. Simply select the object you want to outline, then click the outline stroke button.

Refer back to Figure 9.30 and notice the shadows, highlights, and details in the gecko. Let's add some of these details to our fish.

stop

Figure 9.35 To add an Action that's a simple menu item, click the "stop" icon, then choose Insert Menu Item from the submenu.

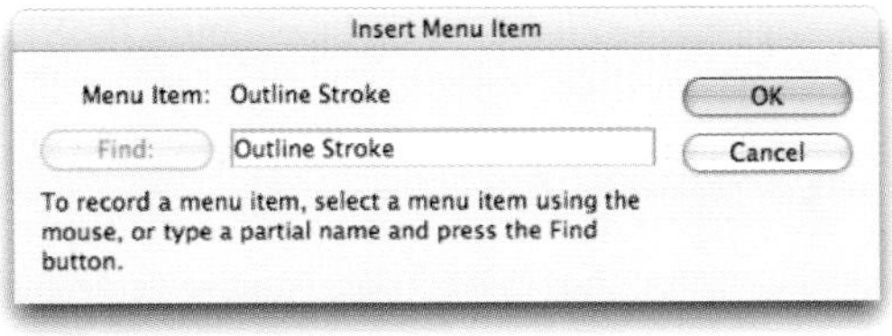

Figure 9.36 When this box pops up, just go to the menu item you want to insert. Its name will appear in the Menu Item field. Then click OK.

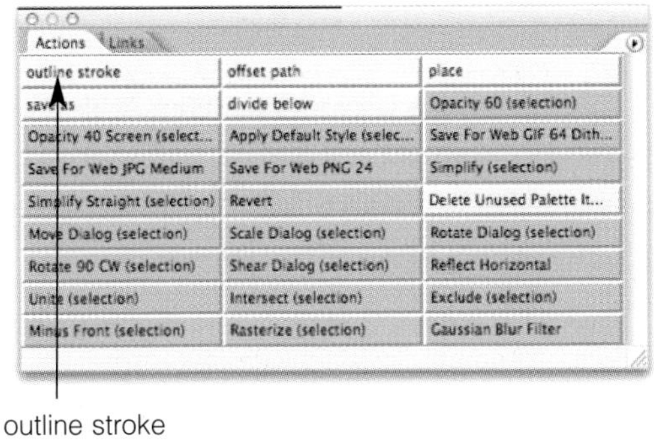

outline stroke

Figure 9.37 When you choose Button Mode you'll see your new Action added to the palette.

While David uses a Wacom tablet and a pressure-sensitive pen to draw these shapes, you can be equally successful using your mouse. The key to making them semi-transparent is to choose Multiply from the Transparency palette as the blending mode after you've drawn them.

The Multiply blending mode makes the selected object transparent and adjusts its color to reflect the interaction of the multiplied object with the color of any objects it overlaps.

Go ahead and create some shadows and spots. You might want to add some secondary waves within the ocean, or some coral or seaweed. With each element you create, and while it's still selected, use the Transparency palette to play with the various blending modes to see which ones create an effect you like (Figure 9.38).

DIY:
LIVE TRACE

Illustrator CS2's Live Trace function provides the ability to transform a bitmapped image into vector shapes. It's like having Streamline at your fingertips, eliminating that middle step between optimizing your scan in Photoshop and creating the colors, lines, and details in Illustrator.

Live Trace deserves your attention. Aside from this DIY, you should spend some time playing with what it can do to black-and-white, grayscale, and color images.

For now, however, we're going to use the settings that David might specify.

1. Open a new Illustrator file and place the "blanket.tif" file you'll find in the "brooks" folder on your DVD (Figure 9.40).

One of the nice features in the Adobe CS software is that all the programs are able to read

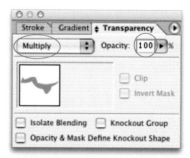

Figure 9.38 Using the various blending modes and transparency in the Transparency palette creates a wealth of interesting interactions between overlapping colors.

Figure 9.39 This finished fish uses all of David's very cool tricks. Not bad!

Figure 9.40 Open the "blanket.psd" file to experiment with the Live Trace feature.

each other's file formats—you don't have to save a Photoshop image as a TIFF or EPS file before bringing it into Illustrator (or InDesign, for that matter).

Notice the Control bar at the top of your document window. There's an opportunity to click Live Trace there, which will perform the default Trace Action on your image. Next to that is a drop-down menu with several presets. If you can't see the Live Trace options, make sure your image is still selected.

The top option—Custom—will trace your image using the last options you used. If you haven't used Live Trace yet, it will be traced using the default options. At the bottom of the list you can choose to alter those options.

NOTE: These options are also available under Object ➡ Live Trace ➡ Tracing Options.

---

2. While your placed image is selected, slide down to Tracing Options at the bottom of the list to open a dialog box where you can change the default settings to something that will work better for this image (Figure 9.41).

3. Use the settings in Figure 9.42.

   Leave the color mode setting to Black and White for this exercise. Later, if you want to place a color image, you can play with the color settings.

NOTE: Don't check the Preview button until after you've established your settings; it slows things way down. When you're experimenting, however, you'll want to keep it checked so you can see what the different settings do.

Figure 9.41 Select Tracing Options from the Live Trace pop-up menu in the Control bar.

MODE:	black and white
THRESHOLD:	128
BLUR:	0
FILLS:	no
STROKES:	yes
MAX STROKE WEIGHT:	1 px
MIN STROKE LENGTH:	5 px
PATH FITTING:	2 px
MINIMUM AREA:	3 px
CORNER ANGLE	20

Figure 9.42 Use these settings to trace your placed bear image.

Threshold refers to how light or dark your lines will be; a lower number recognizes fewer pixels, and results in a thinner line, while a higher number gives you a thicker line.

Blur allows you to eliminate stray bits, if the image is sketchy. This one isn't, so we don't need to blur it.

On the Trace Settings side of this dialog box, the **Fills** option is usually set by default. We don't want that here, so uncheck it. The Strokes setting will automatically become checked.

Max Stroke Weight refers to how thick a line needs to be in pixels for Live Trace to trace it as a path. For our purposes, a setting of 1 px is perfect.

Min Stroke Length determines how large or small a piece of the image has to be before Live Trace includes it in the tracing, or ignores it. Set this field to 5 px.

Path Fitting establishes how tightly Live Trace will adhere to the original image. Lower numbers result in a more precise tracing, while higher numbers smooth things out. The default setting is 2 px, and we'll leave it at that.

Minimum Area is an important one to pay attention to. Again, the smaller the number here, the more detail will remain in the tracing results. Higher numbers ignore small areas and will delete those portions of the image from the results. We want to keep the details, so change that setting to 3 px.

The default for **Corner Angle** of 20 is fine for now. It refers to how sharp a corner has to be for Live Trace to consider it a corner point versus a curve point.

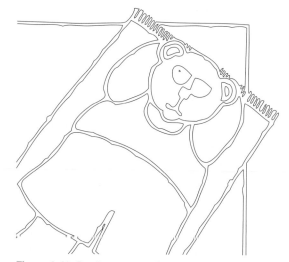

Figure 9.43 Preview your settings to see what's going to happen to your bitmap art as it's transformed into vector art.

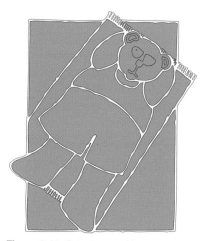

Figure 9.44 Select everything except the outer edge of your image and change the fill color to anything you want. Note that the ears and nose and sunglasses have disappeared. You'll need to pull them back to the front.

4. Once you've entered the specifications and previewed the image, click Trace. At this point you won't see much difference from the original image, other than it's now outlined. You can't manipulate the vector paths until you expand the image.

5. Use either Object ➡ Expand, or Object ➡ Live Trace ➡ Expand As Viewed to break the image into individual vector paths.

Our image is now a group made up of several individual objects.

6. Select the image and ungroup it a couple of times to make sure each piece is a discreet element (Object ➡ Ungroup, or Command Shift G/Ctrl Shift G).

7. While the image is still selected, deselect the outer edge by holding the Shift key as you click on it.

8. Fill the remaining selection with a color so that when we fill the outer shape, we'll have some contrast (Figure 9.44).

9. Select the outer shape and fill it with black.

Now you're ready to add your personality to the image using David's techniques.

Have fun!

Figure 9.45 Have fun adding your own personality to the bear image.

KEY POINTS

- Create a Custom Swatch Library by deleting all the colors in the Illustrator default library, creating new colors, and using the Swatches palette submenu to save it.

- Save Custom Swatch Libraries in Illustrator's Swatches folder.

- Open saved Swatch Libraries from the Window menu or the Swatch palette's submenu.

- Create custom Actions by either recording a set of steps, or inserting a menu item. This is especially handy for creating shortcuts for items that have no key-stroke options.

- Set your Live Trace options using the Control bar, or Object ➡ Live Trace ➡ Tracing options.

- Use the Custom Live Trace option to trace something using the same settings you used previously, or the default settings.

- Save your settings in the Tracing Options dialog box to use again. Your saved preset will be placed at the bottom of the preset list.

- Preview your settings only after they've been established to save time.

- Expand a traced object using Object ➡ Expand, or Object ➡ Live Trace ➡ Expand as Viewed.

ON YOUR OWN:
SHAPES AND OUTLINED STROKES

There are several funky black-and-white Photoshop files on the DVD. Find them inside the "brooks" folder in a folder called "fun images."

Choose one and make it your own by using David's techniques to create positive spaces, add color, Outline Strokes, and then create dimension and texture using the Multiply blending mode and transparencies, just as we have in these exercises.

If you're feeling really ambitious, re-create an existing book cover with your own illustration.

10 MARK COLLINS

Distorting Gradients • Illustrated Edges • Opacity Masks

Creating edges as filled objects, rather than stroked paths, adds a sense of whimsey to Mark Collins's illustrations, whether for serious or light subject matter.

Mark Collins always wanted to be an illustrator and credits his success as a professional to two influences: *Mad* magazine's Mort Drucker, and his dad, who supported Mark's decision to go to art school.

"My dad is actually pretty conservative, so it was surprising that he was okay with me pursuing a career in the arts. I don't think he was happy in his job, and he didn't want that for his kids."

Growing up in a suburb of Philadelphia as the oldest of two brothers and a sister, Mark's only exposure to art of any kind was his private collection of *Mad* magazines. As a result, there's a Mort Drucker-esque, highly graphic influence readily apparent in Mark's illustrations, especially his caricatures of famous personalities.

Al Hirschfeld, a regular illustrator for *The New York Times*, was another influence.

"It's not that apparent in my work, but it's there," Mark says.

He's also a fan of Ren & Stimpy and the Powder Puff Girls, and continues to watch them even though his thirteen-year-old son, Austin, has outgrown them.

"They do such great things with patterns and line. It's wonderful stuff!"

Mark went to the Art Institute of Philadelphia, graduating with his A. S. in Specialized Technology (Design) in 1983.

Figure 10.1 Mark's illustrative style, as well as his sense of humor, stem from an early love affair with *Mad* magazine.

"At that time, they were pushing us away from illustration and toward design. People were saying that illustration was dead, and photography was the wave of the future."

Despite the advice of many professors and industry analysts, Mark insisted on taking illustration and painting courses along with his design requirements.

After graduating, Mark rekindled a relationship with a woman whom he'd met in college but never dated—Mindy.

They married shortly after that, and created the design firm of Big Ideas Graphics (BIG) in Mt. Laurel, New Jersey Their work included creating logos, ads, and brochures, and a lot of work for other design studios and ad agencies, as well as casinos.

Figure 10.2 Mark attributes his skill as a caricaturist to influences like Mort Drucker and Al Hirschfeld.

Figure 10.4 The painting courses Mark took in college provided him with the skills to create realistic highlight and shadow areas.

Figure 10.3 Mark's graphic style of using brush-like black strokes is so flexible that it works for a broad range of subject matter, from kids' books to plumbing magazines.

"Mindy would develop the ideas, select the type, and give me a sketch of what she wanted the layout to look like. My job was to make it look great."

They were very successful, in part because Mark's comprehensive layouts were so polished.

"It definitely helped to have an illustrator on staff, as it were."

It's no surprise that most of the work they did included illustration rather than photography, in direct contrast to what he'd been told in college.

They shared pre-press production chores, and bought their first computer in 1991. Mark didn't intend for it to become his illustration medium until several years later, when he began experimenting with Adobe Illustrator.

"The Pen tool was a killer to learn. But once I understood it, everything fell into place. I actually did try using a Wacom tablet, but it was a disaster. I'm definitely a mouse guy."

In the early 90s, with a new family and diverging interests, Mark and Mindy decided to move

Figure 10.6 This caricature of Brad Pitt features some of Mark's favorite techniques, including a wonderful background he created using different brush strokes and the punk, bloat, and roughen filters.

Figure 10.5 A lot of the work Mark is hired to do is what he considers "spot art." He was aiming for a retro feel in this one, hence the faded look in the colors.

in different directions—she to becoming a school teacher, and he to pursuing his dream of becoming a full-time freelance illustrator. They also moved to Delran, New Jersey to be near Mindy's family and still close to Philadelphia.

He submitted a portfolio of his painted illustrations to artist's rep Deborah Wolfe in Philadelphia and never heard back. In 2000, when he sent her a series of his digital pieces, he got a call from her within a few days. Their relationship continues to grow, and Deborah has no problem finding clients to keep Mark busy.

"I do a lot of illustrating for books at this point, for Oxford Press, and Berlitz. Right now I'm working on 256 images that are due in two weeks."

Other clients include magazines like *Consumer Reports, Muscle Mag International* (twenty-one spot images per month!), *Raley's,* and *Plumbing & Mechanical* magazine.

He is still an avid painter, and continues to show his work at galleries in the North East.

"In my studio, I have a desk for my computer. I swivel around and behind me is my easel!"

While he'd love to earn his living as a painter, his illustration work keeps the chair swiveled facing the computer more often than his easel.

Mark admits to wishing he was as proficient with Photoshop as well as he is with Illustrator, but he says whenever he looks at what some Photoshop artists are doing, he figures he's better off sticking with vector art.

"I'm a designer as well as an illustrator, and vector art is just more 'me' than bitmapped art."

His skills with color and shading, however, do a good job of imitating a bitmapped look. He relies on very complex radial gradients for that effect.

Mark also admits to being a procrastinator.

"I could have two months to do a job, and I'll wait until two days before it's due to start. I need that pressure, I think."

What Mark doesn't enjoy, though, is chaos. "He who travels lightest travels fastest" is one of his mottoes. Everything in his home studio is in its place, and Mark would sooner throw old things out to make room for new things before buying another file cabinet.

"I did finally get an external hard drive so I would have room for all the digital work, though."

DIGITAL DECONSTRUCTION: FROGPOT

Mark created this whimsical piece for *Insight* magazine, and it's a great example of many of the techniques that define his style (Figure 10.7).

The first thing that catches your eye, aside from the calligraphic brush-like black strokes that Mark uses, is the subtle yet accurate use of color blending from one tone to another. Getting a radial gradient to work, as it does here specifically with the boiling water and in the electric stove element, is tricky.

Marks achieves this by implementing two techniques: pushing the gradient color stops to one end or the other of the gradient bar, and by altering the gradient with the Gradient tool so that the center is some distance away from the actual object he's working on.

Figure 10.7 This illustration is a great example of the techniques Mark has developed and that characterize his distinctive graphic style.

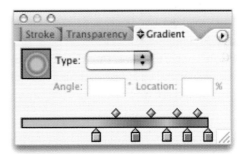

Figure 10.8 The gradient Mark created for the water requires both multiple shades of blue to imitate ripples, and pushing the color stops to the end.

Figure 10.9 Mark created the water in three parts to better control how the gradient affected various areas within the round pot shape.

He creates separate objects for each piece, even if he'll be applying the same gradient to each, as in the water inside the pot. This trick allows him more flexibility in controlling how the gradient fills each area within the "whole."

Once he's developed his shapes, he uses the Gradient tool to place the center point of the radial fill (which is the left side of the gradient bar) some distance away from the actual object, and then drags it to the outer edge of the shape.

The other area of this illustration where this technique is most evident is in the burner underneath the pot. In this case, the electrical element is three separate objects with a gold-to-orange radial gradient. The darker red area closest to the pot is actually a two-color gradient going from black in the center, to the glowing-ember red at the outside (Figure 10.10).

"I used to rely on blends, creating an inner shape and an outer shape and color, and then using Smooth Color (Object ➡ Blend ➡ Blend Options) to create them. Once I figured out how to do it with a gradient, though, it made life a lot easier!"

Mark is able to achieve these effects without relying on some of the more sophisticated features the recent CS versions of Illustrator provide.

"I don't use anything that didn't exist in Illustrator 9. I don't use transparencies or blending modes."

Part of that is because Mark wants to keep his work, like his life, simple and efficient. He's also concerned with reproduction issues. He's noticed that sometimes, when his images have been placed into a QuarkXPress document for instance, the gradients shift. He uses Object ➡

Figure 10.10 The black-to-red gradient connecting the pot to the burner was created with a gradient that Mark manipulated with the Gradient tool. To get this effect, he had to start his drag approximately five inches above the actual object.

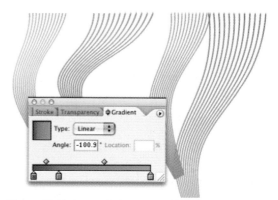
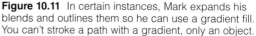

Figure 10.11 In certain instances, Mark expands his blends and outlines them so he can use a gradient fill. You can't stroke a path with a gradient, only an object.

Figure 10.12 Using the edges of his black shapes as cookie cutters (Object ➡ Path ➡ Divide Objects Below) to eliminate portions of shapes ensures perfect registration between two areas of color.

Expand to turn his gradients into individually colored paths or shapes as a way to prevent that problem.

Because Mark is so sensitive to the quality of his line, he usually expands everything he creates. The steam rising from the pot was created by blending two lines a specific number of steps. Mark expanded the blend (Object ➡ Blend ➡ Expand), increased the line weight a bit, and then outlined the paths (Object ➡ Path ➡ Outline Stroke). Once his paths were turned into objects, he could fill them with a linear gradient (Figure 10.11).

One of the other very clean and precise things Mark makes use of is Object ➡ Path ➡ Divide Objects Below (Figure 10.12). By using the edges of one shape as a sort of cookie cutter for shapes below, he ensures perfect registration between two colors. (See also Chapter 3, Jack Tom).

There are a lot of interesting techniques in this piece. Let's take a closer look at the gradients, since they're quite unusual, and very effective.

DIY:
RADIAL GRADIENTS

Forcing a gradient to extremes is one trick Mark uses. Another is to transform an object filled with a gradient to distort it.

1. Open a new document in Illustrator. Make sure the paper orientation is horizontal and set the color mode to CMYK.

We're going to create Saturn with its rings. The thing to remember here is that in order to get the radial gradient to distort into an oval, we'll start with circles and then use the Free Transform tool to turn them into ovals.

Figure 10.13 Create your version of Saturn using some of Mark's gradient tricks.

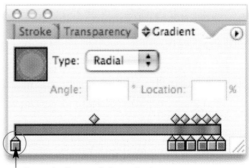

Figure 10.14 Select the two outer circles and make them a compound path (Command/Ctrl 8), then fill them with a radial gradient.

center color in a radial gradient

Figure 10.15 In order to get the gradient to fill the area we need, you have to move all but the center color (the left color stop) off to the right of the gradient bar.

2. Create three concentric circles. To make sure they're aligned to each other, select them all and use the Align palette.

   Make the outer two circles a compound path. Select both of them and type Command/Ctrl 8 (Object ➡ Compound Path ➡ Make).

   The inner circle will become the planet.

3. Open the Gradient palette if it's not already open. It's usually grouped with Transparency and Stroke.

One of Mark's hallmark tricks is to really force the colors of a gradient to one end or the other of the gradient bar (Figure 10.15).

4. Select Radial for the type of gradient you'll be constructing. By default, the gradient sets itself to black and white. We need to change those color stops, and add a few more.

5. Click the white tab, then go to the Color palette and change the mode from Grayscale to CMYK.

   Select or create a warm gray.

6. Click the black color tab in the gradient bar and again change the mode in the Color palette to CMYK.

   Select or create another warm gray.

7. Add several more analogous colors and move the tab stops for all but the first (at the left) as far to the right as you dare (Figure 10.15).

   If the compound path wasn't selected when you started constructing this gradient, select it now and click the gradient fill to apply it. If it was selected, the gradient fill should already be in place.

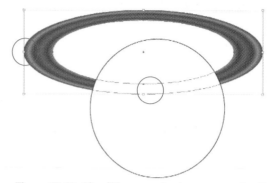

Figure 10.16 After filling your circular compound path with your gradient, use the Free Transform tool to squish and drag it into an exaggerated ellipse.

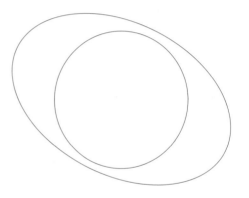

Figure 10.17 Create an ellipse that will act as the fill for your actual planet. Rotate it slightly with the Rotate tool.

8. If you have black strokes assigned to this object, change them to None.

9. Select the Free Transform tool in the Toolbar. Grab the bottom center control point and drag up to change the circle into an ellipse.

   Drag from one of the side points to distort it further (Figure 10.16).

Creating the planet itself uses the same principles. In order to make the subtle variations in the planet's surface, however, we'll need to create a mask. The back shape, an ellipse, will contain the radial gradient; the front shape, the circle, will be the mask.

10. Create an ellipse that's about twice as wide and only slightly taller than the planet, then rotate it slightly with the Rotate tool (Figure 10.17).

11. Create a new gradient. According to reference images, the planet itself is pale yellow with pink and mauve bands of color evenly distributed across the gradient.

    Once the ellipse is filled with the new gradient, select the Gradient tool and click once toward the bottom of the ellipse to offset the gradient's concentric circles (Figure 10.18).

12. Use the Free Transform tool to squish the ellipse. This will distort the actual gradient for more dramatic stripes.

13. Send this ellipse to the back.

14. Select both the planet and the gradient-filled ellipse and make a mask (Command/ Ctrl 7, or Object ➡ Clipping Mask ➡ Make).

At this point, you have both the shapes you need: the planet and the rings. The trick is to position them so that the planet is within the

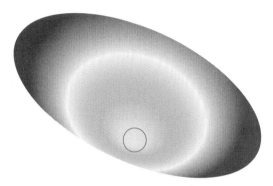

Figure 10.18 Click once in your gradient to offset the concentric rings.

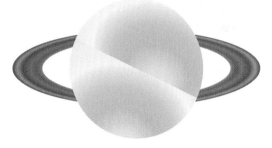

Figure 10.19 If you snip a gradient-filled shape in half, you end up with two separate filled objects.

rings. This requires cutting either the compound path (the rings) and deleting the portion that goes behind the planet, or snipping the planet in half and sending the upper portion to the back.

In truth, if you snip the planet and its mask, the gradient will split into two separate pieces (Figure 10.19). We'll snip the rings instead. This works better, since it's a compound path.

15. Select the rings and cut them (Command/Ctrl X).

16. Add a new layer above any you've been working on and paste the rings in front (Command/Ctrl F). Make sure to reposition them so they surround the planet.

17. Use the Scissors tool (not the Knife or Slice tool) to snip the bottom portion of the rings into pieces, and use the Direct Selection tool to delete it (Figure 10.20).

Don't panic! All you need to do now is connect the two endpoints on both sides of the rings where you deleted the center piece.

18. Select the Pen tool and click on one point to select that path, and then on the other endpoint to complete the shape.

Add a point in between these corners, convert it to a curve point, and adjust it to fit the curve of the planet (Figure 10.21).

19. Repeat this for the other side so both edges of the rings conform to the edge of the planet.

20. To make it more dramatic, add a black background, and rotate both the planet and the rings.

Save your file. We'll be coming back to it.

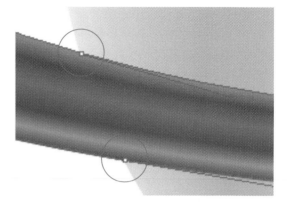

Figure 10.20 You'll need to snip the rings in four places: top and bottom at the left side of your planet, and top and bottom at the right. Select and delete the middle portion (use Command/Ctrl Y to access Outline view if you have trouble finding the edges).

Figure 10.21 Connect the two open endpoints at one side and then the other to get rid of the weird gradient band across your planet.

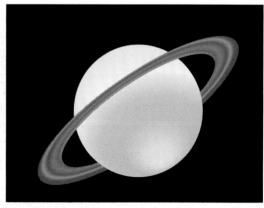

Figure 10.22 Add a black background and rotate your planet to make it look more realistic.

DIGITAL DECONSTRUCTION: PLUMBING

In this cover for *Plumbing & Mechanical* magazine, Mark had to develop an image that included just about every plumbing fixture and tool one could think of.

It's a dense cover, filled with a variety of shapes and colors, and includes a fairly complex background of water and splashes.

Mark draws every element he intends to include in his final image in his preliminary sketch. He also takes the time to indicate the various line weights and shapes he wants for each object and detail.

While this image is very complex with hundreds of individual pieces, Mark insists he had a great time creating it. It took him about three days to complete.

You've already seen how well Mark manages his radial gradients, and they are used here quite liberally. Note the showerhead; he used the same free transform trick you just learned while making the rings of Saturn to distort the gradient.

The part of this illustration that is most fascinating, because he's used it for just about every object, is the way he creates his black lines.

Mark draws every outline as a black shape. He doesn't create a path and make it thick, nor does he create a path and outline it to achieve this effect. He draws every edge around the shape of the line with the Pen tool.

"It's tedious. I scan my sketch and then replicate every edge with the Pen tool. I can't get the look I want with a calligraphic brush, and an outlined stroke can be too sterile, so I literally illustrate the line. It's a nice effect."

Figure 10.23 This cover illustration for *Plumbing & Mechanical Monthly* has everything, including the kitchen sink.

Figure 10.24 This detail of the image shows the thick and thin line Mark creates as shapes using the Pen tool (above).

When you select the "lines" you can see they are really shapes (left).

The only object in the illustration that doesn't use this constructed shape-as-line technique is in the red tubing; here Mark used offset paths of increasingly darker reds to create the rounded effect (Figure 10.24).

DIY:
ILLUSTRATED EDGES

You played with different edge techniques in both Kenny Keirnan's chapter, and in David McCord's. Now we'll experiment with creating an edge as a shape. The trick to success with this technique is to remember that because the line itself is a shape, you aren't going to surround the entire object with a path. Rather, you'll draw your path almost to the beginning, as if you were going to complete the shape, and then backtrack the way you came instead.

1. Create a new Illustrator document and use File ➡ Place to create a Template layer using "scissorsketch.psd" for your template image. It's located in the "collins" folder on your DVD.

   Make sure there's a second layer to draw on.

2. Set your colors to black fill with no stroke, and select the Pen tool.

The outer edge of the handle is all one shape. The inner edge is a second shape, and the little triangle shadow at the top is a third shape.

3. Start working your way clockwise around the left handle, from point A, creating anchor points where you need them. Keep to the outside of the pencil lines.

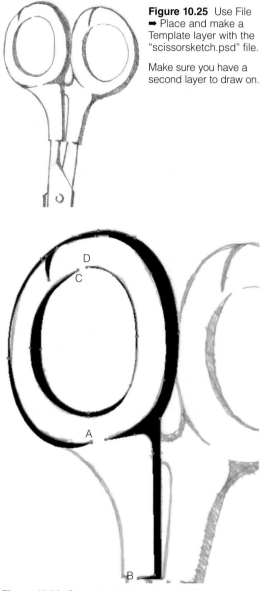

Figure 10.25 Use File ➡ Place and make a Template layer with the "scissorsketch.psd" file.

Make sure you have a second layer to draw on.

Figure 10.26 Start at point A and create the outer edge of the handle. When you get to point B, reverse direction and place anchor points to define the inner edge, ending back at point A again. The inner shape of the handle is created the same way.

NOTE: If the black fill gets in the way of seeing the template, use Command/Ctrl Y to toggle to Outline view and back again. Since you made the scan a Template layer, you'll be able to see it in Outline view. Remember, to create a template select the layer and choose Template from the submenu.

4. When you get to a natural turning point (point B), reverse your direction and work your way back around the handle, keeping to the *inside* of the pencil line this time. Ignore the triangle shadow at the top left— that's its own shape. Close the path when you get back to point A.

5. Create the inner handle shape the same way, starting at point C working counterclock- wise, and reversing direction at point D.

   Remember you can "break" the curve han- dles by holding the Option/Alt key, and clicking and dragging the end of the *handle* (not the point).

6. Create the triangle shadow as another solid shape.

7. Using this technique of drawing around the outer edge first, then reversing direc- tion and creating the inner edge, complete the right handle.

Hide your Template layer from time to time (Command Shift W/Ctrl Shift W, or click the eyeball icon in the Layers palette) (Figure 10.28) to study the shapes you're making; make sure they're gorgeous. Remember, any shape will be smoother with fewer, rather than more, anchor points.

8. Now that you have the hang of it, complete the scissors.

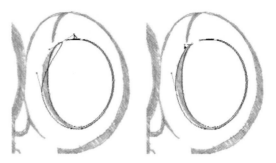

Figure 10.27 Reverse directions when you're working with a curve point, at the corner finish dragging the point—it might create a backwards loop (above left). Hold the Option/Alt key, click the handle, and drag it back where it belongs (above right).

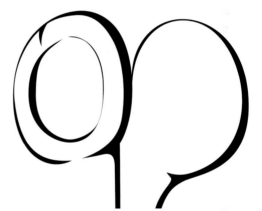

Figure 10.28 Hide your Template layer from time to time (Command Shift W/Ctrl Shift W) to make sure your shapes are beautiful.

Wherever you have two shapes coming together, zoom in (hold Command Spacebar/Ctrl Spacebar, then click and drag a rectangle around the area you want to zoom in on) to make sure the lines meet at each edge. It helps to be in Outline view (Command/Ctrl Y) to really see what's happening.

While we didn't look too closely at the way Mark uses color, other than his dramatic radial gradients, you might want to take the time to add color to these scissors (Figure 10.29).

The easiest way to do that is to create a new layer and drag it beneath the layer you drew your edges on. Use the Pen tool to draw the shapes within the black "edges."

Since in many areas the black will cover the edges of the colored shapes, you don't have to be too precise. Let your shapes overlap the black parts.

Don't forget to make compound paths for the handles. Draw the outer shape first, then the inner shape, select both and use Command/Ctrl 8 (Object ➡ Compound Path ➡ Make).

One of the benefits to creating edges this way is the complete control you have over the resulting shapes. When you create a path and outline it, you frequently get more anchor points than you really need. More often than not, adjusting a shape with too many points is more tedious than drawing it from scratch.

Figure 10.29 Add the colored areas on a new layer underneath the layer with your black edges.

Figure 10.30 Creating an Opacity Mask is a nice way to create subtle shading, or to have something fade to white.

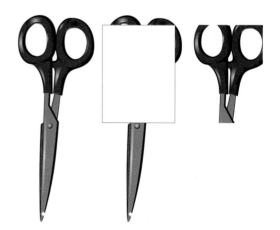

Figure 10.31 A Clipping Mask hides anything outside its shape—in this case, a rectangle.

FYI: MASKS

As you've seen, a mask, or as Illustrator refers to it, a Clipping Mask, is just like cutting a mat for a painting or print. It covers up the areas surrounding your image, and will hide anything that may be drawn or painted in those spaces (Figure 10.31). They are a great way to clean up the edges of an image, or to create an interesting shape for an image rather than an ordinary rectangle. You can also use masks to block out some areas within an image and not others by using them on the layers containing the objects you want to mask, as you did when creating the planet Saturn. You can have multiple masks within a single Illustrator file.

Making a Clipping Mask is very straightforward. Create the shape you want to use as the mask shape—whether it's a circle, rectangle, star, or anything else. Make sure this shape is on top of the elements you want to mask. Select the mask object along with the elements you want it to affect, and type Command/Ctrl 7, or select Object ➡ Clipping Mask ➡ Make. You could also highlight the name of the layer in the Layers palette and click the Make/Release Clipping Path icon at the bottom of the palette. If you've chosen elements from different layers, they will be moved to the layer on which the mask is created.

If you decide you don't want or need the mask, you can eliminate it by selecting it and typing Command/Ctrl 7, or choosing Object ➡ Clipping Mask ➡ Release, or clicking the Make/Release Clipping Path icon at the bottom of the Layers palette. You could also drag the Clipping Mask object in the Layers palette to the trash icon.

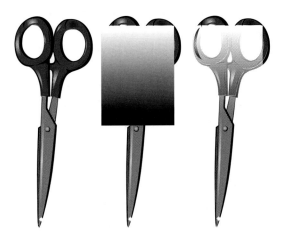

Figure 10.32 An Opacity Mask uses a gradient to change the opacity of the area it covers.

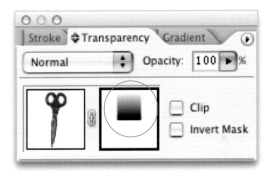

Figure 10.33 Click the mask in the Transparency palette to edit it.

The Opacity Mask feature in Illustrator CS is pretty amazing. Rather than just a shape, it uses a black-and-white gradient to mask what's below it so that it appears to fade out, based on the type and direction of the gradient (Figure 10.32). You won't find it under the Object menu with the Clipping Mask—it's in the Transparency palette.

Mark doesn't use this feature, nor does he need to; however, for our DIY Saturn image, a gradient mask is a nice way to add the shadow to the left side of the planet.

Here's how to make one.

DIY: OPACITY MASKS

Open your Saturn image.

1. Draw a circle the exact size as Saturn, on the same layer, and position it over the planet.

2. Drag a copy off to the right so that they overlap, select both circles and use the Pathfinder palette to Subtract from shape area (it's the second icon from the left in the top row). You should be left with a moon-like shape. Click the Expand button to delete the paths you don't need (Figure 10.34).

3. Fill this with a radial gradient from white in the center to black at the edges.

    Use the Gradient tool to adjust the gradient. Where it's white, your image will be most visible; where it's black, your image will be hidden from view. You might also want to shift the midpoint of the gradient to the right or left.

4. Select Saturn—the ellipse fill and the mask— along with this gradient moon-shape.

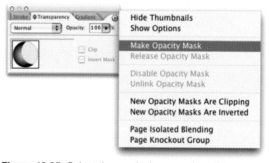

Figure 10.34 Create your mask shape with two over-lapping circles and using the Subtract from shape area pathfinder.

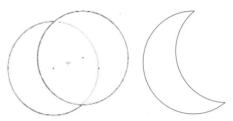

Figure 10.35 Select the mask shape and anything you want it to affect and choose Make Opacity Mask from the Transparency palette submenu.

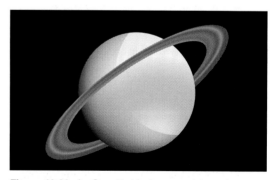

Figure 10.36 An Opacity Mask can create a nice blend between areas.

From the Transparency palette, use the sub-menu and choose Make Opacity Mask (Figure 10.35).

NOTE: If you need to adjust the gradient once you've created the mask, Option/Alt-click on the mask icon in the Transparency palette to focus on it, then use whatever tools you need to make the adjustments. Any changes you make will be automatically reflected in the mask's effect on the objects attached to it. Click back on the left (image) side of the Transparency palette to refocus on the actual image objects.

KEY POINTS

- Adjust radial gradients by setting the center point some distance away from the object you're working on.

- Create dramatic radial gradients by pushing the color stops to one side or another in the Gradient palette.

- Distort radial gradients using the Free Transform tool.

- Create pen and ink-like edges by drawing them as closed, filled shapes, rather than stroked paths.

- A mask object can be any shape, and must be on top of everything you want it to affect.

- A mask will block out the edges beyond its shape. Select all areas of an image you want to mask, along with the mask object, before making the mask.

- You can have multiple masks within a single image.

- Selecting portions of an image on multiple layers to use in a mask will combine them onto a single layer.

- An Opacity Mask is used to have an image fade to nothing.

- You must use a black-and-white gradient for an Opacity Mask. The lighter areas will reveal your image, and the darker areas will hide it.

- Adjust an Opacity Mask's shape or the direction of the gradient by clicking on it in the Transparency palette.

ON YOUR OWN:
POSTAGE STAMPS

Mark's technique for making edges has lots of possibilities. It can be used to define very crisp-looking images, or to give form to more loosely colored objects.

Using this type of edge, create a set of four postage stamps that all have the same theme. There's a template for the size of the stamps on the "collins" folder on your DVD. This template is larger than an actual stamp, but is in proportion. As long as you don't use any ordinary paths to stroke your objects, you can reduce your final stamp images to the correct size for a real stamp without worrying about the strokes becoming too thin to print.

Some themes to consider: Love, Holiday, Nature, Patriotism, Sports, or American Crafts.

CHRIS SPOLLEN

Type Around a Circle • 3D Revolve • Mapping Artwork • Adding Textures

While Chris Spollen still incorporates many of his traditional illustration techniques in his digital artwork, some aspects, like the ability to rotate a stroke into a three-dimensional object, can only be created in Illustrator.

Figure 11.1 Chris's signature style includes high-contrast images that he creates by photocopying a photograph, and then copying the copy until he gets the contrast and texture he's after.

Chris Spollen has been working as a professional designer and illustrator for more than thirty years. His client list is impressive, including *Boy's Life* magazine, AT&T, *MacWorld* magazine, General Motors and Citibank.

Instrumental in his development was professor, mentor, and good friend Murray Tinkelman. Chris studied with Tinkelman while an undergraduate student at Parson's School of Design in Manhattan. As a lifelong resident of Staten Island, Chris didn't have to go far for his training, or his success.

Chris began his illustration career with an eclectic style that mixed traditional media with found images and other two-dimensional pieces. He's perhaps best known for his manipulation of photographs with a photocopier, copying the copies to the point where he created grainy black-and-white images he then used in his final pieces. He still uses found images and his own photography in his digital work, employing the copy machine, and some of Photoshop's Image Adjustments to re-create the look and textures of his nondigital work. His transition to digital image-making is almost invisible.

One significant aspect of his work, whether the final image is created in Illustrator or Photoshop, is his love affair with Adobe Dimensions. In almost every piece he creates, you'll find evidence of the three-dimensional renderings Adobe's Dimensions program makes possible. While Illustrator CS2 includes a 3D effect, Chris still prefers to draw his rockets, towers, and Tiki heads using Dimensions.

The other thing you notice in his work is the preponderance of robots, rockets, cars, and other mechanical things.

In particular, Chris is fascinated with what he calls HPV or Human Powered Vehicles. He and his brother have turned their garage into a model shop where they build bikes that are anything but common. He's also created several sculptures based on his illustrated characters.

Chris believes that good illustration and design come from knowing who you are and what

Figure 11.2 Chris uses a variety of techniques to add detail to his visual messages.

Figure 11.3 Chris's illustrations usually include something he's rendered in 3D using Adobe Dimensions.

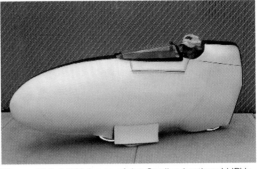

Figure 11.4 Li'l Nel, one of the Spollen brothers' HPVs.

In "Commerce and Technology," Chris's photocopying technique is clearly evident. A photograph of a man in a welding suit was copied several times, and then scanned into Photoshop. Chris used Image ➡ Adjust ➡ Brightness and Contrast to delete detail, then Image ➡ Adjust ➡ Posterize to generate the pure black-and-white image.

He imported that image into Illustrator to use as a Template layer. "I redraw it in Illustrator because I'm a perfectionist and I want to create my own shapes."

Within the man's torso are diagrams and solar system objects. "I have a whole collection of stuff that I save and when I need it, I just open the other file and drag what I want over into the image I'm working on."

The space-age planets and structures in the background are images he created in Dimensions and copied into his Illustrator file. Using Illustrator's 3D Revolve effect, along with some simple gradients or blends would work as well.

Another trick Chris is fond of is adding textures to his work. Turning certain characters from dingbat fonts into outlines, making multiple copies by using the Option/Alt drag shortcut, and then adjusting transparency levels all help

drives you. And, he maintains, that's neither computer, nor software driven. "The talent behind the machine should come through, disproving the idea that computer work is easy or only based on tricks."

His advice: draw, draw, draw. Keep a sketchbook and use it every day. Your talent and skills, digital or otherwise, will grow along with your development as an imagemaker.

to add subtle, yet important texture and detail to an otherwise straightforward image.

In the "Hot Radio" image (Figure 11.5), he's used the "f" character from Zapf Dingbats for the texture at the bottom of the radio, and the "g" and "h" characters for the inside of the tuner window. He added gradient fills behind them, and made the objects transparent to 24%.

And while he is devoted to Dimensions, he used straightforward blends and gradients for the handle, knobs, and buttons. He also added some subtle feathered shadows around them for depth (Effect ➡ Stylize ➡ Drop Shadow).

DIGITAL DECONSTRUCTION: ROCKET COMMAND

The first interesting part of this image is Chris's inclusion of a scanned photograph—Johnny Rocket. When you place a TIFF or EPS file into Illustrator, it's contained within a rectangular frame, even if the background is white.

Chris achieved the silhouette of Johnny's face by drawing a path around it, selecting both the path and the photo, and using Object ➡ Clipping Mask ➡ Make (Command/Ctrl 7).

Once the face was isolated from the background, Chris added the black circle and moved it behind the photograph using Object ➡ Arrange ➡ Send to Back (Command Shift [/Ctrl Shift []). Once that was done, he added the collar and headpiece.

A final step, the type, was created by drawing circle shapes, and using the Type on a Path tool. In order to position the type exactly around the head, Chris used two circles—one for each part of the phrase—and rotated them individually. Then he used the Align palette to

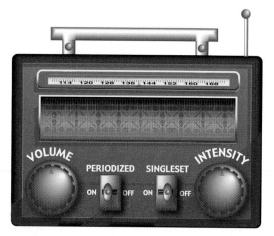

Figure 11.5 Chris incorporated type dingbats to add texture and detail, and the Drop Shadow effect for depth in "Hot Radio," an image he created for a design firm in California.

Figure 11.6 This image recalls trading cards packed with bubble gum and Buck Rogers. It includes several of Chris's trademark techniques.

center them to each other and positioned them around Johnny's face.

The final touches for this center medallion were adding a star shape and some gradient-filled circles along the same paths the type used.

The sky, mountains, and bottom portion of this image all use the same gradient. Chris reversed the gradient in some areas, and determined its length for each area using the Gradient tool.

The details in the type "rocket command" and within the spaceship are particularly intriguing. Chris used Gill Sans Bold, adjusted his point size and letterspacing, then turned the type into outlines (Command Shift O/Ctrl Shift O).

He added triangle shapes at the right and left of the outer letters by drawing them with the Pen tool. He duplicated them using the Option/Alt drag technique and positioned these copies to the left of the "C" and "R." He reflected two additional copies for the right side of the "T" and the "D." He combined them into single shapes using the Pathfinder palette.

Then, Chris found a font with characters that looked like dingbats. He filled them with a slightly lighter orange, turned them into outlines, and placed them over the solid orange ones. A couple of duplicates of the solid type positioned slightly above and below each letter creates a subtle 3D effect.

Chris also used a font for the details in his spaceship. After creating the basic rocket shape and filling it with a red-black linear gradient, he selected some of the letters to use as decorative elements. He turned them into outlines, copied, rotated, and positioned them within the rocket.

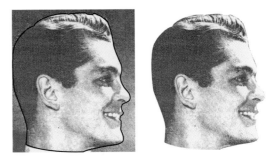

Figure 11.7 Chris drew a path around Johnny's face. He selected the photo and the path, and created a mask.

Figure 11.8 Chris used the Type on a Path tool around two identical circles, then rotated them and used the Align palette to make them concentric (left).

Figure 11.9 The finished medallion includes a star shape and gradient-filled dots positioned along the same path the type used (right).

Figure 11.10 Chris added some triangle shapes to his main font, and used (another font) to create the subtle interior texture.

One key to making this all work easily and quickly is to isolate the object on its own layer, and create it in an upright position. That way, you're able to take advantage of the Reflect tool to create a perfectly symmetrical shape. When you've completed it, you can rotate it to its final position.

Simply draw half of the shape, add the details, and then select them all. Option/Alt click with the Reflect tool, then choose to reflect along a vertical axis, and copy (not OK) to create the other half of your object (Figure 11.11).

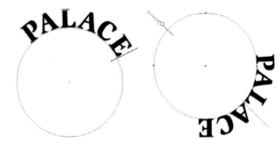

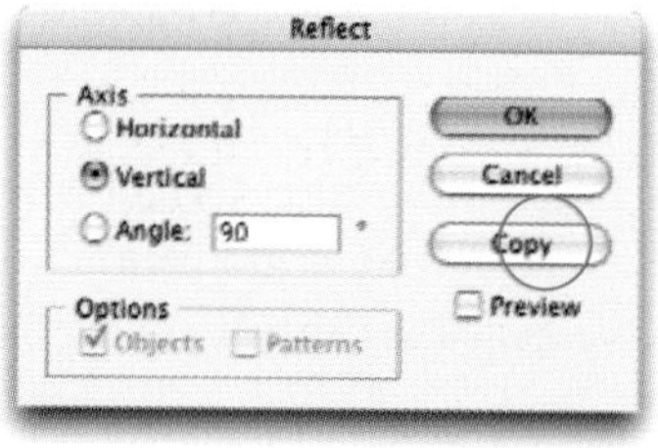

Figure 11.11 Create symmetrical shapes by drawing half, and using the Reflect options to copy it for the other half. Rotate it to the desired position once it's finished.

DIY:
TYPE AROUND A CIRCLE

You've probably already played with using the Text tool to place text along a wavy line, or around a shape. There are a couple of tricks to working with circle shapes in particular that are worth looking at.

1. Open a new Illustrator document and draw a perfect circle, about 3" in diameter. We'll use it to create a logo for an independent movie theater.

2. Select the Type on a Path tool and click on the edge of the circle. The fill and stroke characteristics will be eliminated, leaving the type cursor flashing on an invisible shape.

    Type the word "Palace" (Figure 11.12).

3. While the Type tool is still selected, double-click the word and type Command Shift C/Ctrl Shift C, which will center the type from left to right (Figure 11.13).

4. Use the Selection tool to move the type to the top of the circle; click and drag on the blue guide in the middle of the word.

Figure 11.12 Type your word on the circle with the Type on a Path tool.

Figure 11.13 Use Command Shift C/Ctrl Shift C to center the type.

Figure 11.14 Note how the cursor has a small upside-down T next to it, indicating you can drag your type along a path.

NOTE: If you try to use the Direct Selection tool for this, you won't see the blue guides that indicate the beginning, end, and center of the word on the path: you have to use the Selection tool.

5. Drag a copy of the circle to create the second word.

6. Select the Type tool again, and double-click the word on your copy; change it to "Theatre" (Figure 11.15).

   Use the Selection tool to center it along the bottom edge of the circle.

7. Select both circles and use the Align palette to center them to each other (Figure 11.16).

Now we need to flip the word Theatre upside-up.

8. Use the Selection tool again: click on the center guide and drag up, inside the circle. Your type should flip right-side up.

   Use the center guide to center it at the bottom of your circle if you need to (Figure 1.17).

9. Select the text with the Type tool and adjust the letterspacing (tracking): hold the Option/Alt key and use the right and left arrows to add space between each letter.

   If you need to adjust the spacing between two letters (kerning), place the cursor between them and use the same keystrokes to make your adjustments.

It's not quite finished; we need to make the circle for the word Theater a bit bigger, to create the illusion that the words are within the same circle shape. Right now, it looks like the word Theater is on a smaller circle.

10. Use the Ellipse tool to draw a perfect circle that's larger than the original; its edge

Figure 11.15 Duplicate the original circle and text, and edit the text by double-clicking it with the Type tool.

Figure 11.16 Use the Align palette to center both circles to each other.

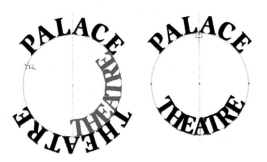

Figure 11.17 After you flip the type to the inside of the circle, use the center guide with the Selection tool to center it at the bottom of the circle.

should touch along the top of the letters in the word Palace (Figure 11.18).

Turn this circle into a guide (Command/Ctrl 5, or View ➡ Guides ➡ Make Guides).

11. With the Group Selection tool (the hollow arrow with the plus sign), select the circle with the word Theatre, then use the Scale tool to enlarge it to match the circle guide (Figure 11.19).

NOTE: If you use the Selection tool to select the circle, you'll be scaling the type as well as the circle. To make sure you don't do that, you need to use the Group Selection tool, which will only scale the shape, and not the type.

---

12. Once things are scaled, you can go to town adding embellishments to this logo. There's a file called "projector.tif" in the "spollen" folder if you'd like to add a Spollen-esque image to it.

DIGITAL DECONSTRUCTION: TECHNOMAN

There are a lot of "found" elements in this detailed illustration (Figure 11.21).

The diagrams make it look very technical, scientific, and rather complicated. Chris scans diagrams he's found into Photoshop and then either uses them as templates and redraws the shapes, or uses the Live Trace function to retain the rough photocopied edge quality.

Several of the details in this image can be easily re-created using the 3D Revolve effect in Illustrator. Let's take a look at the flashlight.

First, it's important to understand how Illustrator creates a dimensional shape. It's

Figure 11.18 Create a circle that's large enough to reach the top of the word Palace.

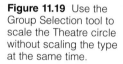

Figure 11.19 Use the Group Selection tool to scale the Theatre circle without scaling the type at the same time.

Figure 11.20 This final logo includes a scatter brush of stars, along with a placed image that was Live Traced to make it look more like a photocopy.

based on the silhouette of either the left or right side of a vertical object. When you select a line and use the 3D Revolve effect, Illustrator literally uses that path to create a blend using hundreds of copies of that path. Each one is also distorted so that they flatten out at the center of the object, and become reversed at the other edge.

Figure 11.22 is an example. The line at the left was created with the Pen tool and then duplicated using the Reflect tool to create the right edge of the shape. The Blend tool was set to a specified number of steps, which created the intermediary strokes between the two edges.

The major difference between the Blend tool and the 3D Revolve effect, however, is the introduction of more true-to-life shading, along with the option to determine the direction of the light source.

In the 3D Revolve options dialog box (Figure 11.23), you can choose the view of your object (in this case, a straight head-on frontal view). You can also determine whether to rotate the line to the right or left of the original, the type of shading desired, and the position of the light source.

Chris created his flashlight using three profiles: the head and body of the flashlight, the rounded area toward the bottom, and the on/off button.

Figure 11.24 illustrates the three paths that had the 3D Rotate effect applied. Because the flashlight is a full 3D object, Chris made sure the rotation was set to 360°, and that the view was from the front (the default view is Off-Axis Front).

After completing these three steps, Chris had to rotate the final flashlight shape to a horizontal position.

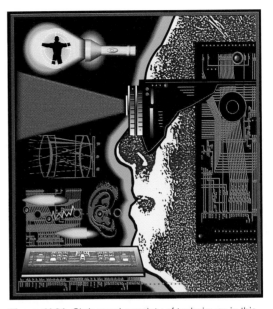

Figure 11.21 Chris used a variety of techniques in this piece, including textured photocopies, technical charts, and 3D effects.

Figure 11.22 The Blend tool creates a transition from left to right edges, approximating a 3D effect.

Rotating these shapes, however, would seriously alter the look of the original rotation (Figure 11.25). Chris used Object ➡ Expand Appearance on each piece to "unlock" the shape from the 3D effect. At that point, he used the Rotate tool to point the flashlight in the proper direction.

To eliminate a 3D effect from an object, use the Appearance palette to select it and drag it to the trash.

DIY:
A SPOLLEN ROCKET SHIP

The 3D effect in Illustrator is fascinating. Let's create some rocket ships of our own, and you'll discover not only how amazing this feature is, but also how very easy it is to use.

1. Start by drawing an elongated oval with the Ellipse tool.

    Delete the right half of your shape by either selecting the anchor point on the right edge of the path and hitting the Delete key, or using the Scissors tool to cut it at noon and 6 o'clock, and deleting the right half (Figure 11.26).

    NOTE: It's important to draw this oval from the top left to the bottom right.
    ---

2. Choose a color for your stroke and set your fill color to none.

3. While it's still selected, choose Effect ➡ 3D ➡ Revolve to open the 3D Revolve Options dialog box. Click More Options to see all the options you will need to use. Make sure to click Preview so you can see what's happening to your curved stroke.

view of 3D shape

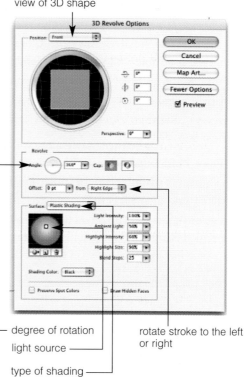

degree of rotation
light source
type of shading
rotate stroke to the left or right

Figure 11.23 The 3D Revolve options.

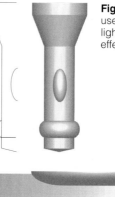

Figure 11.24 The three profiles used to create the final flashlight (left), and the finished effect.

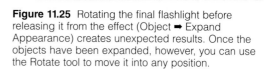

Figure 11.25 Rotating the final flashlight before releasing it from the effect (Object ➡ Expand Appearance) creates unexpected results. Once the objects have been expanded, however, you can use the Rotate tool to move it into any position.

Use these settings to establish the rotation:

Position: Off-Axis Front

Rotate: 360° from right edge.

Feel free to play with the light source location by clicking and dragging the circle in the sphere at the bottom left of this dialog box.

You can also change the Shading Color option from the default of black to something else using the Color Picker. Select Custom, then click on the default red box to access it.

When you like what you've got, click OK.

Now we need some fins.

4. Use the Pen tool to draw a fin shape similar to that in Figure 11.28. Make a reflected copy of it.

5. Selecting each fin in turn, use Effect ➡ 3D ➡ Revolve to generate a fin that's revolved from the Front position (select it from the drop-down menu) with a rotation of 90°. Again, play with the light source.

    Remember to rotate one from the right edge, and the other from the left.

    Arrange the fins to either side of the ship.

Since the fins were drawn after the body of the ship, they're on top in the stacking order of the drawing. Select them and send them to back by either dragging their sublayers below the one with the ship in the Layers palette, or by cutting them and pasting them in back (Figure 11.29).

6. Create a center fin by drawing another shape and rotating it 360° in the 3D Revolve Options dialog box. Position it in the center of your ship.

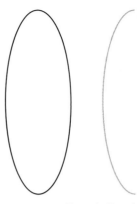

Figure 11.26 Use a half oval shape to generate the body of your rocket ship.

Figure 11.27 Rotate your path into a three-dimensional shape using Effect ➡ 3D ➡ Revolve.

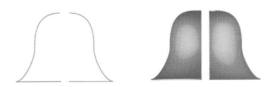

Figure 11.28 Create the fin shape and reflect a copy (left). Apply the 3D Revolve effect to each one separately (right).

Having created this basic rocket, now try your hand at developing other body and fin shapes. See the profiles and results in Figure 11.30 for some ideas.

Now that we have a ship, it's time to add graphics.

DIY:
MAPPING ARTWORK
TO YOUR ROCKET

A Spollen rocket ship isn't complete without some decoration. Let's add some to our own rocket ship using the Map Art feature found in 3D Effects.

Mapping artwork to a revolved shape takes a symbol that you've created and, using the architecture of the rotation, distorts it and adds the appropriate shading so that it appears wrapped around the shape.

1. Start by printing your rocket. It doesn't have to be in color. Sketch right on your hard copy, or use tracing paper, to work out some decorative. Consider adding a name, some simple repetitive shapes (like the dots and stars in Figure 11.31), or even dingbats from an illustrative font like Wingdings.

2. Once you have a good idea of what you want, return to your computer and create your decorative elements on a new layer of your rocket ship file. (You might even want to scan in your sketches to use as a template for drawing them.)

3. Open the Symbols palette.

4. When you're ready, arrange and select the elements you want to include in a single symbol. Then click on the "new symbol" icon at the bottom of the Symbols palette

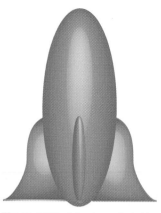

Figure 11.29 A basic rocket ship.

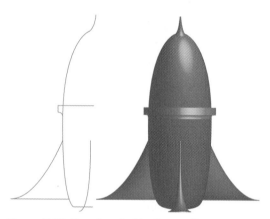

Figure 11.30 Experiment with other profiles to create more sophisticated rockets.

Figure 11.31 Create some decorative objects to use as symbols. These are simple characters and shapes from a dingbat font.

to add it. Repeat this for each decoration (Figure 11.32). If you want a stripe that surrounds the entire rocket, make sure your symbol is wide enough to wrap around the circumference.

5. Open the Appearance palette from the Window menu.

6. Select the body of your rocket and notice that in the Appearance palette, there's a 3D effect noted as an attribute.

   Double-click it to open the 3D Revolve Options dialog box (Figure 11.33).

7. Click on the Map Art button to open the Map Art Options dialog box. At the top left is the menu of available symbols. To the right of that are arrows that will highlight each surface in your selected object in turn.

   Arrange your dialog box so you can see your rocket while you work on it.

   Use the right and left arrows to see which area of your rocket each represents. You'll see a red wire frame pop up in your image at various places (Figure 11.34, right).

   When you get to the surface you want the art to wrap around, select the symbol you want to use from the pop-up menu. The light gray area in the window below represents the visible area of your rocket; move your symbol into that space. (You might want to click on the Preview option to see what's actually happening!)

   Use the symbol's control points to move, scale, rotate, or skew the symbol.

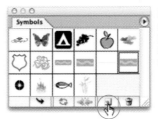

Figure 11.32 Click on the "new symbol" icon in the palette to add your selected objects as a symbol.

Figure 11.33 Edit an object that has been revolved by double-clicking on that aspect of its appearance in the Appearance palette.

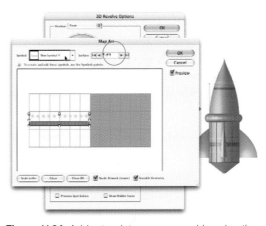

Figure 11.34 Add artwork to your spaceship using the Map Art feature in the 3D Revolve Options dialog box. Note the red grid on the rocket; this indicates the area of the shape you're mapping.

If you want art mapped to several surfaces, select each one from the surface options, then choose your symbol from the pop-up list and position it.

8. Click OK to return to the main 3D Revolve Options dialog box, and click OK again to exit it.

NOTE: In order to create several images on the same surface, they have to be created as a single symbol.

DIY: ADDING TEXTURES IN ILLUSTRATOR

The transparency feature in Illustrator works not only on colors and patterns that you create in any particular file, but also on any images you place in a document. Let's use this feature, along with a mask, to add a scanned image for some texture on our rocket.

Here's an overview of the steps:

First create the mask shape. Use the Pen tool to redraw your rocket (remember, you only have to draw half of it).

Use File ➡ Place to locate the file on the DVD called "crunchy.tif." This is a scan from a book called *Background Patterns, Textures, and Tints* by Clarence P. Hornung, published by Dover.

Once it's in place, set its transparency to 25% and send it to the back (Object ➡ Arrange ➡ Send to Back or Command Shift [/Ctrl Shift [, or Command/Ctrl X, Command/Ctrl B.)

Drag your outlined rocket shape on top of the crunchy texture. Select both the ship shape and the texture and create a mask (Object ➡

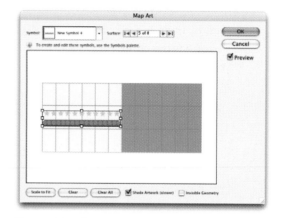

Figure 11.35 The lighter gray indicates the front part of your image. Beware! Some of the areas you can map may be on the inside of the object and won't be visible no matter what.

Figure 11.36 The transparent map texture on Chris's rocket (left) was created in Photoshop. You can create the same effect in Illustrator as well (right).

Clipping Mask ➡ Make, or Command/Ctrl 7). Finally, drag the masked object on top of your original 3D rocket.

Ready?

1. Add a new layer and use the Pen tool to re-create the outline of half your rocket (①).

2. Select your rocket profile and use the Option/Alt key when you click with the Reflect tool to create a copy (②).

3. Select any points at either side of a shape and use Command/Ctrl J to join the points with a straight line (indicated with the arrows), or Command Option Shift J/Ctrl Alt Shift J to unite two points into one (indicated with dots at the top and bottom of the ship) (③).

4. If necessary, select all the parts of your rocket and turn them into a single shape by Option/Alt clicking on the Add to shape area icon in the Pathfinder palette (④).

5. Locate the "crunchy.tif" file on the DVD using the Place command from the File menu.

   Once the file is in place, send it to the back (Command Shift [/Ctrl Shift [, or Command/Ctrl X, Command/Ctrl B.) (⑤).

6. Position the outline of your ship over the texture. Select both the texture and the path and make a Clipping Mask (Object ➡ Clipping Mask ➡ Make, or Command/Ctrl 7) (⑥).

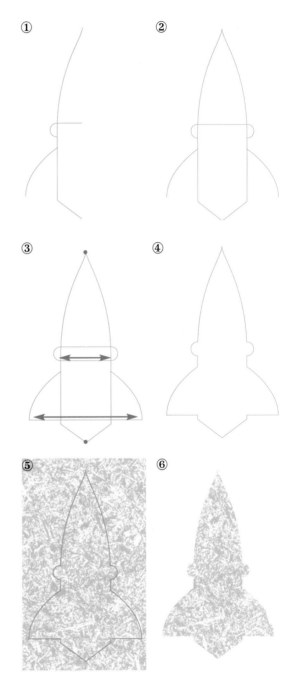

Figure 11.37 Create the outline of your rocket to use as a mask shape for the texture.

NOTE: You can also select the layer's name in the Layers palette and then click the Make/Release Clipping Path icon at the bottom of the palette.

---

7. Drag this shape over your original 3D rocket and set its mode to Multiply in the Transparency palette.

Voila!

You can generate your own textures by scanning simple things like a crumpled piece of paper, a piece of lace, or a burlap bag. Save the scan as a TIFF file to place in Illustrator images. You might want to try creating a bitmap (black-and-white) version of your texture so you can change its color from within Illustrator, the way Rocco Baviera does.

KEY POINTS

*   To create type around a circle that's right-side up at the bottom, you need to flip it upside-down with the Selection tool.

*   Use the Selection tool (not the Direct Selection tool) to adjust type along a path.

*   Enlarge or reduce the path for type using the Group Selection tool to select it.

*   Enlarge or reduce the path *and* the type using the Selection tool.

*   Drag shapes from the top left corner when using them for revolved objects.

*   Double check the Offset edge in 3D Revolve Options to make sure you aren't inverting your shape.

*   To create a decorative stripe to use as art for mapping, you need to create several copies of the objects and add them as a single element to the Symbols palette.

- Edit 3D objects by double-clicking the effect in the Appearance palette.

- Set the mode of texture images to Multiply to have them affect elements below.

ON YOUR OWN:
SPORTS

The 3D Revolve feature lends itself well to creating round shapes, like baseballs and basketballs and footballs.

Experiment with this feature by creating a magazine ad or a poster that advertises a sporting event or TV sports channel. See if you can add texture and/or images to revolved shapes to make them look more realistic. Work within a standard 8.5" x 11" vertical format.

 DANIEL PELAVIN

Creating Letterforms • Type Trix • Creating Graphic Styles

Design skills and illustration talent combine to create forceful visual communication in Daniel Pelavin's work. His attention to detail and creative approach to typography are a hallmark of all his work.

Daniel Pelavin has enjoyed a very successful thirty-year career as a designer, illustrator, and type guy. He's been drawing both images and letterforms since he was old enough to hold a pencil.

So why did he ever consider becoming a lawyer?

"Senior year at college, all my friends took the LSAT's so I did too. I did well, and was accepted into law school. The summer before I was supposed to start, I got an apprenticeship at a design studio in Detroit. It changed my life."

His passion and talent for design and making images led him to Cranbrook Academy of Art in Michigan, where he completed his M. F. A. in design. He explored moving to the west coast, but decided to move east instead. His current home and studio are in Manhattan, where he lives with his two talented daughters.

Daniel's traditional work began as tightly developed silkscreens, relying on his skills with drafting tools, an X-Acto knife, and the manipulation of rubdown type (called "press type" or "transfer type"). Moving to the computer, and Adobe Illustrator in particular, to generate images was a natural extension of his approach to illustration and design. As he says, "Illustrator serves those who wish to take a risk and possibly create magic." And that he does.

Daniel's unique style pays tribute to the artistic influences of old matchbook covers, enamel signs, and packaging design from the 1890s to

Figure 12.1 One of Daniel Pelavin's original silk screen posters, created for *The Mother Goose Collection* in 1990.

the 1950s. His work has a distinct Art Deco style, even though each piece of work is unique to the needs of his clients.

He describes his creative process as:
1) accept assignment;
2) research necessary reference material;
3) procrastinate until the latest possible moment (preferably the morning of the day rough sketches are due);
4) submit five to ten incomprehensible scribbles; and
5) using client's choice as a guide, complete tight, grayscale or color art in Illustrator.

What you don't see in the process is the way ideas based on his research simmer in his mind until they all come together in a series of rough sketches. After discussing them with the client, Daniel tightens them up in Illustrator.

Figure 12.2 Cover for *Ad Week* magazine.

Daniel's faculty with some of Illustrator's less obvious features, like Offset Path, the Pathfinders, and his skill with gradients, lend great detail to his work, even if it's a logo that will never be reproduced at larger than a two-inch square. Attention to stroke weight and the balance between positive and negative space helps him to create intricate and compelling images. One gradient option that Daniel doesn't use much, however, is the gradient mesh.

"I use it when I need to." How often is that? "Once, for an image of some marshmallows."

Daniel's skill and innovative work have earned him recognition from a variety of venues, including the American Institute of Graphic Arts (AIGA), the Society of Illustrators, *Print's Regional Design Annual*, *Communication Arts* magazine, the Society of Publication

Figure 12.3 Build a Better Burger point-of-purchase display for Sutter Home Winery.

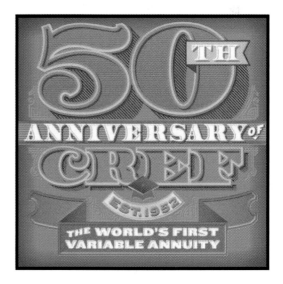

Figure 12.4 This design features some classic Pelavin typographic treatments.

Designers, and the Art Directors Clubs of Boston, New York, San Francisco, and Washington D. C., among others.

Daniel's advice: "You can't be a great designer today without using a computer, but you can't be a great designer just because you know how to use a computer."

DIGITAL DECONSTRUCTION: LOST ANGELES

The published cover for this book was produced by creating meticulous drawings for each color on separate mylar overlays. The version approved by the art director used black, maroon, tan, and red spot colors. But Daniel had a better idea, so he created this digital piece to showcase his vision, as well as his proficiency with Illustrator.

For the original project, Daniel began with pages and pages of rough sketches because "drawing is good for the soul." In this case, he generated at least eight full pages of ideas (Figure 12.6). After conferring with the art director, he created a very tightly drawn sketch to the finished size (Figure 12.7).

Because Daniel's early training included a lot of drafting, his final sketch is meticulous in the rendering of the lines, shapes, and curves he wanted to define his elements. For this project, he only needed to scan it and bring it into Illustrator as a template layer to trace.

For the sky area at the left, Daniel created two colored strokes, then used the Blend tool to create intermediate steps, producing a smooth transition in both color and shape. The stroke weight is an important factor in making a smooth blend without producing more vector

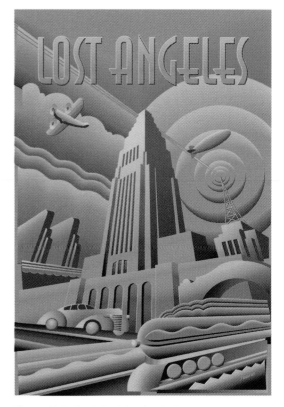

Figure 12.5 Daniel's vision for the book cover.

Figure 12.6 Daniel used these sketches to talk with the art director.

information than is absolutely necessary. In this case, the strokes are 2.45 points wide.

For the clouds, he created two filled shapes—one to define the outer/upper edge of the cloud, and another, darker, one, to define the end of the gradient area within the cloud. The Blend tool created intermediary shapes that morphed between the two original shapes, as well as graduating the color from light to dark.

The sun shape was created using a combination of both techniques. He created two stroked circles, and blended them as a specified number of steps. Note in the outline detail that his ellipses are actually two shapes, creating sharp highlights at the top edges, and more dramatic shadows at the bottom.

By contrast, the buildings are quite simple; basic rectilinear shapes filled with gradients. He customized his gradients by adding several color stops.

On the subject of color, this illustration uses only six colors—custom colors that Daniel saved as swatches, so he could use them over and over again.

Finally, the type was turned into outlines and duplicated two times to create the three-dimensional effect. (Daniel designed this font and called it Anna, to celebrate the birth of his daughter.) The back-most characters are stroked with his lightest gold, and a weight of 2.5 points. The middle characters are identical to the top; they've been offset slightly, and have a stroke of 1.25 points, matching their brown fill, so they're slightly larger. The topmost characters are filled with a simple three-color gradient and no stroke.

Figure 12.7 The technically rendered final sketch.

Figure 12.8 The original, printed version.

Figure 12.9 Detail of the sun's blended strokes, in Outline View (Command/Ctrl Y).

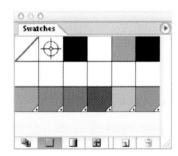

Figure 12.10 Daniel created a simple, six-color palette for the entire illustration.

Designing a font is no small undertaking, and although Daniel has designed several, he more often will design just the letters he needs for a particular job. A solid understanding of the anatomy of type, and its history, is something every designer and illustrator should have. Most of the illustrators in this book also have a design background, and so are all sensitive to the appropriate and inappropriate uses of type. Daniel is no exception, and as evidenced by the work included in this chapter, is frequently called for jobs that require an elegant typographic solution.

"I don't always design the type I need. I have some favorite fonts I use a lot, those that have a lot of variations, and lend themselves to the different techniques I use in my work."

DIY:
CREATING ORIGINAL
LETTERFORMS

While we can't get into an entire discourse on the elements of designing type, it is appropriate to take a look at how letters can be constructed. Since Daniel is a bit of a purist when it comes to how he works, let's take a look at Century Gothic, a font where the strokes making up each letter are all the same weight, and the rounded areas of the letters are all created using perfect circles.

1. Open "centgoth.psd" from the "pelavin" folder on your DVD as a template.

    Show your rulers (Command/Ctrl R).

    Drag two guides from the top ruler; one to establish the baseline and the other to mark the cap height for each row of letters (Figure 12.12).

Figure 12.11 Three-dimensional type was created by duplicating each letter twice, and altering the stroke and/or fill of each.

Figure 12.12 When you're about to create something as technically demanding as letters, it makes sense to set up Illustrator and your document to be as technically perfect as possible.

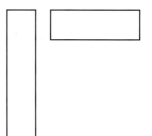

Figure 12.13 Create rectangles that will be copied and used for all your vertical and horizontal strokes.

2. Turn on Smart Guides from the View menu. This feature will help you align elements to one another perfectly.

NOTE: The key to making Smart Guides work effectively is to drag objects from the edge or a point, since they work relative to the position of the cursor, not the object you're moving or creating.

---

3. Using the Rectangle tool, draw a rectangle the exact width and height as the letter I. This will serve as your "master" vertical shape, and you'll duplicate it several times to create the upright strokes for the letters we need (Figure 12.13).

4. Use the Rotate tool to create a horizontal rectangle. Option/Alt click on the selected rectangle you already made, set it to rotate 90°, and click Copy (not OK). You'll use this rectangle for the cross-strokes where they're needed.

At this point, you might want to set the fill to none and the stroke to black so you can see what you're doing. Later, you can toggle to Outline view (Command/Ctrl Y) to make sure things are accurately aligned.

5. Start by constructing the T. Drag a copy of the vertical rectangle on top of the T in your template (Figure 12.14 ①).

6. Drag copy the horizontal rectangle and position it at the top of the vertical one.

   Use the Align palette to center these two shapes to each other and to align them at the top edges. Adjust the width of the top bar to match your template. (Figure 12.14 ②).

7. Use the Pathfinder palette to unite these two pieces into one; select them both and

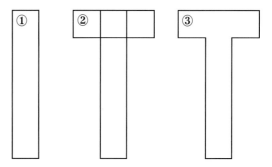

Figure 12.14 Use a copy of your upright stroke shape and your cross-stroke shape to create a T.

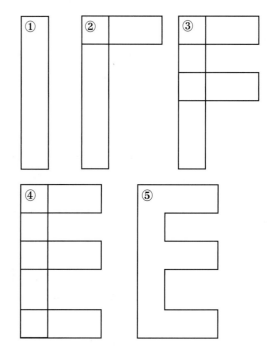

Figure 12.15 Assemble the E, taking care to align the center stroke in the correct position by using your template as a guide.

Option-click the "Add to shape area" icon in the Pathfinder palette—it's the first one in the top row.

Reverse your fill and stroke so that you've got a black letter with no outline (Figure 12.14 ③).

8. The next easiest letter is the E. Again, drag a copy of the vertical rectangle (Figure 12.15 ①).

9. Add a copy of your horizontal rectangle and position it over the E in your template. Use the Direct Selection tool to shorten the horizontal piece (Figure 12.15 ②).

    Select both rectangles and use the Align palette to ensure they're aligned at the top and left side.

10. Drag a copy to the middle of the vertical rectangle, and another to the bottom, using the template as a guide to position them (Figure 12.15 ③ and ④).

11. Unite these four shapes using "Add to shape area" from the Pathfinder palette. Hold the Option/Alt key as you click on the icon to expand the shape in one step (Figure 12.15 ⑤).

12. The Y is not difficult, either. Start with a copy of your vertical rectangle and position it over the Y in your template. Use the Direct Selection tool to shorten it (Figure 12.16 ① and ②).

13. Make another copy of your vertical rectangle and position the top of the rectangle at the top of the left angle in the Y. Use the Direct Selection tool at the bottom edge and drag it to the right to create the angle. Then drag the bottom edge up to match the template (Figure 12.17).

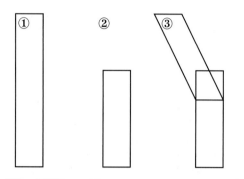

Figure 12.16 The Y uses three copies of the vertical rectangle, with some modifications.

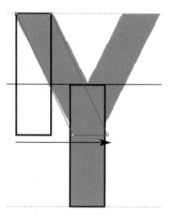

Figure 12.17 Use the Direct Selection tool to move the bottom edge of the angled stroke over to meet the stem.

Figure 12.18 Reflect your angled piece and unite these three pieces for the Y.

14. Use the Reflect tool to copy this vertically for the other piece (Figure 12.18 ④). Make sure all the anchor points are solid so you're not reflecting just a portion of the shape.

NOTE: Using your Arrow keys are a real time-saver when you need to make small adjustments on the position of an object. If your keys are moving things too far, open General Preferences from the Illustrator/Edit menu (Command/Ctrl K) and change your Keyboard Increment to a smaller number.

---

15. Unite these three pieces using the Pathfinder palette, again expanding the shapes into one object (Figure 12.18 ⑤).

The P is a bit challenging since it involves curves. Luckily, they're based on ellipses.

16. Start with a copy of your vertical rectangle.

17. Add two horizontal rectangles, using the template to position them, and reduce their length. Aim to make their right edges end exactly where the curved portion starts (Zoom in using the Command and Option/Ctrl and Alt keys, and dragging a marquee around the area you want to focus on.

18. Create an ellipse with the Ellipse tool. Try to start from the center of the shape (hold the Option/Alt key) and drag it out so that it meets the top and bottom of your two horizontal pieces, and matches the rounded bowl at the right.

    If you don't get it right the first time, try again. You can also use the Scale or Free Transform tool to make adjustments.

19. Select the left point of your ellipse (9 o'clock) and delete it with the Delete key.

Figure 12.19 The P begins like the E. Shorten your horizontal rectangles, then add a circle to match the outer curve for the bowl (rounded part).

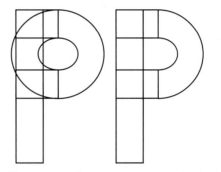

Figure 12.20 Create a second circle for the inner part of the bowl, then snip both circles at noon and 6 o'clock. Delete the left halves.

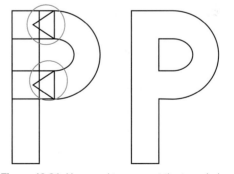

Figure 12.21 You need to connect the two circles at their left points. Use the Pen tool.

That will eliminate half your ellipse and leave you with the right half.

20. Repeat this with a smaller ellipse to match the inner portion of the bowl of the P.

Now you need to connect the end point of the larger ellipse to the end point of the smaller one at the top and at the bottom to create a complete shape.

21. Select the Pen tool and click once on the upper end point of the larger ellipse, then click down and to the left. Finish by clicking on the upper end point of the smaller ellipse (Figure 12.21).

Repeat this for the bottom points.

Not too bad!

22. Select all the parts for your P and unite them using the Pathfinder palette (Figure 12.21).

23. If you haven't filled your letters with black and eliminated the stroke, do so now.

24. Arrange your letters to spell the word TYPE (Figure 12.22).

Save your file!

Obviously, this was a fairly simple exercise in creating letterforms. You used two basic shapes to develop three letters, and most of the fourth.

As you can see from the template, creating the remaining characters wouldn't be difficult. If you decide you want to do that, start by creating the circle shape that you would use for the C, D, G, O, and Q (use the O as your guide, and don't forget to make it a compound path when you're finished).

Figure 12.22 Arrange your letters to spell the word "TYPE."

Figure 12.23 If you want to keep creating characters, make sure to start with "master shapes" that you can copy so your stroke weights are consistent.

You can use the P you already made for the basis of the R. The key is to create an element and use copies of it wherever possible to retain a visual consistency, as well as a mechanical one, among all the letters you construct. (There's a video demonstration in the "pelavin" folder on your DVD that provides more tricks for constructing letters, if you're interested.)

DIGITAL DECONSTRUCTION: SPORTS ILLUSTRATED COVER

Attention to detail is one of Daniel's trademarks. His decorative elements and textures add depth to his designs. This cover, for *Sports Illustrated*, uses a variety of techniques that create an Art Deco feel.

We're also treated to some of his elegant typographic tricks, including distorted type along paths, and his signature embossing effects.

The decorative border around this design is particularly intriguing in its apparent complexity. In fact, it was deceptively easy to create.

Daniel used the Blend tool to create the spikes that frame the page. Starting in one corner with a truncated triangle, he created a second shape—an elongated triangle—some distance away. The Blend tool created the intermediary steps. He used the same technique for the dotted border.

Each area of type has been treated to a different technique, reminiscent of circus posters of the eighteenth and nineteenth centuries.

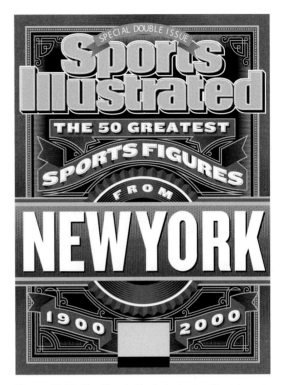

Figure 12.24 The *Sports Illustrated* cover Daniel created for art director Steve Hoffman.

Figure 12.25 Elegant but simple shapes are used as detail around the border.

DIY:
DIMENSIONAL TYPE

Daniel's treatment of "The 50 Greatest" lettering, in particular, is worth a closer look. He's used drop shadows, an embossed effect, and an interesting striped background. The font is Knockout, one of Daniel's favorites, designed by Jonathan Hoefler (*https://www.typography.com/*).

This effect can be created two ways. First, let's look at constructing it from scratch.

1. To create this effect, start with one of the letters you just made.

    For now, don't use the P because a letter with a counter can create difficulties when you're just starting out.

2. Drag a copy of your letter (hold the Option/ Alt key as you drag).

    Change the fill of the copy to none and the stroke to black.

    Assign it a stroke weight of 9 points (Figure 12.27).

3. Use Object ➡ Path ➡ Outline Stroke to turn the outline into paths.

4. Use the Direct Selection tool to delete the outer edge, retaining the inner shape (Figure 12.28).

This shape will become the gray area within the white letter.

5. Align this shape with the copy of the outlined letter (from Step 1), making sure it's centered.

    Fill it with gray (Figure 12.29).

6. At this point, you can fill the original black letter with white. You might want to add a

Figure 12.26 Reverse the fill and stroke colors of one of the letters you created in the previous DIY.

Figure 12.27 Apply a thick stroke to a copy of your type.

Figure 12.28 Outline the stroke of your letter and delete the outer path.

Figure 12.29 After deleting the outer edge, fill the inner shape with gray. Position this shape inside the original character.

Figure 12.30 Create a copy of the inner gray shape, offset it to the left, and fill it with white.

black stroke for now, too, so you can see what you're doing.

7. Select the inner shape and drag a copy up and to the left. Fill this shape with white so it partially blocks out the gray beneath, creating an embossed effect (Figure 12.30).

8. Select your original character and make a copy of it (Command/Ctrl C). Paste this copy behind the original (Command/Ctrl B) and then nudge the copy down and to the right to create the drop shadow; use your down and right arrow keys to move the selected objects (Figure 12.31).

   Fill this with black and delete any stroke color you may have.

   Name this layer "solids."

Now for the dramatic black stripes.

9. Create a new layer by clicking on the "create new layer" button at the bottom of the Layers palette and name it "stripes."

10. Copy and paste your original letter onto the "stripes" layer. Use Command/Ctrl F so it maintains its original position.

    Lock the "solids" layer to keep the next steps from getting in the way of what you've already done.

11. Create a 45° stroke over the widest area of the largest letter with the Pen tool (hold the Shift key to constrain the angle). Give it a stroke of 9 points, then move it off to the left edge.

12. Use Object ➡ Path ➡ Outline Stroke again to change this path into a shape. Fill it with red for now so you can see it (Figure 12.32).

Figure 12.31 Paste a copy of your letters behind everything and offset them to create a black shadow.

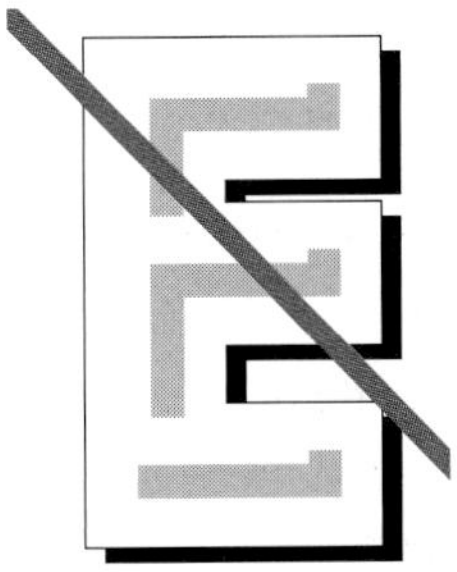

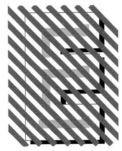

Figure 12.32 Create a 45° stroke and outline it. Make it extra long to be sure it will cover the entire letter.

Figure 12.33 Copy it across your type using the "Command/Ctrl D" shortcut.

Subtract from shape area

Figure 12.34 Turn your letter into stripes by using the Subtract from shape area pathfinder.

13. Drag a copy of this shape a small distance away from the first—try to make the distance between each the same as their thickness.

   Hold the Shift key as you drag to constrain the move to the left or right.

14. Use Object ➡ Transform ➡ Transform Again (Command/Ctrl D) to continue making copies of the shape all the way across your letter (Figure 12.33).

15. Select one of the stripes and use Select ➡ Same ➡ Fill Color to select all of them, without selecting the letter (or use the Magic Wand). Group this selection (Object ➡ Group, or Command/Ctrl G).

16. Now select both the stripes and the type. You can do this easily by locking your "solids" layer, and then typing Command/Ctrl A (Select ➡ All).

17. Open your Pathfinder palette from the Window menu and, with everything still selected, click the "Subtract from shape area" button (the second from the left on the top row).

   Expand your shape by clicking the Expand option in the Pathfinder palette.

NOTE: You can use any of the Pathfinder options holding the Option/Alt key to have them expand automatically.

   Add a black fill and no stroke to the stripes (Figure 12.35).

18. Use the Layers palette to drag the "stripes" layer underneath "solids" so the stripes are behind your letter. Nudge the stripes lower and to the right of the original.

Figure 12.35 After using the Pathfinder, your letter will actually be stripes, cropped to conform to the letter's outline. Fill them with black.

Figure 12.36 Rearrange your layers so the stripes are under the original lettering, and add your background.

19. Add your colored background by drawing a large rectangle in the "stripes" layer. Send it to the back by using Object ➡ Arrange ➡ Send to Back (Command Shift [/Ctrl and Shift]) (Figure 12.36).

There are several interesting techniques used to create this stylized lettering. Any one of them would be a great way to spice up otherwise ordinary type.

One of everyone's favorites is to create type that looks like neon tubing (Figure 12.37). Here's another quick exercise to show you one way to do that.

DIY:
NEON TYPE

Create a new document and open the Character palette (Command/Ctrl T).

1. Type the word(s) you want, and set your font and point size. These examples were set in 72 point Folio Light (Figure 12.38).

2. Turn them into outlines (Command Shift O/Ctrl Shift O) and ungroup them (Command Shift G/Ctrl Shift G) (Figure 12.39).

    Reverse the fill and stroke so the letters are outlined, with a fill of none.

3. Thicken the stroke weight so there are no spaces in the middle of the letters—that is, so that they look like solid shapes, rather than outlines (Figure 12.40).

    Change the stroke to the color you want.

4. Copy the letters and paste in front (Command/Ctrl C, Command/Ctrl F), then change the weight of their strokes to 1 point.

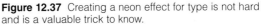

Figure 12.37 Creating a neon effect for type is not hard and is a valuable trick to know.

Figure 12.38 Start with a word set in a fairly thin sans-serif font.

Figure 12.39 Turn your type into outlines using Command Shift O / Ctrl Shift O and ungroup the letters.

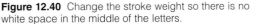

Figure 12.40 Change the stroke weight so there is no white space in the middle of the letters.

Figure 12.41 Paste a copy in front, and reduce the stroke weight to 1 point.

Figure 12.42 Move this copy slightly away from the original so you can see both in Outline View (Command/Ctrl Y).

Change the stroke color to white (Figure 12.41).

5. Move this copy slightly away from the original letters: switch to Outline View so you can see what you're doing (Command/Ctrl Y) (Figure 12.42).

6. Create your blends one letter at a time, deselecting everything between each step.

    Remember, the best blends are made when you click on the same relative point in both shapes. If you click on the top left corner of the first letter, make sure you click on the same point in the second (Figure 12.43).

7. Select one set of letters and realign them with the other set (Figure 12.44).

DIY:
USING THE APPEARANCE PALETTE

There are other ways to play with type and objects by creating graphic styles, saving the style, and then applying it to an element in your image.

This technique is a real time saver, especially if you create something you'd like to use in more than one project.

Here's how it's done.

1. Open a new CMYK Illustrator document, and open the Appearance palette from the Window menu.

2. Draw a straight line with the Pen tool.

    Assign the path a dark stroke color, and a weight of 18 points.

Check the Appearance palette (Window ➡ Appearance). You should see the characteristics of your stroke reflected in the list (Figure 12.45).

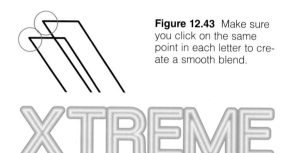

Figure 12.43 Make sure you click on the same point in each letter to create a smooth blend.

Figure 12.44 Realign your letters once all the blends are complete.

Figure 12.45 Use the Appearance palette to see the characteristics of a selected object.

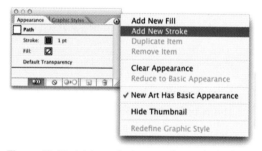

Figure 12.46 Add new instances of your stroke from the Appearance palette's submenu.

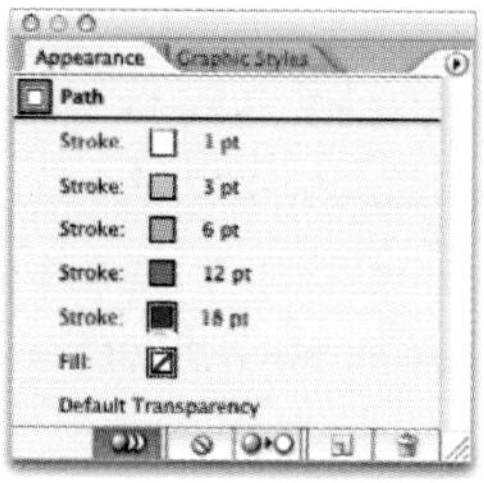

Figure 12.47 When you've finished adding all your strokes, your Appearance palette should look like this.

3. From the Appearance palette submenu, choose Add New Stroke. By default, this will place a new stroke appearance above the first one.

   Assign it a slightly lighter color, and a weight of 12 points.

4. Add another new stroke from the Appearance palette submenu.

   Select it and then assign it a lighter color. Set the stroke to 6 points.

5. Repeat Step 4, assigning an even lighter color, and a weight of 3 points.

6. Finally, add one more stroke from the submenu, make it white, and 1 point thick.

Your Appearance palette should look like the one in Figure 12.47.

7. Open the Graphic Styles palette—it's usually grouped with the Appearance palette—and drag your line into it (Figure 12.48).

8. Create some type, and while it's selected, click on your new graphic style.

DIY:
MORE GRAPHIC STYLES

You may have noticed that the style you just created only altered the stroke of your text. To create a style for the fill, you need to use a shape as your basis.

1. Draw a rectangle with the Rectangle tool. Fill it with a basic color.

2. Use the Appearance palette submenu to add a new fill this time, instead of a stroke. Change the color of this fill.

You won't see your original fill until you modify the new one.

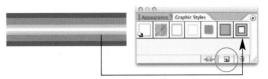

Figure 12.48 Drag your stroke to the Graphic Styles palette or select it and click the New Graphic Style icon at the bottom of the palette.

Figure 12.49 Select the baseline of your type and click on your new style to apply it.

Figure 12.50 You need to modify the new fill so we can still see the original color around the edges.

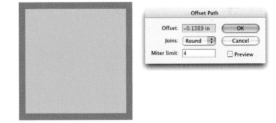

Figure 12.51 Use the Effect menu items to modify each instance of your fill. Make it smaller using Effect ➡ Path ➡ Offset Path.

Since we can't make the rectangle smaller using the Stroke palette, we're going to use the Effect menu instead.

3. While your rectangle is still selected, go to Effect ➡ Path ➡ Offset Path.

    Offset your path with a negative number to make the new fill smaller than the first (Figure 12.51).

4. Now go to Effect ➡ Stylize ➡ Feather and slightly feather the edges of your inner shape (Figure 12.52).

Let's add a third fill and modify it.

5. Add a new fill from the Appearance palette's submenu.

6. Use Effect ➡ Path ➡ Offset Path to make this third rectangle smaller. I used -.3"

You can also use transparency and blending modes to alter your style.

7. Change the color of this fill, then use the Transparency palette to change it, and set it to Multiply mode (Figure 12.53).

8. Add one final fill using the Appearance submenu and, again, change the fill color.

    Use Effect ➡ Path ➡ Offset Path again to make the rectangle smaller.

9. Then try Effect ➡ Distort & Transform ➡ Roughen to make this inner shape jaggedy.

10. Finally add a drop shadow using Effect ➡ Stylize ➡ Drop Shadow.

NOTE: Even though some of the same effects are available from the Filter menu, you must use the Effect menu for it to work in a graphic style.

Figure 12.52 Use Effect ➡ Stylize to add a feathered edge.

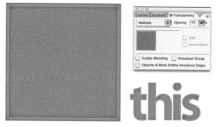

Figure 12.53 Use transparency and blending modes to alter the look of a fill.

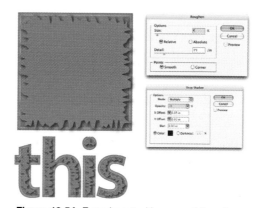

Figure 12.54 Experiment with some of the other Distort & Transform options under the Effect menu.

As you can see, there are many ways to affect the appearance of a fill: transparency, fill colors (including gradients and patterns), and any of the options under the Effect menu.

When you've completed your style, select the rectangle and drag it to your Graphic Styles palette so you can apply it to something.

If you want to save the style for use in other Illustrator images, you have two choices:

Save the file you've been working in. When you want to use the style again, open this file, copy the rectangle, and paste it into a new document. Then drag it into your Graphic Styles palette.

Or, you can save the entire Graphic Styles palette as a Library.

1. Select Save Graphic Style Library from the Graphic Styles submenu.

2. Illustrator should automatically navigate to the Graphic Styles folder within the Illustrator application folder.

3. Name your library and click save.

4. To use it again, use the Graphic Styles menu to Open Graphic Style Library. Choose "Other Library" to locate and open it.

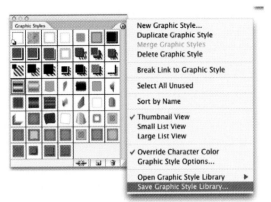

Figure 12.55 Save your graphic styles into a new library using the Graphic Styles submenu.

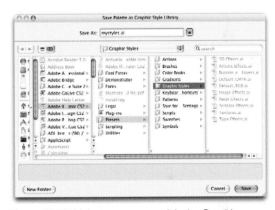

Figure 12.56 Make sure you save it in the Graphic Styles folder within the Illustrator application folder so it becomes available as a library the next time you need it.

KEY POINTS

*   To use Smart Guides effectively, make sure you're dragging a path or shape from an edge or anchor point.

*   When designing letters, use basic shapes and duplicate them to ensure uniformity.

*   Use your arrow keys to fine-tune the position of things. You can change the amount something moves with your arrow keys in General Preferences (Command/Ctrl K, or from the Illustrator/Edit menu).

- Hold your Option/Alt key when using the Pathfinder filters to "Add to shape area" and expand in one step.

- If you're creating a letter with a counter that won't turn "transparent," try making it a compound path. If it still doesn't work, open the Attributes palette and reverse the Even-Odd Fill Rule.

- Create graphic styles as strokes or fills using the Effect menu and the Appearance palette.

- You must use the Effect menu, rather than the Filter menu to create graphic styles.

- Edit graphic styles by double-clicking the effect in the Appearance palette.

- Save your graphic styles as a library using the Graphic Styles palette submenu.

ON YOUR OWN: POSTCARDS

Daniel's graphic style is elegant in its simplicity. Using some of his techniques, create a postcard for your favorite vacation spot.

While you certainly don't have to design your own font, pay attention to the typefaces you select so they work well with the design, and complement the subject matter (for instance, using Zapf Chancery wouldn't work too well on a postcard touting a trek across the Sahara).

Create some graphic styles of your own and apply them to your type. You can use a stroke, or a rectangle. Just remember to make any/all transformations using the Effect menu, or it won't work as a graphic style.

The finished size of a postcard is 5.75" x 4".

THEIR SPIRITS ARE THERE
NATIVE VOICES ECHOING
ONONDAGA LAKE

13 FROM OVEN TO TABLE

Soft Proofing • Commercial Printing • Transparency • Overprinting and Knockouts
Print Options • Color Separation

Once you've got something ready to print, it's important to pay attention to a few last details so you can avoid any issues with your output, whether it's being printed on your own printer (soft proofing), or going to press for commercial reproduction.

It's important to understand that what we see on our monitors is being displayed in red, green, and blue dots (RGB). This color space, frequently referred to as the "additive primaries," creates colors as one or more is added to the other. When 100% of all three is present, we see white. When they are all absent, we see black. Some colors that we can create on-screen cannot be reproduced on paper.

When we look at a printed page, on the other hand, we are looking at the "subtractive primaries" of cyan, magenta, yellow, and black (CMYK). This color space is impossible to reproduce on a computer monitor since it operates using the exact opposite principles. When all colors are 100% present, we see black (a dark brown, really), and when they are all absent, we see the color of the paper—be it white, lime green, or mauve. Many of the colors we can print can't be accurately displayed on a monitor.

The entire range within any color system is called the "gamut" (pronounced GA met).

And speaking of paper colors, that will also affect how something looks when it's printed. Because printing inks are slightly transparent, a full-color image printed on yellow paper is going to look a lot different from the same image printed on white.

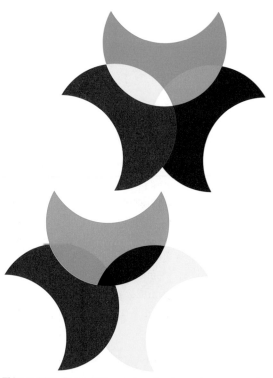

Figure 13.1 The additive colors (top)—red, green, and blue—overlap to produce intermediary colors of cyan, magenta, and yellow. The subtractive colors overlap to create red, green, and blue.

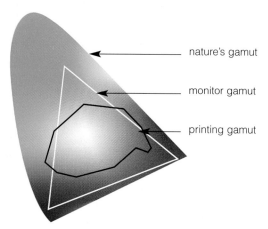

nature's gamut

monitor gamut

printing gamut

Figure 13.2 There are more colors in nature than can be reproduced either on a monitor, or on a piece of paper. Notice that some colors in either gamut can't be reproduced by the other.

SOFT PROOFING

The term "soft proofing" is what we do when we print something on our desktop printer, whether it's an inkjet or laser printer. Typically, these printers use at least cyan, magenta, and yellow inks, if not all four (including black) to re-create your Illustrator image.

A typical inkjet printer might print at a resolution of 300 dots per inch—something like 8,415,000 dots across an 8.5" space. If you do the math, you realize that to print a full 8.5" by 11" image, the printer is creating about 28,000 tiny dots in order to re-create your illustration. The results look almost as good as a photograph, although it's important to recognize that the colors will shift from what you see on the screen to what gets printed.

The type and quality of the paper you're using also make a huge difference in your results. Softer, more porous papers absorb ink, while the ink sits on top of highly polished or coated photographic paper.

In any case, what you get when printing to an inkjet or laser printer is very different from what your image will look like when printed in mass quantities using offset lithography.

COMMERCIAL PRINTING

Art that consists of all the colors in nature, whether created using pigments, photography, or software, is called "continuous-tone" art.

One of the first things to recognize is that offset lithography—the most common commercial process for reproducing print pieces—can only print solid colors.

In order to create a gradual blend of colors, from one to the next with all the variations in

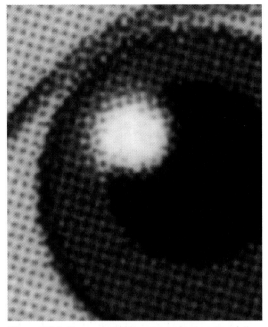

Figure 13.3 To re-create the range of colors in a full-color image, it's separated into the four process colors, and screened to re-create subtle variations.

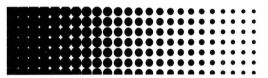

Figure 13.4 A flat PMS color can be reproduced in various tints using screens to create dots of various sizes.

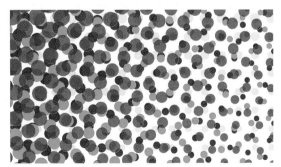

Figure 13.5 To create a full-color image, all four colors are screened and overlapped. The result is called a halftone. Black-and-white photos are also treated this way to accurately reproduce hundreds of grays.

between, each color is broken down into various sized dots. Larger dots create more intense color, and smaller dots create paler versions.

When using the Pantone inks, the process of using paler versions—or tints—of a solid color (that is, using smaller dots), is called "screening."

If you're printing a full-color job, the result of screening the image into dots is called a "halftone." The four process colors are each screened separately, with the dots at different angles so that they create a flower pattern (Figure 13.5), rather than overlapping each other. If the screen angles aren't set accurately, the result is called a moiré pattern (Figure 13.6).

Depending on the size of the screen (higher numbers create better-quality reproduction) or the distance between the viewer and the image, these dots blend to create the illusion of continuous-tone color. The quality of the screen used is referred to as dots per inch, or dpi. This shouldn't be confused with ppi, pixels per inch, which is something you need to take into consideration with bitmapped images.

So, in essence, we have three different factors to consider when dealing with creating color images with Illustrator: what we see on the screen, how it will be printed—soft proofing, or offset—and the screen or printer resolution, dpi.

The good news is that because Illustrator is a vector-based program, you can enlarge or reduce your image at any point without compromising quality.

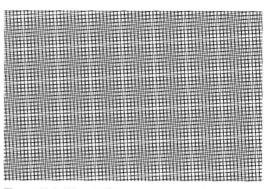

Figure 13.6 When halftone screens are misaligned, a moiré pattern is created. This can also happen when you scan a printed image, and then print it again.

Figure 13.7 We can create transparent objects using effects like drop shadow, feather, and glow, and when we set a solid color to less than 100% in the Transparency palette.

TRANSPARENCY

Since Illustrator version 9, we've been able to set the color of objects to less than 100 percent, thereby creating transparencies. This is a wonderful option, but not without its own set of limitations.

First, let's take a look at the different ways Illustrator can create transparency.

When you use the Transparency palette, you can adjust the intensity of a color from 100% to 0%.

Transparent objects are also created when you use some of the effects, like drop shadow and feather, and inner or outer glow. These effects create the illusion that your color is fading to nothing around the edges.

Creating an Opacity Mask is another way to utilize the transparency features in Illustrator.

It's easy to start thinking that when you place a transparent object over another color, it's sort of like putting a piece of colored cellophane over your image, or creating a wash of color as you would with thin paint. In fact, Illustrator is actually changing the colors behind the scenes.

When you save an Illustrator file in its native AI format, any transparencies you've used remain "live," that is, you can still edit them when you reopen the image.

If you save your file in EPS format, Illustrator actually creates two versions: one that retains the editability of your transparencies that only Illustrator can open, and another flattened version to use in a page layout program like QuarkXPress or InDesign (although you can place and edit Illustrator transparencies in InDesign). In the flattened version, any areas

Figure 13.8 Once an image file containing transparencies is saved as an EPS file to use in another program, like QuarkXPress, the transparency is flattened into solid colors.

Figure 13.9 Effects like flattening a glow, feather, or drop shadow actually create bitmapped images.

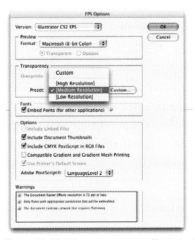

Figure 13.10 When you save an Illustrator file in EPS format, you're asked to set the quality of your transparency.

containing transparency are rasterized—that is, they are converted into pixels.

You can flatten your transparencies in Illustrator, or they will be flattened automatically when you save your file in EPS format, or print your image.

You may have noticed the option to set the resolution of your transparencies in the EPS Save dialog box—that's what determines the pixels per inch Illustrator will use to rasterize transparent areas.

By the same token, if you choose to flatten your transparency before you save your file, you can do so using Object ➡ Flatten Transparency (your object needs to be selected, first). Again, you'll be asked to set the quality of the resolution for the rasterized area. Once you flatten any transparencies this way, however, they are no longer editable.

You can create a custom flattening option using Edit ➡ Transparency Flattener Presets. Before you do that, however, it's important to note that another place where you establish at what resolution images are rasterized is found under the Effect menu.

Any changes you make using Effect ➡ Document Raster Effects Settings stay in effect for all subsequent new images. At the very least, although it will increase your file size, you should be working at a medium resolution. The only exception to this is if you're working on files that will be used on the Web. Set your resolution to High (300 ppi) only if your image is going to be reproduced using a commercial printing method.

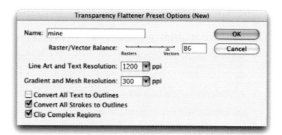

Figure 13.11 You can create your own transparency flattener options using Edit ➡ Transparency Flattener Presets.

Figure 13.12 Image quality and file size are both increased when you use a raster resolution higher than the default "screen" (72 ppi) option. It's important to check these settings if your file is going to a commercial printer.

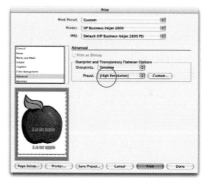

Figure 13.13 In the Advanced pane of the Print dialog box, choose "Simulate" to get an approximate idea of what objects that print on top of others will look like.

OVERPRINTING AND KNOCKOUTS

Two colors that overlap, whether they have a transparency of less than 100% or not, are considered an "overprint"—that is, one color prints on top of another. On your monitor, you typically see one solid color on top of another. In fact, since commercial printing inks are slightly transparent, the colors may affect each other when the file is printed. You can get a feel for how this might look by selecting "Overprint Preview" from the View menu, or by printing with the overprint "simulated." If the overprint item is black, you won't see a huge difference, and in fact, your black will be richer in color than if it was just black ink on white paper.

To soft-proof an image that gives you a facsimile of what you'll get when the file is printed on a commercial press, you need to navigate your way to the Advanced option in the Print dialog box. Select "Simulate" in the Overprint options pop-up menu.

On the other hand, a knockout area is one where any color behind another object is deleted from the image. This essentially exposes the top object directly on the paper, rather than over another color ink.

A great example of a knockout is white type on a black background. Unless you're using a white PMS ink in addition to your four process colors, you can't get white type without creating a knockout area (or, more accurately, type that's the color of the paper you're printing on).

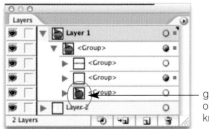

Figure 13.14 Unless you're printing with white ink, white type must be knocked out of the surrounding color.

Figure 13.15 Illustrator provides the option to knock-out portions of an image so the background objects show through them.

grouped objects for knockout

Figure 13.16 Select everything you want to be included in the knockout, and group them.

DIY:
KNOCKOUT GROUP

Illustrator provides an additional knockout feature that allows you to have background objects "show through" foreground objects, as in Figure 13.15.

Take a look at how that's done.

1. To make this work, you'll want to create an interesting background pattern or texture.

   Lock this layer.

2. Add a layer above your background texture or image and create something simple, like the apple in Figure 13.15.

3. On the same layer, add the element(s) you want to act as "windows" to the background.

   If you choose type, as in this example, turn it into outlines (Command Shift O/Ctrl Shift O, while the baseline is selected). Copy and paste these type outlines in front.

4. Set the fill transparency of your "window" object(s) between 50% and 0%, and add a stroke to create definition if the image or text extends beyond the underlying image—as with the "A" in this example.

5. Select everything on this layer (Command/Ctrl A will work as long as the background layer is locked), and group it (Command/Ctrl G).

6. In the Transparency palette, make sure your options are visible: select "Show Options" from the submenu.

7. Select the group—not the layer—that you want to make a knockout group, and check "Knockout Group" in the Transparency palette.

Figure 13.17 Make sure your Transparency options are showing, select the group you want to affect, and check the Knockout Group box.

Figure 13.18 Elements in a Knockout Group can include transparency, gradients, and blending modes as well.

Figure 13.19 If your objects fall outside the new document size, just select them and move them back into place.

You can also use gradients and blending modes to affect how the background shows through.

This is a pretty cool option and one you should remember. You never know when it will come in handy.

THE PRINT DIALOG BOX

Before you print an Illustrator document, you need to coordinate the document size with the size of the paper you'll be using.

Typically, your document size is 8.5" x 11" unless you specify something different in the New Document dialog box.

If you've designed something that isn't going into a page layout program like InDesign or QuarkXPress, you may need to change your document size. For example, a business card doesn't have to be positioned within an 8.5" x 11" page size.

File ➡ Document Setup provides the opportunity for you to change your document size to something more appropriate for the job.

NOTE: When you make your document smaller, it's possible that the objects in your image may fall outside the new page boundaries. Simply select everything and move them back where they belong.

If your image is larger than the standard 8.5" x 11" paper that most printers use, you can resize it to fit within the file (select all, and use the Scale tool to click and drag every element to a smaller size. Hold the Shift key to constrain the proportions).

If you want to print your document at the full size on 8.5" X 11" paper, then you'll need to

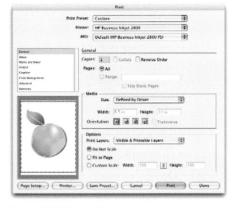

Figure 13.20 The General pane in the Print dialog box provides the most basic choices, including the printer, how many copies you want, and the size and orientation of your paper.

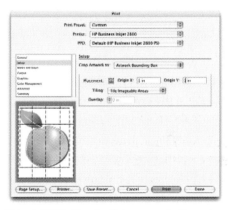

Figure 13.21 Use the Setup pane to tile an image that's larger than the paper size. It will print on several pieces of paper that you can then assemble into a single piece.

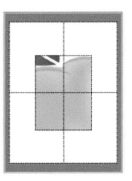

Figure 13.21 Setting the Crop Artwork to "Crop Area" will delete any portions of your image that fall outside the document dimensions.

tile the image. You make that specification in the Print dialog box.

The second step before actually printing your document is to make sure your color mode is set to CMYK. Use File ➡ Document Color Mode to change it, if necessary.

Now you're ready to print.

When you choose Print from the File menu, Illustrator presents you with a new and streamlined Print dialog box. The options here reflect Adobe's response to professional printers who requested a more simplified process for proofing and color separations. They also make soft proofing easier, and more accurate.

The **General** pane is where you make the choices appropriate for proofing an image. Choose your printer, determine how many copies you want, the paper size, and your page orientation. Use the preview field to move your image around within the page. You can also check "Fit to Page" here to reduce an image larger than the paper size, or to enlarge one that's small.

You'll notice at the bottom left of this window you have buttons called Page Setup and Printer. Use these buttons to access any special options your printer offers.

The **Setup** pane is where you can choose to tile your image—having it print on more than one sheet of paper if the image is too large to fit on the specified page size.

You can choose to crop the artwork to the artboard size (your document size), the artwork itself (artwork bounding box), or to crop the image to fit within the paper size. If you want the whole image, choose Artwork Bounding Box.

Figure 13.23 Adding an overlap measurement when you Tile Full Pages ensures a perfect match at the edges of each printed page.

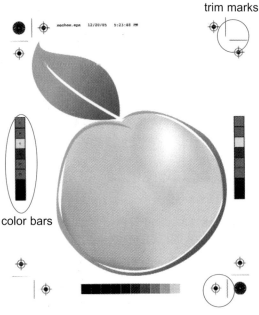

trim marks

color bars

registration marks

Figure 13.24 This is a page printed with all the marks and bleeds.

Figure 13.25 Any areas that print off the edges of the paper are considered bleed.

You can move your image around inside the preview pane at any time. Just click and drag within that area.

When tiling to multiple pages, it's worth the time it takes to move the image, and possibly change your paper's orientation, so the image prints on as few pieces of paper as possible.

When you choose Tile Full Pages, you have the option to determine an overlap—how much extra image you'll get around all four sides that you can then trim to ensure a perfect match between edges.

Marks and Bleed refers to adding printer's marks for registration and cropping, in addition to establishing the amount of bleed needed.

Trim marks are used to indicate where the paper will be cut to create a document the size you want when it's printed on paper that's larger than it needs to be. They're indicated at each corner by thin lines.

Registration marks look like small targets with a crosshair in the middle. These are printed using all four process colors so that if any one of them is out of alignment, you'll be able to see it immediately.

Color bars are used to gauge the accuracy of the color. In soft proofing situations, there's not much you can do since you're limited to your printer's behavior. On a commercial press, however, the various rollers that control how each color prints can be adjusted to increase or decrease the amount of ink that's being laid down.

Bleed refers to any area of the image that will print to the edge of the page. When you're printing something that needs to go right to

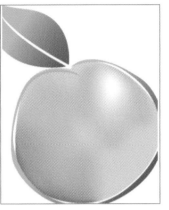

Figure 13.26 Always create extra image area outside the trim if you want your image to bleed so no paper shows at the edges when it's trimmed.

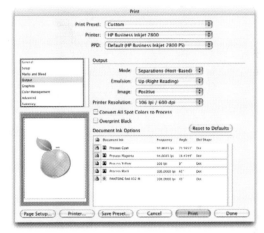

Figure 13.27 The Output pane is where you can determine whether you want to print a composite image (full-color) or separations (a black-and-white page for each color).

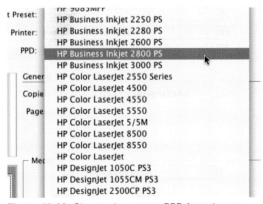

Figure 13.28 Choose the correct PPD from the pop-up menu.

edge, you should add at least 1/8" of extra image at that edge so when the page is trimmed, there's no paper showing accidently.

Use the **Output** pane if you need to print color separations for commercial printing. By default, Illustrator always prints a composite image—that is, in full color. Unless you have a PostScript printer, however, it's unlikely you'd need to do this.

Even though you might never print color separations, it's worth a closer look at the option so you better understand how the four process colors come together to create your full-color image.

DIY:
PRINTING COLOR SEPARATIONS

As mentioned earlier, any full-color image needs to be separated into the four process colors, and each separation is screened to create the different sized dots that make up the tints of color.

1. Open any one of your saved exercises or chapter assignments.

    Make sure the page size is accurate, and the color mode is set to CMYK.

2. Select File ➡ Print (Command/Ctrl P).

3. In the General pane, select the printer you want to print to. In a networked environment, you may have several to choose from.

4. Check your PPD. The PostScript Printer Description contains information about your printer's features. If it doesn't match your printer (i.e., it says "Generic Color" or something nonspecific), use the pop-up menu to scroll to and select your printer.

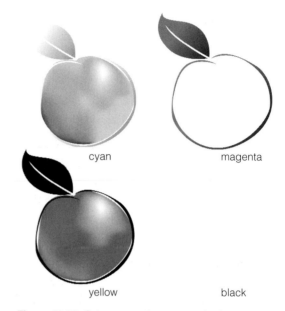

cyan   magenta

yellow   black

Figure 13.29 Color separations create the images needed to print a full-color image on a commercial printing press.

Document Ink Options				Reset to Defaults
Document Ink		Frequency	Angle	Dot Shape
Process Cyan		94.8683 lpi	71.5651°	Dot
Process Magenta		94.8683 lpi	18.4349°	Dot
Process Yellow		100 lpi	0°	Dot
Process Black		106.0660 lpi	45°	Dot

Figure 13.30 Your ink options are preset to create the correct screen angles to avoid creating a moiré pattern when the image goes to press.

5. If your image is too large to fit on an 8.5" x 11" piece of paper, select the "Fit to Page" option. There's no need to print more than four pieces of paper for this exercise.

6. In the Marks and Bleed pane, choose to print trim marks and registration marks.

7. In the Output pane, change the Output Mode from Composite (which is the default) to "Separations (Host based)." This is how a commercial printer would create the film negatives needed to create printing plates.

Take a minute to look at the Document Ink Options. Notice the preset angle for each; this prevents the halftone dots from creating a moiré pattern when they come back together on the press.

8. Click the Print button.

After your document prints, take a look especially at the black page. Typically, there won't be much black within your image unless you used black shapes for any portion or black type. If you created a "rich" black for your blacks, as many illustrators do, you should see hints of your black areas on each of the other three pages.

In the **Graphics** pane, you can eliminate some printing issues by changing the Paths Flatness option from Automatic to something between Quality and Speed. Moving the slider towards Speed will degrade the quality of curved paths, but may eliminate printer issues.

It's important to note that because Illustrator is a vector-based drawing program, the contents of a file are created using a lot of code. Excessive anchor points, each needing to be translated from

Figure 13.31 A rich black—one composed of all four process colors—will create an image on each of the color separations. "Plain" black will only appear on the black separation.

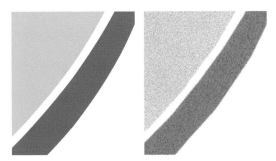

Figure 13.32 Shifting the Paths from "Quality" (left) to "Speed" (right) may get a complicated image to print, but the quality of your curved areas will be compromised.

Illustrator's code to your printer's, can cause serious printing issues. If an image just won't print for you, try setting the Paths Flatness option to "Speed." Your image might print, but the quality of the curves will be degraded somewhat.

NOTE: If you are having printing issues, go back into your image and check for stray points. Go to Select ➡ Object ➡ Stray Points, and then hit Delete to eliminate them. A stray point is one that goes nowhere and isn't part of any real object.

Decide whether to let Illustrator determine the color, or your printer in the Color Management pane, and whether to retain or flatten transparencies in the Advanced pane.

KEY POINTS

- Unless you calibrate both your monitor and your printer, getting colors to print as you anticipate will be difficult.

- The type of printer and the finish of the paper will affect color and print quality.

- Continuous-tone images are broken into dots to create the illusion of color blends or shades of gray for commercial printing.

- The quality of a commercially printed image is dependent on the halftone screens used to break the image into dots.

- Transparency in Illustrator files remains editable until it's flattened, whether by saving the file in EPS version, or flattening it using Object ➡ Flatten Transparency.

- Make sure your transparency resolution is set to the appropriate quality when saving an Illustrator file as EPS.

- An overprint is any area where two colors overlap. Select Overprint Preview from the

View menu to see how these colors will actually affect each other.

- A knockout is any area of an image that has been deleted so the color of the paper shows through.

- Use the Transparency palette to create knockout groups.

- Tile an image that is too large to fit on the printer's paper using the Setup pane in the Print dialog box.

- By default, Illustrator prints a composite (full-color) image. To print separations, use the Output pane in the Print dialog box.

- If an image is too complex to print, change your quality settings closer to "Speed" in the Graphics pane of the Print dialog box.

The gummy candy crawling with flavor!

GUMOEBAS

THEY'LL DRIVE YOU WILD!

Lime

The following images reflect the work of students in the Syracuse University Ad Design and Illustration programs. Each was created as an example of the projects found at the end of each chapter.

Peter Sinclair's use of Multiply blending mode was used in billboards for the zoo (Chapter 2).

Top: **Lauren Katz**

Bottom: **Amanda Cohen**

Peter Sinclair's use of Multiply blending mode was used in a billboard for the zoo (Chapter 2).

T-shirts that incorporate the compound paths in Jack Tom's work (Chapter 3) are shown below.

Meg Paradise

Concept: **Natalie Mammone** Here a solid color is used as the barrier through which the T-shirt's fabric shows.

Concept: **Carolina Mendez** In this shirt, the compound path was a circle in the shirt shape, so the photograph of snow could show through. Carolina then added the wave shape to symbolize her native Puerto Rican beaches.

Custom brushes were used in these invitations based on Colleen O'Hara's style (Chapter 4).

Lauren Zuckerman Lots of custom brushes add definition to loosely created shapes.

Caitlin Douglas The dress and hanger were constructed using custom calligraphic brushes.

Kenny Kiernan's graphic style used in snack food packaging ideas (Chapter 5).

Nicholas Panas (above) The nice contrast in stroke/edge colors create a dynamic tin. **Tim Hsieh** (right) A die-cut window to see the contents inside is a nice touch.
Deirdre Merrigan (chapter title page) A die-cut window along with whimsical gummy creatures and funky type treatment makes this package appealing.

These are examples of using patterns in covers, as illustrated by Heidi Schmidt's work (Chapter 6).

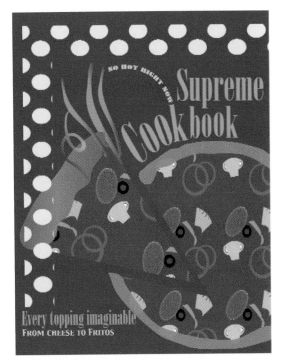

Carolyn Rabiner The pizza toppings are a pattern in this one!

John Intrater The sprinkles on these donuts demonstrate an inventive use for patterns.

Kate Ambis One blueberry pattern was used twice, at different sizes to create texture in the background.

Rocco Baviera's technique of using negative areas to create positive spaces is shown here, along with his droplet trick (Chapter 7).

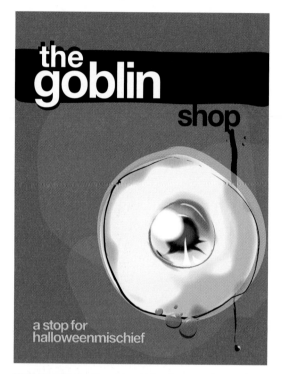

Natalie Mammone The tree is a negative space cut out of the sky.

Nicholas Panas Droplets of blood are a unique twist to Rocco's waterdrop technique.

(right) Concept: **Anna Bratslavskaya** This image makes use of both the negative space in the web and Rocco's cool droplets.

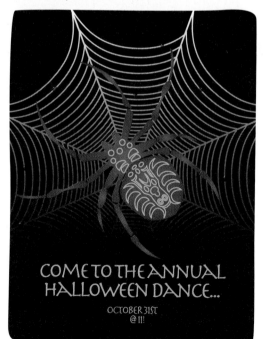

David McCord's technical illustration inspired these images of electric/electronic devices (Chapter 8).

Amanda Cohen

Carolina Mendez Carolina used David's woodgrain technique for the reflection in the glass on this iPod.

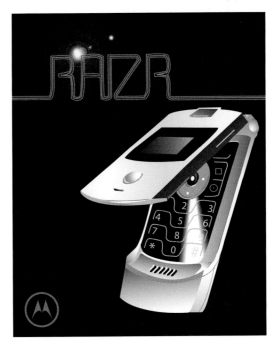

Natalie Mammone

Using David Brooks's LiveTrace technique ensures a nice hand-created quality in these images (Chapter 9).

Caitlyn McCarthy A finished fish image, a la Brooks.

Melissa Evans If you're feeling ambitious, create a new version of an old favorite book's cover.

Everyone loves playing with the 3D Revolve feature, inspired by Chris Spollen (Chapter 11).

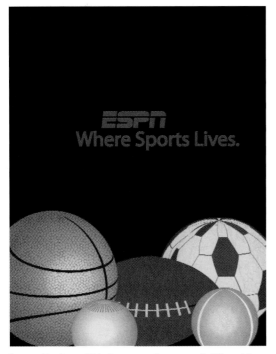

Laura Fontana This image makes use of different textures for each ball.

Oliver Vignola The mapped art for this soccer ball included the team logo.

Lauren Katz The bowl for this image was created using a quarter arc, rotated 380°.